BUILDING DEMOCRACY
IN LATIN AMERICA

BUILDING DEMOCRACY
IN LATIN AMERICA

John Peeler

LYNNE
RIENNER
PUBLISHERS

BOULDER
LONDON

Published in the United States of America in 1998 by
Lynne Rienner Publishers, Inc.
1800 30th Street, Boulder, Colorado 80301

and in the United Kingdom by
Lynne Rienner Publishers, Inc.
3 Henrietta Street, Covent Garden, London WC2E 8LU

Library of Congress Cataloging-in-Publication Data
Peeler, John A.
　　Building democracy in Latin America　/　John Peeler.
　　　　p.　cm.
　　Includes bibliographical references.
　　ISBN 1-55587-758-3 (hc　:　alk. paper).—ISBN 1-55587-781-8 (pb　:
alk. paper)
　　1. Democracy—Latin America.　2. Latin America—Politics and
government—20th century.　I. Title.
JL966.P44　1998
320.98—dc21　　　　　　　　　　　　　　　　　　　　　　97-33554
　　　　　　　　　　　　　　　　　　　　　　　　　　　　　　　CIP

British Cataloguing in Publication Data
A Cataloguing in Publication record for this book
is available from the British Library.

Printed and bound in the United States of America

　　　　　The paper used in this publication meets the requirements
　∞　of the American National Standard for Permanence of
　　　　　Paper for Printed Library Materials Z39.48-1984.

　　5　4　3　2　1

Contents

Tables and Figures

TABLES

FIGURES

Acknowledgments

Among the many people who have helped me through the various stages of this book, I would like to specifically thank my wife, Judith Harris Peeler; numerous colleagues at my university, including Eugenia Gerdes, Thomas Greaves, and Andrea Stevenson Sanjian; and my research assistant, Helen Bayes. Among scholars in Latin America, the following have been particularly helpful: Carlos Acuña, Juan Antonio Blanco, Marcelo Caetano, Manuel Antonio Garretón, René Mayorga, Romeo Pérez, Francisco Rojas, José Miguel Rodríguez, Jorge Rovira Mas, José Luis Vega, Carlos Sojo, Manuel Rojas Bolaños, and Patricio Silva.

Some parts of this book appeared in earlier versions in the following essays. Sections of Chapter 1 are drawn from "Constitution-Building and Democratization in Brazil and Colombia," paper presented at the American Political Science Association, 1994. Chapter 2 has sections adapted from "Elite Settlements and Democratic Consolidation: Colombia, Costa Rica, and Venezuela," in John Higley and Richard Gunther, eds., *Elites and Democratic Consolidation in Latin America and Southern Europe* (Cambridge: Cambridge University Press, 1992); "Decay and Renewal in Democratic Regimes: Colombia and Venezuela," *MACLAS Latin American Essays* 9: 135–152 (1995); and "Early Democratization in Latin America: Costa Rica in the Context of Chile and Uruguay," paper presented at the Latin American Studies Association, 1995.

Preface

This is a book about the struggle to create a humane and democratic political order in a context, Latin America, where such a task has more often than not seemed impossible.[1] Yet the last quarter of the twentieth century has witnessed substantial movement toward that goal in virtually every country of the region. The thrust of my argument is that liberal democracy is both feasible and desirable in Latin America. It is feasible because the Latin American tradition includes ways of thinking and acting (e.g., elite settlements) that are adaptable to liberal democracy. Liberal democracy is desirable in Latin America because it works to protect individual freedom and to restrict the concentration of power.

The genealogy of the concept of democracy is explored in the Introduction. Here, I will simply note that although "democracy" literally means "rule by the people," in this century it has come to be synonymous with "liberal democracy," an increasingly widespread type of polity. A liberal democracy is *democratic* insofar as it chooses its government by popular, competitive election, thereby providing democratic legitimation to the polity. But the people do not rule directly outside these periodic elections. Liberal democracy is *liberal* in that it limits government authority and protects individual rights. It is the best and most durable system yet invented for protecting individuals against government oppression, but liberal democracy is not fully democratic. A key issue is whether it is possible to move toward a more democratic polity without losing the benefits of liberal democracy.

What do we mean by "possible"? It can mean being consistent with prior and predetermining conditions. Some scholars argue that the history and culture of Latin America are such that democracy could never thrive there. Chapter 1 addresses this issue and concludes that democracy can indeed find indigenous roots in Latin America. Others argue that democracy requires a particular class structure without which it will be fragile at best. Dietrich Rueschemeyer, Evelyne Huber Stephens, and John Stephens (1992) have developed such a structural argument with notable sophistication and meticulous research. Structures in general and class structure in particular clearly matter a great deal in determining what is possible. The cases examined here suggest that structures limit possibilities but do not determine outcomes.

Much research on regime transitions has emphasized the importance of statecraft, that is, purposeful action by political leaders to shape outcomes. Guillermo O'Donnell and Philippe Schmitter (1986), for example, in their *Tentative Conclusions About Uncertain Democracies,* sum up many cases in their multivolume study by emphasizing the indeterminacy of transitions from authoritarian rule. Outcomes are not determined by structures; they depend on the interaction of decisionmakers. This book tends to support this perspective, but it does not negate the importance of structure.

I propose that we consider structure and human action as mutually constituting each other. Any social structure, such as an economic system or a religion, sets boundaries on what any given individual can do without incurring costs (e.g., poverty results from refusal to do remunerative work under capitalism, or ostracism results from behavior considered immoral by the dominant religion). Social structures, in turn, are products of the human actions that created them over time. For example, the comprehensive structure that is the capitalist system resulted in part from actions by landowners in seventeenth-century England to change traditional patterns of land tenure. That is, landowners acted to change an existing structure and in the process contributed to the creation of a new structure (capitalism). Action constitutes structure; structure limits action. Structures do not prevent actions but rather affect the probability of their achieving their purposes. Weak structures are obviously more susceptible than strong ones to change through human action. By the same token, powerful actors (e.g., leaders who can mobilize large numbers or other resources) are more capable of changing structures.

From this perspective, neither structure nor action alone can explain social and political phenomena. It is essential to see the two as interacting through time, mutually shaping each other. Therefore, in this book I eschew the argument about whether structure or action is the better explanation.

Any political system has a broad range of structures—called the regime—that determine which actors actually have governmental authority; how political conflict and cooperation take place; which actors receive or lose resources; and what role, if any, the vast majority of nonpowerful actors play in the political process. Like any other structure, the regime is the consequence of prior action and may be changed by action. But at any given time, the regime constrains elites as well as other actors. Nonelite actors, though having less power than elite actors, nevertheless individually and collectively structure the environments of elites. And, of course, elites continue to be subject to global economic and political structures.

The political system of the United States may be used to illustrate the point. One of the features of the U.S. political regime is the two-party system, which was shaped by the actions of key leaders such as Franklin Roosevelt and Abraham Lincoln. Current leaders such as Bill Clinton and Newt Gingrich must work within the two-party system if they hope to accomplish anything, and voters must vote for Republicans or Democrats if they want to avoid wasting their votes. Thus the structure binds both elites and nonelites. Yet at the same time, Clinton and Gingrich by their actions, and the voters by their votes, are both reproducing and changing the party system. They reproduce it by continuing to act within it. They change it by redefining both the policy commitments and social bases of the parties.

The termination of a regime is a matter of great interest in the study of comparative politics. Regime structures are more durable than lower-order structures, but they are nonetheless subject to change as a consequence of actions. Regime change will occur when some combination of elite and mass action disposes enough power to overcome regime structures. Often, defection of regime supporters will help to shift the power balance and thereby create conditions appropriate to regime change.[2]

Again, let us turn to the political system of the United States for an example. The Civil War was a stupendous struggle for power at both mass and elite levels, which had the result of a sweeping transformation of the country's political, economic, and social structures. The war erupted when the antebellum political coalitions (structures) broke down and realigned as a result of the successful organization (action) of the Republican Party. After the war, an entirely new set of structures emerged that would take the country into the next century.

One additional set of factors in regime termination should be considered: international influences, including direct political or military intervention by a foreign power. The United States terminated several regimes in Central America and the Caribbean by this means between 1898 and 1933, and in the Dominican Republic in 1965, in Grenada in 1982, in Panama in 1990, and in Haiti in 1994. Such influences also include international economic actors such as the International Monetary Fund, which is often in a position to force politically destabilizing policies on Third World governments. Finally, international influences may include worldwide economic or political conditions, such as recession, that function as structural constraints on political regimes.[3] This book will show that such international influences have been very important in shaping the political and economic evolution of Latin America.

In the absence of an extant regime, elite and mass political actors confront a radically different set of conditions. A very important set of constraints on action has been removed: the structures that most directly affect the political elites.[4] The scope for elite choice and action is abruptly increased. Those elites recently dislodged from political power will find their capabilities for action substantially reduced if not eliminated. Other elites will find their capabilities suddenly much stronger. However, this period of increased scope for choice is unlikely to persist long, since actions inherently create new structures.

Further, the destruction of political regime structures still leaves structures intact in other levels and sectors. Sectors of the mass population may well be making demands that newly dominant elites cannot ignore. Aspects of the traditional social structure, such as ethnicity, are unlikely to have undergone fundamental change. The structure of the international economy will in all likelihood be unaffected by the end of the political regime in one country, but the governments of powerful neighboring states may have strong preferences about the outcome of political struggles in the system in question.

Thus in the wake of the termination of a regime, interaction among political elites—constrained by surviving structures—will create the structures of a new regime. If power in the interregnum is somewhat concentrated in the hands of a single, relatively unified elite, the elite will be able to establish regime structures according to its preference and thereby dominate the regime. Good examples would include the victorious communist revolutionaries in China (1949) and Cuba (1959). More commonly, a winning coalition fragments after the destruction of the old regime. At the same time, elements of the losing elite may still have substantial power, as may other elites who did not participate on either side. The interregnum may therefore witness intense political conflict unconstrained by regime rules. The potential for violence is high, and the risks to both elite and mass actors are substantial. Conflict within the interregnum may produce a single dominant elite or a coalition that triumphs over competitors in relatively short order (Russia, 1917). Alternatively, the interregnum may persist through a prolonged and possibly violent impasse (Mexico, 1910–1934; Vietnam, 1941–1975; Lebanon, 1975–1991).

Interregnum conflicts may lead competing elites to arrive at an explicit or tacit agreement about new regime structures that protect the vital interests of all participating elites.[5] John Higley and Michael Burton (1989) distinguish "elite settlements" (involving an explicit agreement among competing elites about regime rules) from "elite convergence" (reduction of conflict and increasing cooperation within a set of regime rules, without an explicit, comprehensive settlement). The type of political regime we know as "liberal democracy" has usually, if stable, been rooted in such settlements or convergence rather than either unresolved conflict or clear dominance by one elite or coalition.[6] This is not an accident, since liberal democracy implies civil competition for political power within constitutional rules. If one elite is dominant, then competition will not be meaningful; if elites will not be bound by constitutional limits on their competition, they are essentially engaged in civil war, not civil competition.

In this book I show how liberal democracy has in fact emerged in Latin America, consistent with my perspective on the interaction of structure and human action. Demonstrably, democracy was not and is not impossible in Latin America, but neither is it inevitable, as the cases of Paraguay, Mexico, and Cuba illustrate.

Having made the case that liberal democracy is both desirable and feasible in Latin America, I conclude the book with the argument that, ethically, liberal democracy embodies contradictions that lead toward a more equal distribution of resources and broadened opportunities for participation. Liberal democracy presupposes the equality of citizens, but it exists everywhere in a context of greater or lesser economic inequality, which inevitably produces political inequality. Liberal democracy depends for its legitimacy on popular participation, but it depends for its stability on controlling and channeling that participation. Liberal democracy may in fact achieve stability without enhancing equality and participation, but to the extent that it fails to do so, it will continue to embody these contradictions. This set of issues is addressed in Chapter 7, where a strategy for achieving a more profound democracy is laid out. In addition to reforms of liberal democracy at the level of national regimes, I emphasize political decentralization and civil society, democratization of the economy, and international cooperation to achieve increased political regulation of the global economy.

NOTES

1. This book deals with the conventional political region of Latin America, that is, the independent countries that were formerly colonies of Spain or Portugal, plus Haiti.

2. Przeworski (1991) has analyzed the logic of this process in great detail.

3. Note that these international influences result from actions of other governments, but they function as structures within the society at hand. The actions of X thus constitute structures for Y.

4. A change of political regime will not necessarily have affected lower-level structures controlling everyday life or even local political institutions, unless a popular uprising has taken place. Thus the majority of the population may be relatively unaffected by a regime change.

5. See Higley and Burton (1989); Higley and Gunther (1992); and Peeler (1985).

6. There are some major exceptions to this, perhaps most notably Third Republic France (1875–1940) and Chile (1932–1973), which both persisted for a long time without either settlement or convergence.

Introduction: Basic
Issues of Democratic Theory

The purpose of this Introduction is to set the context for the study of democracy in Latin America by acquainting the reader with some of the seminal thinkers and fundamental issues in the study of democracy. We begin with the ancient Greeks and pass swiftly through some of the high points in the history of Western political thought.[1] Considerable attention is devoted to major controversies of the twentieth century, including the issue raised by our exclusive focus on Western thought: is democracy appropriate only within the sphere of Western civilization, or is it in some measure a universally valid aspiration? In Chapter 1, we specifically address the question of whether democracy is culturally alien to Latin America.

The classic arguments about democracy usually turn in one way or another on whether to accord primacy to the achievement of genuine popular sovereignty, as the word itself implies, or to emphasize limiting the authority of the government and protecting the rights and liberties of citizens. The two emphases are not in conflict if the government in question is not under popular control (e.g., an absolute monarchy), but by the late eighteenth and early nineteenth centuries liberals were as worried about popular abuses as monarchical abuses. As liberalism increasingly assumed a democratic guise during the nineteenth century, critics pointed out that the liberal version of democracy fell far short of the democratic ideal of rule by the people. But in practice, what could "rule by the people" mean?

DEMOCRACY IN THE CLASSICAL EXPERIENCE

The modern practice of democracy has developed from a dialectic between the idea of absolute popular rule, with neither limits nor delegation of authority, on one side, and the idea of limited government respectful of popular rights on the other. Both concepts have their roots in ancient Greece. Plato (*Republic and Laws*) and Aristotle (*Politics* and *The Constitution of Athens*) offered typologies of regimes in which democracy was defined as a constitution in which the (poor) mass of the population (the demos) ruled. The ancient Greek concept of "the demos" was distinct from the modern idea of "the people": when the Greeks talked about the rule of the demos, they meant rule by the many over the few, by the poor over the rich.[2] Aristotle and later Plato distinguished democracy from a more desirable, balanced constitution in which neither the poor majority nor the rich minority dominated.

The Athenian democracy, with its restricted demos, was the historic high point of the radical concept of democracy, but the concept of the balanced constitution continued to be influential in subsequent centuries. The Roman Republic was founded on just such a balance between a popular Assembly and an aristocratic Senate, and it sought—unsuccessfully in the end—to constitutionally restrict the concentration of power in any magistrate. Republican Rome was also the cradle of the concept of law as a rational code binding officials as well as subjects. The concept of "natural law" holds that the world is inherently rational, that correct reasoning enables humans to understand this natural rationality, and that they may then shape their own conduct and their own "positive" law accordingly. Imperial Rome, in five centuries, sucked the life from both the Republican constitution and the Roman concept of law, but without formally abolishing either.

The emergence of Christianity within the empire, and its adoption as the official religion after Constantine, radically recast these classical political ideas. Originally, of course, Christianity was a religion of the poor and the oppressed. Christian scriptures convey a positive view of the poor as especially deserving of God's love and of justice on earth. Even when Christianity became the established church of the empire and ceased to be a religion of the downtrodden, a succession of minority currents continued to raise issues of social justice.[3]

The church as a whole, however, evolved into a hierarchical institution closely allied to the secular rulers, which played the principal political role of legitimizing those rulers and the secular order in general. In return, the rulers protected and enriched the church. A central underpinning for this new political role of the church was a very negative view of life on earth, a view that resulted from the context of corruption and political decay of the late Roman Empire. If the world in general is a beastly place, if people in general are corrupt, and if the church must act in that world, then it must know the rules and to some extent follow them.

This negative perspective on this world was exemplified by St. Augustine, whose conception, in *The City of God,* of a corrupt "Earthly City" as a metaphor for life in this world inverted the classical idea of the polis as the highest form of human life. From Augustine's perspective, life on earth was inherently sinful; only salvation through Christ could give access to the virtuous "Heavenly City." This pessimistic view of human nature, so uncharacteristic of the classical Greeks and Romans, has since remained central to the political outlook of the Western world. Because human beings are seen as basically sinful, they—and the institutions they create—are not to be trusted.

THE RULE OF LAW IN THE MIDDLE AGES

After the final destruction of the Western Roman Empire in the seventh century, economic power and political authority were fragmented, while the church retained its unity. Political thought tended to reflect this situation. For the most part, secular rulers could not realistically expect to exercise absolute control over their subjects, whether they were peasants, merchants, or knights. Instead, the feudal system that evolved in Western Europe was a complex network of rights and obligations. Monarchs had a right to obedience for certain purposes, if the ruler also fulfilled her or his duties to the subjects.

Moreover, rulers were held to be subject to the authority of the Pope and the bishops of the church as representatives of God and enforcers of God's law. Thus the medieval conception of kingship was emphatically limited. Royal authority was legitimate only if the monarch met his or her lawful obligations, respected the rights of subjects, and obeyed and protected the church.

The most systematic formulation of this medieval approach to political authority was that of St. Thomas Aquinas (*The Summa Theologica*). Aquinas relied extensively on a long-neglected Aristotle to propose a revaluation of the political: denigrated by Augustine, the secular political order was seen by Aquinas as good. He departed from Aristotle in that he attributed the goodness of the secular political order to God's will. Similarly, Aquinas adopted the idea of natural law, so important to the early Romans, but changed it by equating it with God's will. Aquinas used these and other ideas from classical times to systematize the medieval worldview. He defended the idea of a limited and lawful kingship and even affirmed (as had Aristotle) the right to resist tyranny (i.e., unlawful rule). The church was at the peak of its power in Aquinas's day, and he strongly defended its right to instruct and even control secular rulers. Thus, with Aquinas, the medieval tradition of limited and lawful secular rulers reached its apotheosis under the overall dominance of a unified Roman Catholic Church.[4]

Even as Aquinas was writing, though, cracks were appearing in the monolith that was the church. The church's political standards were, of course, frequently defied even when it was at the peak of its power. But during the Renaissance, the church itself became increasingly corrupt and increasingly party to abuses of its own political principles. The Renaissance popes were secular princes who dominated the politics of a fragmented Italy and played a significant role on the larger stage of western Europe. Like other princes of the era, they tended to seek absolute power and to deal ruthlessly with their internal and external enemies. Machiavelli's famous treatise, *The Prince*, exemplifies the new viewpoint in its emphasis not on natural law, but on principles by which the prince may best safeguard his own interests. The medieval idea of limited and lawful authority was largely left behind. Increasingly, in Mediterranean Europe, obedience to church teachings was no longer taken for granted. People could choose to be practicing Catholics or to be secular. The politically active could choose to support the church's influence (i.e., to be pro-clerical) or to oppose it (i.e., anticlerical).[5]

At about the same time, the church's corruption led, especially in northern Europe, to the irrevocable religious schisms known as the Reformation. In contrast to the secularism of the southern European Renaissance, the driving motive of the Reformation was religious: to purify the church of its corruption and of centuries of doctrine and practice without scriptural foundation, or, failing that, to separate from the church entirely. The Reformation, like the Renaissance, had complex and somewhat inconsistent political effects. The destruction of the Catholic religious monopoly certainly increased the stature of the individual believer who, in most Protestant doctrines, was no longer seen as needing the intercession of priests for access to the grace of God. However, the erosion of the church's ability to constrain secular princes meant that the way was clear for the development of modern state sovereignty and absolute monarchy. Renaissance princes of such countries as England, Sweden, and the Netherlands harnessed the Reformation to serve their interests by breaking their subjection to Rome and establishing official Protestant churches.[6] In Protestant areas, then, without the unified church to enforce it, the old idea of natural law declined in importance and began a long transformation.

In parallel manner, the loyally Catholic monarchs of France, Austria, Spain, and Portugal actually used their new importance to a beleaguered Catholic Church to enhance their own powers at the expense of nobility and bourgeoisie and indeed at the expense of the church itself. Assuming the role of defenders of the Catholic faith, these kings and queens systematically undercut medieval rights and asserted effective control over the appointment of bishops in their realms. Thus, at the very time of the voyages of discovery, medieval traditions of limited government were being submerged in the Iberian mother countries. However, Catholic natural law doctrine never became as marginal in these Catholic bulwarks as it did in Protestant regions.

THE MODERN WORLD ORDER: CAPITALISM AND CONTRACT

These changes in ideas were of course the counterparts of fundamental transformations taking place in European society, polity, and economy. Of all the complex changes that occurred in the early stages of the creation of modern European society, two are most relevant to our concerns, and they are in some tension with one another: first, the emergence of the modern state and with it the modern idea of sovereignty; second, the emergence of capitalism as the dominant mode of economic practice. Instead of a territory and population regulated by a complex of overlapping rights and obligations in which the monarch was as much bound by law and custom as her or his subjects, Renaissance monarchs had increasing success in claiming absolute and exclusive control over territory and population. That is, they successfully claimed to be *sovereign*. Sovereignty entailed the claim of an absolute right to make laws governing the people in a certain territory, and it further entailed the claim to exclude any competing authority from that territory and population. The former claim was the essence of Renaissance absolutism; the latter was the foundation for the modern system of relations among sovereign states.[7]

Unlike the medieval world, with its overarching agreement on natural law and its respect for customary limits on authority, a world of sovereign states was potentially anarchic in that the sovereign ruler of each state was theoretically free to do anything. At the level of relations between states, this dilemma led to the emergence of international law, first systematically formulated by Hugo Grotius. At the level of relations between sovereign and subjects, there was a divergence between those countries where absolutism was not seriously challenged and those where it was. In the former cases (especially France, Spain, Portugal, and Austria) law and political theory tended to base royal authority on divine right, or the supposed will of God that the monarch rule and that subjects submit. However, this argument did not in the end prevail everywhere: especially in England and the Low Countries (Belgium, Luxembourg, and the Netherlands), the combination of traditions of limited government, powerful economic interests opposed to the monarchs, and strong dissenting religious sentiments permitted successful resistance to absolutism.[8]

England and the Low Countries successfully limited absolutism in part because of the second major change just mentioned: the emergence of capitalism. The economy of much of medieval western Europe was based on custom and legal regulation, with the market playing a secondary role. The absolutist monarchs of the Renaissance and early modern periods tended to continue this orientation in the form of mercantilism, or centrally licensed and regulated trade. But in England and the Low Countries, the class of merchants and craftspersons was strong and resistant to state control of their enterprises.

Since the efficacy of both natural law and custom as restraints on royal authority had eroded, some other justification was needed. For increasingly trade- and market-oriented societies, the idea of contract was intuitively sensible. Unlike natural law, contracts are acknowledged to be conventions agreed to and changeable by the parties. Unlike customary rules, contracts are relatively explicit in their terms. In a market setting, contracts are an everyday occurrence. It seemed natural, then, to think of the political order as also governed by contract.

The idea of a social contract was used in the seventeenth century both to justify limits on governmental authority and to justify absolute authority. All contractarian arguments posited an original, pregovernmental "state of nature," in which people existed free of governmental controls but also were exposed to risks of aggression from other people who were also free of governmental controls. The solution—and the origin of all legitimate government—was a social contract among the people to set up a government to protect them. All parties to the contract would agree to give up their "natural right" to take what they needed, in return for being assured that others would do the same.

The critical innovation of all contract thought was that authority was derived, not from divine ordination or natural law or custom, but rather from the—at least implicit—consent of the governed. There were, however, wide differences concerning what this consent was supposed to have authorized. Thomas Hobbes (*Leviathan*) held that the original consent was irrevocable and the authority granted was absolute. In this he sought to support the claims of the English king Charles I to absolute authority, but his support was rejected by most royalists because they did not wish to grant that royal authority could be based on popular consent, even in the remote and metaphorical sense used by Hobbes. His argument was thus, however philosophically elegant, historically a blind alley.

John Locke (*Second Treatise on Government*) in England and Benedict de Spinoza in the Netherlands[9] represented the main channel of social contract thought. Each depicted the hypothetical social contract not as an irrevocable agreement to grant absolute authority to a sovereign but rather as a revocable agreement to set up a limited government to serve the interests of the parties to the contract, by protecting their natural rights. If those holding authority derived from the contract violate its terms—and thus the rights of the parties—the latter may justly remove them.

It must be emphasized that neither Locke nor Spinoza was in practice a radical democrat, in that neither advocated direct rule by the people. Rather, they stood for rule by the representatives of the people, and they placed great emphasis on the obligation of government to protect the property of citizens. Both must thus be understood as defending the interest of the emerging capitalist class in limiting the right of government to interfere with individual liberty—particularly but not exclusively economic liberty. Nevertheless, their principle that legitimate authority derives from the consent of the governed and their rejection of hereditary rank laid the foundation for modern democratic thought. Since Locke, the mainstream of democratic theory has emphasized limited government and individual rights, and although accepting the principle of popular consent, has rejected direct popular rule in favor of representation.

Some predecessors and contemporaries of Locke and Spinoza, in the turbulent contexts of the Reformation, the Dutch struggle for independence from Spain, and the revolutionary struggle in seventeenth-century England, articulated a more radically democratic political vision. The Dutch Anabaptists, or Mennonites, can certainly be included here, as can some Protestant nonconformists in England. The best-known such group would be the English revolutionary group called the Diggers (see Walzer, 1965). Far from being contractarian, the Diggers, like the other religious democrats, reverted to the idea of a divinely ordained order in which all were equal in God's sight and therefore merited equal rights on earth.

The social contract approach also produced a radically democratic theory, that of Jean-Jacques Rousseau (*The Social Contract*; see Barker, 1947). Postulating the conventional state of nature, Rousseau differentiated himself from both Hobbes and Locke. He accepted Hobbes's argument that the insecurities of the state of nature can be corrected only if all parties to the social contract surrender all their natural rights, but he nevertheless held that it would be irrational for anyone in a state of nature to yield all natural rights to a sovereign, since the person would thereby continue to run all the risks of the state of nature relative to the sovereign. This was precisely Locke's key argument against Hobbes. Rousseau therefore agrees with Locke that the social contract must vest sovereignty in the people themselves, rather than in a magistrate set above the people by their consent. However, he holds that any scheme of representation must eviscerate popular sovereignty, which truly exists only at the moment of election of representatives; thereafter, effective sovereignty lies with the representatives, not with the people.

He thus poses himself the problem of how all of the people can be at the same time absolutely sovereign and absolutely subject to sovereignty. In brief, his answer is that this can occur only if all persons constituting the society surrender all their natural rights to a sovereign composed precisely of all persons constituting the society. Thus, each person would simultaneously be absolutely subject to the sovereign and would participate on an equal basis with all others in that absolute sovereignty. Rousseau's second and crucial stipulation is that all citizens participating in sovereign decisionmaking must have regard only for the common good, not for their own private interests. This is essential because once private interests shape choices, some citizens will prevail over others. This line of argument is summarized in Rousseau's concept of the general will, which amounts to that which all the people would will if they each thought only of the common interest. Rousseau has thereby created an abstract model of the conditions for true democracy, a model far more systematic and rigorous than anything previously seen.

Of course, Rousseau is also sensitive to the criticism that his model has no connection with reality. Much of the treatise is taken up with what is to be done in the event that citizens fail to put aside their private interests. The first contingency is honest disagreement among the truly public-spirited about what the general will requires; in this case, based on the premise of the equality of citizens, the minority will accept that they were in error and support the majority. The next contingency occurs when a minority (or even one person) does not accept the general will as articulated by a public-spirited majority. Here, the obdurate minority has put its private perspectives and interests above the general interest and may be overruled by the majority. But it is also conceivable that the majority of citizens would be so corrupted that they would act on their private interests rather than the interests of all, thus establishing a majority tyranny. In this instance, it is legitimate for a minority who understand the general will to impose that will on the ignorant majority. Following this logic to its conclusion, Rousseau comes to the final contingency, in which all citizens are ignorant of the general will and act tyrannically in pursuit of their particular interests. There is no answer within the terms of his argument; he is forced to fall back on the classical tradition of the quasi-divine legislator, not part of the community, who imposes the general will on an ignorant and corrupt society. Thus far has he brought us from his model of a perfect democracy. One might consider his argument a reductio ad absurdum for radical democracy.

Social contract thought thus produced a diversity of approaches. Hobbes and Rousseau were absolutists, the former in defense of an absolutely sovereign monarch separate from the people, the latter defending—at least in the abstract—an absolutely sovereign people. Spinoza and Locke (followed by the founders of the United States, notably Thomas Jefferson and James Madison) saw the social contract as, in effect, a constitution limiting and controlling governmental authority and protecting individual rights. The latter stream has been more influential, shaping the modern concept of democracy as necessarily constitutional and respectful of individual rights. The thrust against unlimited popular sovereignty was only implicit in Locke, since he was primarily concerned with guarding against monarchical tyranny, but became explicit among the political leadership of the nascent United States. Madison, for example, in *The Federalist Papers,* No. 10, defended the checks and balances of the new constitution as structurally retarding majority tyranny.[10]

The obviously artificial convention of the social contract was increasingly abandoned in the course of the eighteenth century. What replaced it was an acceptance that political organization was neither divinely ordained nor contractual but rather conventional, evolving gradually within a particular historical context.[11] The argument for limited government and individual rights was cast less in terms of contractarian rights and more in terms of prudence. Thus, Adam Smith's famous defense of laissez-faire economic policy (*An Inquiry into the Nature and Causes of the Wealth of Nations*) held simply that all of society would be better off if government refrained from controlling the economic decisions of individuals pursuing their own individual self-interests. In political discourse, the shift to prudential argument was slower, perhaps because the notion of inalienable natural rights was too useful to give up.[12] Earlier in the eighteenth century, Montesquieu (*The Spirit of the Laws*) studied the checks and balances of the English constitution without relying on the device of the contract, and David Hume systematically refuted contractarianism (Barker, 1947). By the 1790s, Jeremy Bentham (1988) and James Mill (1992) had developed the ideas of utilitarianism, which sought to evaluate good and bad in terms of whether a thing caused pleasure or pain, or more broadly, whether it was useful. The utilitarian calculus could be applied at the level of the individual or aggregated to the societal level, where the public interest was defined as "the greatest happiness of the greatest number."[13]

Many of these postcontractarians shared a paradoxical assumption that has become central to modern democratic theory: that human individuals, left alone to pursue their own interests, will serve not only themselves but the public interest better than if the best-intentioned government tried to control them. Prefigured by Hume, the archetype of the argument was provided by Adam Smith; it was echoed by the utilitarians and by Jefferson and Madison.

By the middle of the nineteenth century, the doctrine even had a name, "liberalism," and it received its fullest articulation in the work of John Stuart Mill.[14] Mill's classic, *On Liberty,* defended the proposition that the suppression of free speech was never justifiable because all society would benefit from the free exchange of ideas through which we progress toward truth.[15] Even in the hypothetical extreme case in which the whole truth were known, Mill argued that dissenting views should not be suppressed because the very need to defend truthful ideas would sharpen the faculties of those who hold them and thus help them achieve more of their potential as human beings.

Mill wrote in a context of the wrenching social, economic, and political change associated with the peak of the Industrial Revolution in England. Economic and political liberalism served the broad interests of the emerging industrialists. Both internally and internationally, English industrialists of the early nineteenth century were in a comparatively advantageous position to compete with craftspeople at home and abroad and thus generally advocated a reduction of government economic regulation. These same industrialists were often men of modest origins who lacked the franchise under the old patchwork of electoral laws of England. Thus their interest was served by the defense of the right of dissent, or freedom of speech. And initially, their interest was served by broadening and rationalizing the franchise, at least so as to include themselves. But democracy was no part of their intention. Liberalism evolved from its inception as a doctrine of limited government. Its rejection of hereditary privilege led it inexorably toward liberalization of the franchise, but that tendency made limited government all the more necessary, now as a hedge against majority tyranny as well as the more traditional monarchical tyranny that had preoccupied Locke. Alexis de Tocqueville's book *Democracy in America* exemplifies this deep liberal preoccupation with majority tyranny.[16]

John Stuart Mill confronted this preoccupation head-on in two of his later essays and in the process helped eliminate the last ideological barriers to democratization of the franchise. In *Representative Government* he extended the argument of *On Liberty,* holding that society would benefit by expanding the franchise because a broader range of ideas would be heard and that individuals would benefit as the exercise of citizenship developed their human capacities. In answer to the argument that workers were incapable of the responsible judgment required of voters, he answered that the very exercise of citizenship was what was necessary to develop that capacity. In *The Subjection of Women,* he applied the same argument to the question of women's suffrage, thereby becoming one of the first prominent male advocates of women's suffrage.

However, even though Mill provided an important philosophical underpinning for a democratized franchise, he still remained an advocate of limited government and of safeguards against majority tyranny. Thus in *Representative Government* he advocated giving the educated plural votes, as a means of balancing the weight of the ignorant majority while the latter are developing their citizenship capacities. As exemplified by Mill, liberalism by the late nineteenth century was increasingly committed to a democratic franchise but also to a continuation of the characteristically liberal restrictions on government power that would now serve to limit the power of the majority to truly rule. Even though the franchise would not approach universality until the 1920s and 1930s, the form of twentieth-century democracy was evident by the 1880s in Britain, the United States, and a few smaller countries: a liberal polity, democratically legitimated.[17] Democracy as we know it in the twentieth century involves the limitation of government authority and the protection of rights, a fundamentally liberal orientation. Mechanisms of democratic consent centered on elections serve to legitimate the right of these liberal regimes to rule, but as Rousseau pointed out, the people are meaningfully sovereign only on election day.

The chief nineteenth-century dissenter against this emerging liberal political economy was Karl Marx.[18] His basic concern, of course, was the critique of the capitalist mode of production and not an analysis of democratic theory per se. But Marx saw the emerging theory and practice of democratic politics in his day as intimately related to—in the last analysis, determined by—the structure of power in the economy (i.e., control of the means of production by a capitalist ruling class in all the advanced, industrializing countries of Europe and North America). Thus, the basic determining reality of modern society was its capitalist economy. Other aspects of society, such as schooling, religion, and politics, would tend to serve the interests of the capitalist economy and the capitalist class who controlled it. This is not to say that all dissenting ideas and heterodox practices would be suppressed (obviously, Marx's were not) but rather that they would lack material support, be portrayed as irrational or inconsistent with (capitalist) reality, and only in extreme cases be directly repressed.

Capitalism, in Marx's view, produced liberalism as its central theory of economics and politics. With its emphasis on individualism, on free competition and discourse within a broad legal order, and on limited state authority, liberalism was well suited to the legitimation of capitalist practice. In the political realm, the principle of equality of citizens was combined with a limited state and toleration of economic inequality to produce a political system in which the majority of citizens could be coopted into supporting an order in which capitalists remained dominant. Limitation of state authority would deprive a potentially hostile majority of a key instrument to regulate and control capitalism. In any case, Marx believed that the state was little more than "the form in which the individuals of a ruling class assert their common interests,"[19] having some autonomy relative to individual capitalists but serving the overall interests of capitalism. For example, key state functions would include enforcing capitalist property laws, guaranteeing the sanctity of contracts, and repressing working-class resistance.

In short, Marx believed that the democratic theory and practice emerging in his lifetime were mere illusions serving the interests of the capitalist ruling classes. As long as capitalism continued as the dominant mode of production, it could not be otherwise. Of course, Marx expected that capitalism would be driven by its own internal contradictions toward a final revolutionary confrontation in which the working class would finally seize control of economy and polity and impose (through a "dictatorship of the proletariat") a classless, communist society. Such a society would be without the internal contradiction between ruling class and exploited class; it would indeed be classless. Building on the immense productive capacity developed by capitalism, communism could establish a society of perfectly distributed plenty. The coercive function of the state as agent of the ruling class would be eliminated, and the state as such would, in Friedrich Engels's phrase, "die out."[20] The new society would presumably still have a politics concerned with decisions about collective action but would no longer need a state with coercive power to enforce class exploitation.

This vision, albeit not very thoroughly developed, contradicts the liberal approach to democracy on several points. First, Marx flatly denies that democracy can coexist at all with the inequality and exploitation essential to capitalism. For him, to apply the term to the elected, constitutional regimes emerging in his time was worse than a misnomer; it was a mystification. Second, like Rousseau, Marx rejects the notion that a true democracy could be characterized by limited authority. In the transitional stage of the dictatorship of the proletariat, that class (presumed to represent the overwhelming majority of the population at the time of the revolution) would simply impose its will on the defeated capitalists. In the projected classless, communist society, there would be no state whose authority must be limited and no reason to limit the scope of the (noncoercive) collective choices the people make.

Third, again like Rousseau, Marx makes a clear distinction between the "true," or "objective," interests of people and what they may believe their interests to be. Marx obviously knew that many—even most—proletarians of his day were not revolutionaries. They tended to accept to some degree the ideas and institutions of capitalism, including those of liberal democracy. This fact did not, for Marx, invalidate his thesis, since he expected that the historical development of capitalism would exacerbate its internal contradictions, leading the workers increasingly to see the need for proletarian revolution and the validity of a radically egalitarian vision of democracy in communist society. In contrast, political liberalism from Locke onward takes citizen beliefs as given and in principle vests ultimate sovereignty in the collective expression of those beliefs (i.e., in elections).

All his life, Marx struggled to bring about the revolutionary conditions that he thought were inherent in the capitalist system. Toward the end of his life, he and his followers had increasingly to confront serious anomalies. Capitalists and associated states proved far more intelligent and adaptable than he had earlier expected, continually ameliorating the worst contradictions of capitalism and coopting the workers with concessions such as social services and expansion of the franchise. Correspondingly, the workers were not becoming more revolutionary. Thus, although the fundamental critique of capitalist political economy might continue to be valid, the specific historical expectations were increasingly cast into question. Marx, Engels, and the next generations of Marxists sought to deal with these problems. Marx, for example, came to accept the possibility that the working class might actually come to state power by electoral means in special cases such as Britain.[21]

The points to be explained break down into two categories: (1) Why hasn't the working class become revolutionary? and (2) What is to be done about that? On the first question, the key contribution is probably that of Antonio Gramsci (1971), who argued that capitalists had largely avoided the threat of revolution by establishing an ideological hegemony over the working class, such that workers come to accept and enact the fundamental values of capitalism and are thereby inoculated against revolutionary ideas. This is clearly an elaboration of Marx's ideas, but Marx had expected the hegemony to break down more easily than had in fact been the case.

"What Is to Be Done?" was of course the title of one of Lenin's most important writings, addressing precisely the question of how to proceed with a revolutionary agenda in the face of a nonrevolutionary proletariat. Lenin argued for, and succeeded in establishing, a "vanguard party" consisting of a small cadre that understood the true interests of the proletariat and would take the leadership of the revolutionary struggle. The revolutionary struggle, in short, would not wait upon the emergence of a revolutionary consciousness among the mass of workers. Rather, the party would undertake to shape that consciousness in the course of its struggle for revolution. Under the harsh, authoritarian conditions of imperial Russia, moreover, the party had to be not only small but secretive. It was operationally decentralized into local cells to frustrate police penetration but was nevertheless highly centralized in terms of doctrine and policy. Thus, Lenin's vanguard party, ruled by principles of "democratic centralism," became one major Marxist response to the conditions of twentieth-century capitalism. This approach conceded nothing to liberal conceptions of democracy; rather, democracy was to be found through adherence to the true or ultimate interest of the proletariat, to be realized in the fullness of time.[22]

The principal Marxist alternative to Lenin's approach was articulated by the German revisionist social democrat Eduard Bernstein (1961). His argument, based principally on German circumstances, was that conditions in the late nineteenth century were so fundamentally different from what Marx had expected that an explicit revision of Marxist thinking was necessary. Specifically, he held that the emergence of modern liberal democracy and the welfare state rendered revolution both unnecessary and unlikely in advanced industrial society. Rather, socialists should devote their efforts to building a mass working-class base organized into labor unions and social democratic political parties, with the objectives of exerting political pressure for the humanization of capitalism in the short run, and in the long run gaining political power through electoral means and with it the capacity to bring about a peaceful transition to socialism.

Marx's radical critique of capitalism (and, incidentally, of liberal democracy) thus led, on one extreme, to the antiliberal democratic centralism of Lenin (and ultimately to Stalinism) and, on the other, to the fundamental acceptance of liberal premises embodied in Bernstein's revisionism. Many other currents of Marxist thought existed between these extremes, such as Gramsci. The problem for Marxists concerned with democracy has continued to be how to move toward Marx's vision of a true democracy while avoiding the contradictions of both liberalism and Stalinism.

THE MODERN DEMOCRATIC REPUBLIC

The advent of the twentieth century roughly coincided with the emergence in western Europe of political sociology as a distinct academic field, and in the United States we find the somewhat parallel evolution of political science. In each case, the development signified a heightened commitment to the accumulation of "scientific" knowledge about politics. Scholars on both continents tended to emphasize objective observation and theory building while making less explicit reference to questions of value. In Europe, in place of the old liberal faith in progress, we find newly skeptical analyses of the equivocal consequences of modernization[23] and several studies emphasizing the fundamentally elitist character of political parties and other institutions, even in ostensibly democratic settings.[24] A similar spirit was evident in the United States when Woodrow Wilson showed how the practice of government in the late nineteenth century corresponded only imperfectly with constitutional norms, or when Thorstein Veblen called attention to the existence of a powerful and prosperous upper class in a supposedly egalitarian society.[25]

In terms of the issue of democracy, the culmination of this pre–World War II trend in political studies was the wide-ranging *Capitalism, Socialism and Democracy* by Joseph Schumpeter. In the context of a careful and jaundiced review of the prospects of both capitalism and socialism and their relationship to democracy, Schumpeter proposed a simple operational definition of democracy as a system in which the rulers are chosen by the people in periodic, competitive elections. He thereby hoped to obviate what he saw as useless philosophical speculation about the meaning of true democracy, choosing instead to define democracy as, in effect, that political system used by countries conventionally called democracies. This empirical and conventional approach would dominate postwar political science, particularly in the United States.

The wartime experience of fighting Germany, Italy, and Japan and the subsequent Cold War against the Soviet Union and international communism had the effect of focusing the attention of political scientists, in the United States and its allies, on democracy as an issue, as distinct from authoritarian and "totalitarian" regimes. This last category (exclusively exemplified by Nazi Germany, the Soviet Union, and other postwar communist countries) was said to be characterized by extreme concentration of power and the exertion of nearly complete control over almost the totality of life. Totalitarian regimes were thus held to be analytically distinct from authoritarian regimes, which exhibited less concentrated power and less complete control. In contrast, democratic regimes were seen as having relatively dispersed power and a relatively narrower scope of political control. Thus, under the pressure of military and political struggle, the liberal, limited-government approach to democracy that was already well institutionalized at the turn of the century was given new life, but the alternative radical vision was discredited by being linked to Nazism and communism.[26] The earlier arguments of Veblen, Robert Michels, Gaetano Mosca, and others, that power in democracies was less dispersed than it appeared, were problematic to the new paradigm and thus tended to be treated as merely quaint dissenting voices.[27]

The new democratic theory and related empirical studies displayed several general characteristics. First, they were preoccupied with stability as a goal and were thus essentially conservative. David Easton (1953, 1965) produced a pathbreaking adaptation of systems analysis to the study of politics, in which a stable system was taken as the norm. Gabriel Almond's use of structural-functional analysis (Almond and Powell, 1966) similarly assumed stability as a goal and treated political instability in the developing countries as pathological. Maurice Duverger's study of political parties and party systems (1962) is notable for its argument that two-party systems are preferable to multiparty systems because they better promote political stability.

A second general characteristic of studies of democracy of this period was that they emphasized "pluralism," or the relative dispersion of political power and participation in decisionmaking. David Truman (1951), following the earlier work of Alfred Bentley, developed a theory of politics as the interaction of organized interests, wherein the government's role was to provide the arena for the interaction and to register the outcome of power struggles among groups. Robert Dahl produced the concept of "polyarchy" to signify a political system in which participation was relatively high and power relatively dispersed among competing organized interests. He intended polyarchy to be roughly synonymous with the contemporary practice of democracy and to distinguish this practice from ideal democracy, which he held to be virtually unattainable.[28]

The pluralist model of democracy was essentially liberal in its emphasis on limited government and political competition. However, its preoccupation with stability gave its liberalism a conservative tone, a tone intensified by the pluralists' relative inattention to how economic and social inequalities might vitiate or eliminate the benefits of political equality. Various scholars emphasized these points in taking issue with the pluralist mainstream of the discipline. C. Wright Mills (1956) developed the thesis of "the Power Elite," a set of individuals who collectively held the reins of institutional power in government, the defense establishment, and private enterprise, thereby directly challenging the central proposition of pluralism, the broad dispersion of political power. Peter Bachrach (1967) criticized Dahl and other pluralists for their insensitivity to the effects of social and economic inequality on political power. Dahl himself, after about 1970, increasingly recognized the validity of some of these criticisms and devoted much of his attention to how polyarchy could become more democratic, how the premises of equality and popular rule could be brought closer to reality. Among his key proposals was a substantial decentralization, not only of political power but especially of economic power.[29]

RENOVATING DEMOCRACY

Dahl thereby joined an extensive movement beginning in the late 1960s to think anew about democracy, to take seriously the goals of genuine equality and effective participation. The backdrop to this new theoretical direction included developments in the pluralist democracies and around the world. The 1960s saw the emergence of new movements in the United States and in Europe that posed radical challenges to the status quo. In the United States, the civil rights movement evolved toward a more militant black nationalism, and the Vietnam War provided an initial focus for an increasingly sweeping critique of American society by the New Left. The New Left had its counterparts in all the major countries of Western Europe. The thrust of these new critical movements was to question the authenticity of democracy in the context of social and economic inequality and exploitation, to question the premises of the Cold War and its emphasis on national security, and to demand fundamental democratization in the distribution of power and the practice of politics.[30]

Even as the New Left and black nationalism were on the march in the industrial democracies, marxist revolutionary movements were posing parallel challenges to regimes in Latin America, southeast Asia, and elsewhere, calling into question the capitalist world order on whose exploited periphery they found themselves. The movement against the Vietnam War in the United States and other industrial democracies increasingly assumed an anti-imperialist character that meshed with these challenges being posed from the periphery. From the standpoint of democratic theory, the key issue was how democratic a country could be if its government was the sponsor of oppressive regimes that repressed popular revolutionary movements.[31]

In this worldwide political context, an extended conversation about the renovation of democracy began in the 1960s and continued through the 1980s and into the 1990s. Out of a large and diverse literature, four outstanding examples will be cited here.[32] In the 1960s, C. B. Macpherson (1973, 1977) began a long-term project of retrieving core democratic values from a moribund liberalism. Arguing that liberalism as a political-economic doctrine had its roots in the "possessive individualism" of Hobbes and Locke and that even the humanistic, developmentally oriented liberalism of John Stuart Mill failed to resolve the fundamental tension between that possessive individualism and the ideal of democracy, Macpherson developed a model of "participatory democracy" that would actively encourage widespread participation in political decisionmaking for the principal purpose of fully developing the human capabilities of the citizens. His project was premised on "a view of man's essence not as a consumer of utilities but as a doer, a creator, an enjoyer of his human attributes."[33] He believed that a high level of participation was both necessary to and a consequence of a major reduction in the level of inequality in society. He did not believe that revolution was very likely in advanced industrial societies and thus thought that changes in both participation levels and inequality would have to come gradually, by effective use of points of weakness in the system.

Benjamin Barber (1984) developed a similar argument. Barber held that at a deep philosophical level, liberalism is hostile to democracy and that liberal democracy is consequently "thin democracy," dependent on limited participation and the exercise of control. He advocated "strong democracy," or "politics in the participatory mode where conflict is resolved in the absence of an independent ground through a participatory process of ongoing, proximate self-legislation and the creation of a political community capable of transforming dependent, private individuals into free citizens and partial and private interests into public goods."[34] Barber and Macpherson differed in some important respects. Barber was more cautious than Macpherson about the implications of capitalism for strong democracy, though he did call attention to ways in which modern monopoly capitalism may jeopardize strong democracy (p. 253). Most importantly, whereas Macpherson's developmental justification for participatory democracy contained at least the implication of a teleology, Barber sought to develop a model "without independent ground," that is, without presuppositions of what truly free and participatory citizens would decide (p. 129). Thus two renovators of liberalism came out on opposite sides of an old controversy: should the beliefs and perceived interests of citizens be taken as given, or is there a standard by which it may be decided whether they are fully in possession of their human faculties and hence deserving of full citizenship?

Carol Gould (1988) made an argument for a comprehensive expansion of the scope of democracy. Holding that democracy is justified as the institutional form of decisionmaking that best provides equal rights to the conditions of self-development, she argued that the fullest possible participation should be extended in social and economic realms as well as in the political. By emphasizing the right to the conditions of self-development as the principal justification for democracy, Gould aligned herself with Macpherson's focus on the development of individual powers.

Further, in a treatment of "Democratic Personality" (chap. 11), she argued that two personality traits lend themselves to democracy: democratic agency and the disposition to reciprocity. By democratic agency, she meant a disposition to initiate joint action with others to some rational purpose determined by an understanding of common interests. Democratic agency is distinguished from passivity, or an absence of initiative. The disposition to reciprocity is an ability to understand another's perspective as equivalent to one's own—an expectation that the other will have the same ability and that actions with respect to one another will therefore be reciprocal. There is, in short, "a shared understanding by the participants that their actions are reciprocal" (p. 290). By arguing that these personality traits lend themselves to democracy and that democracy itself is principally justified by its ability to afford equal rights to the conditions of self-development, Gould implicitly affirmed these traits as both means to, and ends of, democracy. In short, personalities congruent with mutual reinforcement will be best served by democracy.

Macpherson, Barber, and Gould each criticized contemporary liberal democracy for its failure to provide for true equality of participatory opportunities. For each, the economic inequality associated with capitalism was central to the problem. Thus the contradictions between the twin progeny of liberalism, capitalism and democracy, have reached a crisis.

There are, moreover, other inequalities in modern societies that also obstruct the possibility of full democracy. Ann Ferguson (1991) explored, with particular reference to the United States, a feminist-socialist perspective on democracy. In addition to advocating "a feasible democratic socialism," Ferguson argued for six feminist values that would make for a *feminist* democratic socialism: (1) eliminating gender dualism; (2) setting up a nonracist and nonethnicist society; (3) maximizing democratic parenting; (4) promoting sex for pleasure; (5) promoting committed sexual relationships; and (6) guaranteeing gay and lesbian rights (pp. 220–221). Ferguson's perspective reminds us that there is more to achieving full democracy than ending capitalism.

REVALUING DEMOCRACY

During much of the 1970s and 1980s, while Macpherson, Barber, Gould, and Ferguson were criticizing existing liberal democracy and calling for its renovation and full democratization, scholars and political leaders of the Latin American Left tended likewise to evaluate democracy negatively for the Latin American context. Emphasizing the meaninglessness of participation in the absence of real choice and the political implications of extreme economic inequalities, many critics judged liberal democracy to be fraudulent and called for socialist revolution as a prerequisite to the establishment of true democracy.[35]

Also in the 1970s, most countries of Latin America (excepting only Venezuela, Costa Rica, and Colombia)[36] saw the establishment of military dictatorships, often overthrowing precarious elected governments. These military regimes were accepted and even encouraged by most U.S. administrations of the period (excepting only Carter—ambivalently) as serving U.S. national security interests by repressing potential communist insurgencies (Schoultz, 1981, 1987). This policy received its most explicit public articulation in a polemical article by Jeane Kirkpatrick (1982), which criticized Carter's preoccupation with human rights and argued that it was justifiable for the United States to support authoritarian regimes in the struggle against communist totalitarianism because the former could be democratized from within, whereas the latter could not.

However, by the mid-1980s widespread and severe economic crisis (associated with the massive growth of international debt in Latin America and the rest of the Third World) had combined with growing popular resistance to repression to bring an end to almost all military regimes across the continent. The opposition to military regimes in many Latin American countries focused attention on the task of restoring democracy and in the process built new ties of cooperation between previously antagonistic groups.[37] The driving conviction of this shift was that, whatever its shortcomings, liberal democracy could serve to protect human rights and provide a civil arena for political debate. In light of the success of the military regimes in repressing both violent and nonviolent opposition, those on the left increasingly forswore violence and pressed for democratization.

Impelled by, and to some extent impelling these developments, the Reagan administration shifted its policy to open support for transitions to democracy, putting pressure on its principal clients in Latin America—military officers and economic elites—to facilitate transitions to democracy. This shift in Reagan's policy was furthered in the late 1980s by the rapid changes in Soviet society and foreign policy implemented by Mikhail Gorbachev after 1985, culminating in the end of Soviet hegemony in eastern Europe and the end of the Cold War itself. A U.S. foreign policy premised on anticommunism was no longer relevant. Moreover, the effective end of Soviet competition with the United States in the Third World meant that the latter held most key economic cards (e.g., effective control over the World Bank and the International Monetary Fund [IMF]). Even Cuba, closely allied with the Soviet Union, found its Soviet subsidies steadily diminishing. With such economic leverage, the United States was able to promote democratization with some confidence that the resultant governments would not pursue economic policies inimical to U.S. interests.[38] Repeatedly during the 1980s, Latin American presidents elected on populist platforms abruptly reversed themselves and implemented orthodox neoliberal austerity policies in order to get help from the IMF with their economic problems.[39]

Thus, by the late 1980s, both the Latin American Left and the North American Right found themselves supporting democracy in Latin America, albeit for contradictory reasons and with conflicting objectives. These contradictions and conflicts would continue to drive developments during the 1990s.

DEMOCRATIC DYNAMICS: UNDERSTANDING REGIME CHANGE

Most of the theories discussed in this chapter deal with the question of what true democracy is. As one might expect of a body of theory emerging from stable liberal democracies, little attention has been paid to questions of political change: What conditions bring about change? How does change take place? With regard specifically to democracy, key issues of change obviously deal with the rise and fall of democratic regimes. It is also important to attend to the question of change within a democratic regime.

To the extent that North Atlantic political theory has dealt with these issues, it has tended to make a structural argument; that is, change will occur in a political regime only when, and to the extent that, overarching social, economic, and political conditions permit or encourage it. Marx's theory of proletarian revolution as a product of objective economic conditions was the archetype of this sort of argument, and Barrington Moore's classic book *The Social Origins of Dictatorship and Democracy* also adopted this strategy.[40] Nonmarxist political sociologists have usually pursued a similar but more static approach. For example, Seymour Martin Lipset was the first of many scholars to analyze aggregate social and economic data to find a pattern of correlations between overall levels of "economic development" or "modernization" and the presence of democratic political regimes.[41] The attempt on the part of the United States to understand and counter revolutionary insurgencies produced a spate of studies emphasizing the economic, social, and even psychological conditions for the emergence and survival of guerrilla movements.[42] Recently, David Easton (1990) attempted an analysis of "higher-order structures," or those relatively unchanging political patterns that condition and constrain political action and even other structures. However, the attempt is plagued by conceptual and logical problems and, though suggestive, remains inconclusive.

Mainstream North Atlantic social science has tended to view regime change as a problem best avoided. A variety of major studies in the 1960s treated political stability as a central goal of policy,[43] and Samuel Huntington's classic and highly influential work *Political Order in Changing Societies* (1968) argued that modernization and economic development would tend to lead to political instability, and that that was a serious problem. Gabriel Almond, Scott Flanagan, and Robert Mundt (1973) edited a volume that paid explicit attention to political crises, which they defined as periods when normal structural constraints on choice are weakened, permitting wider than usual political choice for elites and hence greater possibilities for change. But in paying attention to change, Almond and his collaborators nevertheless saw stability as the norm, only punctuated by crises, periods of significant change.

The most specific and substantial attention paid to the problem of change in general and of the rise and fall of democratic regimes in particular has come from students of the Third World in general and from Latin Americans and students of Latin America in particular. This should not surprise us, since political instability and change are far more characteristic of the region than stability. In the late 1970s and early 1980s, reflecting the resurgence of authoritarian regimes in the region, there was much preoccupation with the fall of democracies; this focus was exemplified in an influential multivolume collaborative work entitled *The Breakdown of Democratic Regimes*.[44] During the early 1980s, only three Latin American countries—Venezuela, Costa Rica, and, by some criteria, Colombia—remained liberal democracies. These cases were compared by Peeler (1985, 1992). However, even as the former book was being published, events in Latin America were transforming the political landscape, as country after country made the transition from authoritarian to democratic governance. Several large collaborative studies sought to focus attention on transitions to democracy and on the phenomenon of democracy in developing countries.[45]

Unlike previous structurally oriented analyses, the books discussed in the previous paragraph, although not denying the importance of structures in constraining behavior, emphasized the importance of political action, choice, and indeterminacy. The importance of elites was stressed in both regime breakdowns and in successful transitions. John Higley and Michael Burton (1989) developed the concept of the "elite settlement" as one of the principal means by which new democratic (or other) regimes could be established and stabilized. Higley and Richard Gunther later edited a comparative volume (1992) on this subject.

Karen Remmer, among others, criticized this emphasis on autonomous political action as a theoretical abdication, a failure to think rigorously about the causes of political behavior.[46] An important aspect of this structuralist perspective is a renewed emphasis on institution building, including the issue of parliamentary versus presidential constitutional structure.[47]

CONCLUSION

In this Introduction I sought to provide the uninitiated reader with a brief survey and guide to the major theoretical issues in the study of democracy. A mode of governance that is clearly rooted in Western liberalism, liberal democracy nevertheless makes universal claims to its validity as a principle of political legitimacy and as a procedure or structure for public choice. The legitimacy principle of popular consent has historically been contested by alternative principles, but in the twentieth century all such alternatives have faded away. However, liberal democracy has also been contested by those who accept the legitimacy of its principles but who see shortcomings in its implementation of those principles. As we look into the next century, though, it appears that no coherent, practical alternative to liberal democracy is on the horizon; what we can expect are a variety of continuing attempts to preserve it against relapses of authoritarianism and to renovate and improve it. Latin America will surely be one of the principal arenas of these struggles.

NOTES

1. This chapter will focus on the European, or Western, political tradition, with its roots in classical Greece and Rome. This is not to deny that other cultural regions have also produced ideas consistent with democracy. For example, consider the egalitarianism of classical Islam or Buddhism or the emphasis on decision by consultation and consensus in many African societies. Still, democracy as we have come to know it in the twentieth century is unequivocally linked to European roots.

2. Of course, women, slaves, and foreigners were entirely excluded from consideration. See Finley (1980, 1983, 1985).

3. See, for example, Hengel (1974); Gager (1975).

4. Aquinas benefited from the scholarship of the Muslim world, which had saved many classic texts, such as Plato and Aristotle, and had translated them into Arabic. After the fall of the Roman Empire, these same texts had been unknown in Western Europe. Aquinas had access to translations of Aristotle from Arabic into Latin, and Aristotle had a major influence on his political argument.

5. Cf. Kristeller (1961).

6. Cf. Tonkin (1971).

7. See, for example, Miller (1990).

8. See Hill (1965, 1972, 1980); Walzer (1965).

9. Spinoza (1951). For Locke, Hume, and Rousseau on social contract, see Barker (1947).

10. See also Jefferson (1974); Pole (1987).

11. If U.S. leaders still used contractarian thought, it was because they were precisely faced with a situation that required overthrowing tyrannical rule and agreeing on a new political order. A generation later, the same situation would confront the leadership of Spanish America.

12. Note Jefferson's use of the contract concept in the Declaration of Independence and Thomas Paine's use of it in both *Common Sense* and *The Rights of Man*. Cf. Mary Wollstonecraft's counterpoint in *A Vindication of the Rights of Woman*.

13. See also Goodin (1995).

14. John Stuart Mill (1975, 1994).

15. Cf. Adam Smith (1952). It is no accident that a key liberal slogan has advocated a "free market of ideas."

16. See also Tocqueville (1980).

17. This formulation is elaborated in Peeler (1985), chap. 1.

18. The best short collection of Marx's voluminous writings is Tucker (1978).

19. Marx, "The German Ideology," in Tucker (1978), p. 187.

20. Engels, "Socialism: Utopian and Scientific," in Tucker (1978), p. 713.

21. Marx, "The Possibility of Non-Violent Revolution," in Tucker (1978), pp. 522–524.

22. However, Gramsci believed that, in a liberal democracy, the vanguard party could potentially operate within the law to develop a counterhegemony that would lay the groundwork for a peaceful takeover of the state through elections.

23. Durkheim (1986); Tönnies (1971); Weber (1983).

24. Michels (1949); Pareto (1984); Mosca (1939); Ostrogorski (1974).

25. Wilson (1885); Veblen (1934).

26. See Friedrich and Brzezinski (1965); Arendt (1951); Kirkpatrick (1982, 1990).

27. Thus, among scholars of American politics, Floyd Hunter (1953) and C. Wright Mills (1956) were widely criticized for an alleged overemphasis on elite control in the United States.

28. Dahl (1956, 1961, 1971).

29. Dahl (1970, 1982, 1985, 1989).

30. Anderson (1995); Bracey, Meier, and Rudwick (1970).

31. Walton (1984); Small and Hoover (1992).

32. Also consult these recent works: Cohen and Arato (1992); Pangle (1992); Putnam (1993); Holmes (1995); Etzioni (1995); Beiner (1995); Van Parijs (1995).

33. Macpherson (1973), p. 4.

34. Barber (1984), p. 132.

35. For example, see Silva Michelena (1971).

36. See Peeler (1985, 1992).

37. Stallings and Kaufman (1989); O'Donnell, Schmitter, and Whitehead (1986); Munck (1989).

38. Hartlyn, Schoultz, and Varas (1992); Pastor (1989).

39. For example, Carlos Andrés Pérez in Venezuela, Fernando Collor de Mello in Brazil, Carlos Menem in Argentina, and Alberto Fujimori in Peru.

40. Moore (1966); see also Skocpol (1994); Rueschemeyer, Stephens, and Stephens (1992).

41. Lipset (1959); Lipset, Kyoung-Ryung, and Torres (1993). See also Cnudde and Neubauer (1969).

42. Wickham-Crowley (1991, 1992) provides a good overview.

43. For example, Almond and Coleman (1960); Almond and Powell (1966).

44. Linz and Stepan (1978).

45. O'Donnell, Schmitter, and Whitehead (1986); Diamond, Linz, and Lipset (1989); Baloyra (1987); Malloy and Seligson (1987); Drake and Silva (1986); Perelli et al. (1995); Mayorga (1992); Tulchin (1995).

46. Remmer (1991a).

47. See, for example, Linz and Valenzuela (1994); Mainwaring and Scully (1995).

1

Democratic Roots in the Latin American Tradition

It is unequivocally true that the dominant political traditions of Latin America have been inhospitable to the development of democracy, even in its less than pure form, the "modern democratic republic," described in the Introduction. This point has been forcefully and elegantly argued by several authors, Claudio Véliz among them.[1] Writing in the late 1970s, when military dictatorships dominated all of South America save Colombia and Venezuela, Véliz argued that Latin America's distinctive "centralist tradition" constitutes a decisive barrier even to liberalism, much less to democracy. Both the political emphasis on centralization of authority in the Crown and the hierarchical yet flexible approach to Catholicism that he labeled "latitudinarian religious centralism" have, in his view, worked over five centuries to render Latin America unreceptive to democratic ideas and practices. He admitted that liberal and democratic ideas had considerable currency in the late nineteenth and twentieth centuries, but he interpreted that period as a "liberal pause" that gave way, in the 1970s, to a resurgence of the dominant centralist tradition. By this argument (and similar arguments of Howard Wiarda and Glen Dealy), democracy is a culturally alien hothouse flower that cannot long survive in the Latin American environment.

The notion that democracy is culturally alien to Latin America implicitly assumes that Iberian civilization has been largely insulated from currents that swept the rest of Europe. That is simply not the case, and it never was. In medieval times, Iberia was on the front lines of the fruitful confrontation between Christianity and Islam. In the Renaissance, Spain and Portugal were the leaders of Europe. Later, both countries were fully embroiled in the political conflicts of Europe, integrated—albeit unequally—into the economy of Europe, and conversant with the intellectual developments in the rest of the continent. Their American subjects were surely more isolated; however, educated people had communications not only with the mother countries but with other lands as well. Liberal economic and political ideas were well known in Latin American cities half a century before independence, and those ideas became just as much part of the Latin American tradition as Véliz's centralism.

In this chapter we argue that democracy does have numerous cultural roots in Latin American history and thought. Though not a dominant theme, democracy as a contemporary political project can and does draw on diverse elements of the Latin American experience. None of the elements cited hereafter is unambiguously democratic in any sense of the word; from the point of view of democracy, each is seriously flawed. Nevertheless, each lends itself to political action by those who would defy or limit authority (one key element of the modern democratic republic) or promote popular participation and political power (the other key element).

ELITE POLITICS AND THE ROOTS OF DEMOCRACY

In both Spain and Portugal, centralism as an ideology of royal absolutism became dominant only in the fifteenth century and was subject, in both kingdoms, to challenge and resistance. At the elite level, a principal focus of resistance to royal authority was the medieval tradition of *fueros,* special privileges and exemptions accorded to the church and its religious personnel, chartered towns, and the nobility.[2] *Fueros* commonly entailed exemption from taxation, as well as other special legal privileges such as ecclesiastical courts with exclusive jurisdiction over clergy. Obviously, a key objective of royal absolutists had to be to restrict and if possible eliminate *fueros;* just as obviously, their beneficiaries would do all they could to maintain them. The issue of such special rights and privileges became an important theme of political discourse throughout the colonial era and continues to have echoes even in twentieth-century politics.[3]

Thus, the practice of absolute royal authority actually carried with it a persistent and widespread assumption that one of the boons most to be desired from such authority was the grant of special privileges and exemptions that, in effect, committed the royal authority to refrain from exercising its full, absolute rights. There was, then, within the Iberian tradition, a concept of rights that limited state actions. In contrast to the Anglo-American, Lockean tradition, these rights were not conceived as prior to the state but rather conceded by the state. But even though the rights were conceded by the monarchies, both the Spanish and Portuguese states found it quite difficult to withdraw or alter them unilaterally. Many political conflicts of the colonial era were over just such attempts by central authorities to change the rules.

Two examples illustrate this point. Francisco Pizarro, conqueror of Peru, was, like other conquistadores, initially vested with the duties of royal governor. The first viceroy, appointed by the Crown in the 1540s to discipline Pizarro, was instead overthrown and killed in battle by the conquistador.[4] Nearly a century later, during the period of Spanish control over Portugal (1560–1640), bands of Brazilian fortune-seekers (*bandeirantes*) raided Jesuit missions in what is now Paraguay, seeking Indian slaves in direct violation of royal policy. Yet the royal government did little to control the raids, except (after prolonged provocation) to authorize the Jesuits to arm the Indians.[5]

Thus, local elites and their followers were most jealous of their autonomy, sought to have it recognized by the Crown whenever possible, and resisted efforts by central authorities to reduce it. Flat rejection of royal authority was rare, but insubordination was common. Often enough, insubordinate elites got away with it, and they might, by appeal to higher authority, actually get a decision reversed. The formula *obedezco pero no cumplo* (I obey but do not fulfill) was sometimes used by colonial officials to indicate that local conditions would not permit implementation of the order, notwithstanding the official's disposition to obey. Moreover, the Crown often neglected to enforce its own policies in marginal areas, effectively requiring autonomy of local elites. As late as the eighteenth century in one of the most isolated backwaters of the Spanish empire, Costa Rica, the governor complained bitterly that no labor was available to till his fields and that he had to do so himself if he wished to survive. There is no indication that the government in Guatemala, the colonial capital of Central America, cared very much about what happened in a place with neither minerals nor agricultural wealth.[6] Costa Ricans even in this century attribute their relatively democratic history to this early neglect and widely distributed poverty.[7]

There is nothing inherently democratic about this tradition of local elite autonomy. Indeed, the autonomy was typically used the more effectively to exploit Indians, Africans, and others not privileged with elite status. This was often true even of the church itself. For example, missions were normally accorded special exemptions from royal regulation of Indian labor, permitting them in some cases to exploit that labor more fully than secular landowners. On a broader scale, the church was often bequeathed land or other property, the income from which was essential to the subsistence of the clergy and the functioning of the institution. The clergy, in short, had an interest in effective exploitation of land and labor.

The church also produced the most eloquent defenders of humanitarian values. The best known is Bartolomé de Las Casas, bishop of Guatemala in the mid-sixteenth century and tireless defender of the native Americans against the depredations of conquerors and colonists. Las Casas's arguments ultimately convinced the Crown to impose new limits and regulations on exploitation of the Indians and to authorize the importation of African slaves as an alternative labor source. San Pedro Claver, active in Cartagena in the late sixteenth century, devoted his life to alleviating the misery of the Africans. In the late seventeenth and early eighteenth centuries, the Jesuits in Paraguay developed a very impressive chain of missions to the Guaraní peoples, devoted paternalistically to their settlement and material prosperity as well as their conversion. Each of these manifestations of ecclesiastical humanitarianism demanded recognition by the central authorities, protection from autonomous action of local settlers, and exemption from secular obligations such as taxation. At the level of policy, the demands were granted; at the level of practice, the results were less reliable.[8]

There was, then, a tradition of limits on and resistance to central authority, albeit not cast in terms of constitutionalism or natural rights. The power of the tradition was evident in more recent phenomena, such as most of the independence movements in Spanish America (with the principal exception of the popular movements of Father Miguel Hidalgo and Father José María Morelos in Mexico, of which more will be said later). Many creole elites (American-born whites) resented the perceived loss of power and privilege emerging from the Bourbon reforms of the mid-eighteenth century (designed precisely to enhance Crown control over the empire), and they frequently saw their economic interests directly threatened by a more efficient central control that might restrict contraband trading, even as they also depended on the Crown for protection against external attack and popular rebellion. This elite ambivalence about central authority was reflected in the political thought and practice of the independence period. Even when creole elites came to reject the legitimacy of royal authority and had to turn for legitimacy to popular consent, they opted universally for constitutionalism rather than pure democracy. In the unique case of Brazil, independence was brought about without eliminating the monarchy, but even there the new imperial regime was constitutional and, in principle, representative.[9] Even though in practice major regime changes were almost always made by force rather than through constitutionally mandated procedures, no basis of legitimacy was ever devised that could replace a constitution grounded ostensibly in popular consent.

The same elite ambivalence toward central authority is evident in major developments in nineteenth-century Latin America. Caudillismo[10] essentially involved the willingness of daring men to disregard utterly any claims of legitimate authority, to seize the government and its benefits for themselves, for no better reason than that they had the power to do so. A successful caudillo necessarily sought to centralize control in order to eliminate possible rivals, but caudillismo itself can never foreclose the possibility or probability of a new rival emerging.[11] Thus, with the definitive elimination of the royal claims to legitimate authority, the caudillos operated—for varying periods and to varying degrees—autonomously as political entrepreneurs, in a competition reminiscent of Hobbes's state of nature and the very antithesis of colonial centralism. Indeed, those who were successful in imposing order often benefited from the support of the propertied classes and the imperial powers (Britain and the United States), whose interests were favored by order. Caudillos are a particularly vivid example of actors who relate in complex ways to their structural environment: they defy structures (e.g., authority claims), constitute new structures (e.g., a new political regime), and are limited by structures (e.g., imperial power).

Caudillismo was also a precursor of democracy in a more direct sense. Caudillos were mostly of humble or, at best, middling origins. Their power lay in their capacity to mobilize and lead other common people. Caudillos and their movements thus embodied democracy in the literal sense that common people were coming to power. That is why some elites of the independence era were frightened of Tomás Boves (royalist) and José Antonio Páez (republican), each a powerful leader of the formidable horsemen of the Venezuelan llanos (plains). Juan Manuel Rosas in Buenos Aires and Rafael Carrera in Guatemala, similarly, were caudillos with strong mass backing who were able to seize and hold power after independence.[12]

Liberalism was the major historic antagonist of caudillismo; the proponents of European and North American ideas of progress sought, like Domingo Faustino Sarmiento, to impose "civilization" on the "barbarous" caudillos.[13] Yet the practice of liberalism, and its offshoot, positivism, showed as much ambivalence toward authority as caudillismo itself. Liberal economic and political thought is deeply distrustful of the capacity of any state to serve the general interest through positive action. Jefferson's dictum, "That government is best which governs least," sums up the basic liberal orientation. Liberals in Latin America most particularly imbibed liberal economic doctrine and consequently sought to promote economies based on free trade. They sought to eliminate government restraints on trade and economic subsidies to inefficient economic activities while encouraging those industries (export agriculture and mining) that could find external markets and attract external investments. Liberals often worked to eliminate forms of property that restricted the free market, such as land controlled by indigenous villages or the church; they thereby promoted a profound concentration of land in the hands of an emerging class of capitalist landowners or foreign corporations such as the United Fruit Company in Central America.

Most Latin American liberals were less deeply committed to the political side of liberalism, with its emphasis on constitutionalism, limited government, and freedom of expression. They usually did articulate such values but often honored them in the breach. Liberals were less liberal in politics for several reasons. First, they had to concentrate power in order to carry out their preferred economic policies. They were, after all, agents of change, actors, and the enforcement of change requires power. Second, the incorporation of positivism into liberal conventions in the late nineteenth century further reinforced pressures toward authoritarianism, since positivism saw progress as depending on a strong state led by people who understood the "scientific" laws of social progress. Thus, the founders of the first Brazilian republic declared their intention to bring "order and progress" to a "New World in the Tropics."[14] Moreover, third, liberals and positivists were creatures of the same societies that produced the caudillos and had, perforce, to behave (in varying degrees) like caudillos in order to get and keep power. Fourth, liberalism was, for many, less a deeply held conviction than a flag of political convenience that would serve to identify them with a particular partisan coalition. Thus, for example, liberal parties in many countries evolved symbiotically with conservative parties, as competing clientelistic coalitions seeking control of the state but without clearly defined policy differences in practice. Finally, for those seeking respectability with the great powers or with large corporations, liberalism was a useful label.[15]

Here the liberals exemplify the interplay of action and structure that is the theoretical ground of this book. They were, on the one hand, actors who sought power in order to change society. They created new structures. On the other hand, they were deeply constrained by the informal rules of the game of caudillismo, the dominant political culture of nineteenth-century Latin America. Further, they had to operate within the structure imposed by a global liberal climate backed by the great powers. Finally, note the relativity of structure: Britain, as the leading great power, might change its policy at will, thereby taking action. But to a Latin American leader or government, any policy of a great power was an unchangeable part of the environment to which it was necessary to adapt; in short, it was a structure.

Several examples can provide a more detailed sense of the diversity and commonality of liberalism in nineteenth-century Latin America. Most observers would agree that the great Mexican statesman Benito Juárez represented the best of Latin American liberalism.[16] A full-blooded native American by birth, Juárez rose to prominence as a liberal leader in the era of the caudillo General Antonio López de Santa Anna and was instrumental in the overthrow of Santa Anna in 1855, after the disastrous war with the United States in which Mexico lost half its territory. Politically, Juárez was committed to constitutionalism and to the liberal ideal of a republic of equal citizens. Ironically, his commitment to economic liberalism led him to sponsor the destruction of indigenous communal landholding in the name of progress. Ousted from power in 1861 by an alliance of Mexican conservatives with the French imperial regime of Napoleon III, Juárez led an insurgency that regained power in 1867 when the United States, freed of preoccupation with its own civil war, pressured the French to pull out.

Juárez's death only a few years later opened the way to the prolonged dictatorship of the other face of Mexican liberalism, Porfirio Díaz (1876–1910). Whereas Juárez was primarily a political liberal and constitutionalist, Díaz proved to be a positivist authoritarian who sought to enhance his personal power by making Mexico attractive to foreign investment and lucrative to those with capital. Concentration of property and income reached new heights, as did political corruption. The excesses of this liberal dictatorship in turn laid the foundation for what is arguably the defining epic of twentieth-century Latin America: the Mexican Revolution.

Similar stories can be told about liberalism elsewhere in Latin America. Many countries experienced an era, in the late nineteenth and early twentieth centuries, of highly elitist constitutional regimes in which substantial opposition freedoms were tolerated and a general tone of civility was maintained for more than one presidential term. These regimes often presided over periods of economic growth and rising standards of social well-being and tended to break down at times of economic crisis.

In Costa Rica, the retirement of military dictator Tomás Guardia in 1882 led to the inauguration of the "Liberal Republic," which would last almost unbroken until 1940. During this period there was only one abortive military regime (1917–1919), elections were regularly held and often won by candidates opposed by the incumbents, and universal public education was given decisive impetus. The relatively strong and stable state was in a much better position than other Central American countries to actually extract benefits to the country from concessions granted to the United Fruit Company and other banana producers. For example, United Fruit agreed in both Honduras and Costa Rica to build a railroad from the coast to the capital; only in Costa Rica was the government able to insist that the job be finished. In Honduras, the rails extended no further than the company's plantations.[17]

Justo Rufino Barrios of Guatemala represents the more despotic face of liberalism.[18] Coming to power in 1873 after a civil war victory over the conservatives, Barrios sponsored a draconian destruction of indigenous communal landholdings as a means of making appropriate lands available for coffee cultivation, which then took off and became the foundation for the Guatemalan economy up to the present time. Politically, notwithstanding its liberal identity, the Barrios regime was a classic self-perpetuating personal dictatorship that lasted over a decade.[19]

The overall legacy of Latin American liberalism for democracy in the region has been ambiguous at best. Its predominantly economic thrust promoted the concentration of property and income and the destruction of indigenous communities. Its positivist variant was openly authoritarian. For the most part, the political commitments of Latin American liberals were weak and inconsistent, usually disregarded when they were inconvenient. Liberals were no more likely than conservatives to be sincere and consistent constitutionalists.[20] Thus, even though liberalism in theory stood for political equality and constitutional government, its inegalitarian economic practice and its inconsistent, often cynical political practice render its legacy suspect.

This section has considered aspects of the Latin American political tradition associated with elite politics that may be used to further democratic ends. The main thrust was on a variety of justifications for the limitation of state authority, whether through the ancient tradition of *fueros,* or the more modern impact of liberalism in its various guises.

THE LATIN AMERICAN CONSTITUTIONAL TRADITION

The predominant interpretation of constitutionalism in Latin America sees the constitution as an inseparable aspect of political independence. The constitution, as a set of rules limiting the authority of the government, is seen as alien to the absolutism of the colonial era. It is my argument, however, that constitutionalism has much deeper Iberian and colonial roots and that those roots are quite distinct from the Anglo-American constitutional tradition.[21] Within the Western intellectual tradition, there are at least three distinct lines of constitutional thought: Roman, medieval, and contractarian/liberal.[22] These threads are woven together to form the Latin American constitutional tradition, a key structural element shaping twentieth-century political practice.

The pronounced legalism of the Iberian tradition has its roots first of all in Rome. The Iberian peninsula, of course, was ruled by the Romans for several hundred years and received from the Romans more than just its languages. The Romans were the first to develop legal thought to a high level, particularly during the republican period, when the governance of the city was regulated by elaborate legal norms allocating powers to the Senate, the Assembly, and consuls and other officials. Even as the republic was breaking down under the weight of warfare and conquest, the expectation that public officers' actions would be clothed in law was maintained. Throughout the life of the Roman Empire and throughout its territory, the law was an essential instrument of rule. Even on the increasingly frequent occasions when emperors were forcibly overthrown and replaced, their successors were always careful to arrange the legal underpinning of their tenure. It was for this purpose that republican institutions such as the Senate were maintained long after they ceased to have an independent role. As much as any other indicator, the decline and fall of Rome may be marked by the decay of its rule of law. The ideal, nevertheless, survived in Iberia, as well as elsewhere.

While the church carried on and adapted the Roman legal tradition after the fall of the empire, a quite distinct political practice emerged in western Europe in medieval times. There were enormous variations, of course, but the general structure of the situation was marked by secular decentralization of authority matched with religious centralization in the hands of the papacy. The popes claimed supremacy over all secular authorities in Christendom, but church doctrine also allowed secular authorities substantial autonomy as long as they acknowledged papal authority and the governing principles of natural law as taught by the church.[23]

Secular decentralization and autonomy meant that in any given population and territory, a variety of entities (e.g., cities, guilds, knightly or priestly orders, estates) were recognized (by tradition, supplemented by written documents) as having rights to autonomy and the right to consent to measures, such as changes in taxes, that would affect them. Correspondingly, these recognized entities had obligations to their feudal lords and monarchs. The political rulers (lords and monarchs) also had obligations as well as rights. Their principal obligation, beyond keeping the peace, was to respect the traditional rights of their subjects. The political theory of Aquinas and others made clear that rulers who did not meet their obligations were tyrants (i.e., unlawful rulers) who might legitimately be resisted by their subjects.

In short, if the Roman tradition emphasized the importance of a comprehensive, written law that is applicable everywhere, medieval tradition emphasized the importance of traditional law that sets the boundaries of authority. Traditional law differs from place to place, though it must operate within the structure of natural law. For example, English common law and its constitutional tradition are rooted in medieval thought and practice.

Iberian societies had their forms of this medieval political pattern.[24] In particular, the regional nobility and the towns developed quite substantial autonomy, and corporate modes of consultation between monarch and subjects, such as the Castilian Cortes, did develop. However, centuries of battles with the Moors gave a decisive advantage to the monarchs of Portugal, Castile, and Aragon, as Christian armies slowly and with great difficulty expelled the Muslims from the peninsula. Thus, medieval traditions limiting royal authority, which laid the foundation for the English constitution, had become marginal to political practice in Iberia by the fifteenth century. Still, the norm of legal autonomy for recognized collectivities was never totally lost and, indeed, became more relevant in the New World because of the distance and time involved in exercising central control.

The contractarian, or liberal, approach to constitutions is the most familiar to U.S. readers, but it is clearly the least important source of constitutionalism in the Iberian tradition. Reflecting the decay of medieval society and the emergence of the individualistic and competitive mentality that would be essential to capitalism, contractarianism had its strongest roots in England (Hobbes and Locke) and was part of commonsense discourse in the English colonies in the seventeenth and eighteenth centuries. The central idea was that political authority is based upon a contract among the people of a society; the very idea of a contract implies agreement of the parties to abide by its terms. Whereas the Romans founded political authority on law and worried not overmuch about origins, and the Middle Ages founded authority on natural law and God's will, contractarians founded it on popular consent. This radical innovation was not completely absent from Iberian discourse (consult Spanish theologian and philosopher

Francisco Suárez, for example), but it never became the dominant mode of political discourse as in British North America and was indeed actively repressed by the Bourbons in the eighteenth century in Spain and Spanish America (Brading, 1987, p. 116).

Contractarian thought did come to the fore in Latin America—and, indeed, in Iberia—in the early nineteenth century. Spain and Portugal absorbed it as part of the effects of the French Revolution and the Napoleonic conquests, which tended to emphasize a version of contractarianism adapted from the radically democratic but illiberal *Social Contract* of Rousseau. These effects were also felt in the New World, but in addition, the emerging Latin American countries had before them the obvious example of the United States. The idea of a political community establishing itself by mutual agreement in the form of a constitution was obviously the best—if not the only—available device for claiming political legitimacy after asserting independence. The earlier Roman and medieval traditions were of some utility in the struggle for independence, for example, allowing municipal authorities to act autonomously in a situation in which central authorities were in no position to enforce the law or allowing an assertion of independence in response to allegedly illegal acts by central authorities. But precisely because these earlier traditions had been actively used by imperial authorities, they were not easily adaptable to an assertion of independence.[25]

The distinctive manner in which Latin Americans appropriated contractarian thought was, however, decisively shaped by the persistence of the older traditions. Colonial political organization, for example, had nothing to do with contractarianism, but it was deeply legalistic in a way reminiscent of the Roman Empire. Every measure taken had to be clothed in law to be valid. Real conditions, however (e.g., poor communications, diversity of local circumstances), often made it impossible to implement fully policies handed down from the center. This basic contradiction generated the widespread use of legal casuistry designed to stretch the interpretation of the law to include actions actually taken. Similarly, after independence, it has been deemed essential in all countries, almost all the time, to have a constitution as the ground of legitimacy, but these constitutions almost always have in their texts provisions for their emergency suspension, in whole or in part (Loveman, 1993).[26] The most arbitrary and repressive acts are typically rationalized casuistically as consistent with the constitution. Or, as was common in the recent transitions from authoritarian regimes in the 1980s, such acts were legally pardoned ex post facto.[27]

Another important feature of Latin American constitutionalism drawn from the earlier traditions is corporatism.[28] Contractarian thought is individualist in its essence, positing a society constituted by virtue of an agreement among egoistic individuals. By contrast, the medieval tradition is corporatist. Humans are construed to be inherently social, and the various collectivities to which they belong thus have a much more fundamental status than in contractarian thought. But these collectivities are only legitimate if they contribute to the overall collective good of the society. They must, in short, be recognized as legitimate by the supreme political authority if they are to be tolerated and participate in public affairs.[29] One of the principal functions of constitutions in nineteenth- and twentieth-century Latin America has been to ratify decisions made by rulers as to which groups or sectors shall be recognized as legitimate interlocutors in the political process. The twentieth-century expansion of political participation from the narrow elitism prevalent in 1900 to virtually universal citizenship as we approach the year 2000 is seen much more in terms of incorporating identifiable collective actors than of extending rights to individuals.[30]

Within the contractarian tradition dominant in the United States, a constitution is supposed to define with some precision the limits on authority and the obligations enforceable on the various parties to the contract. But even though Latin American constitutions assume a conventionally contractarian form, their deeper significance is better understood in terms of Iberian/Roman legalism and medieval corporatism. In the legalistic tradition, all public actions must be within the law to be recognized as valid. Therefore, those who wish a course of action to take place will quite logically want to include it in the constitution as an obligation of the government. This is done not in the expectation that putting it in the constitution will make it happen, but rather to provide advocates with a powerful lever to use in their future struggle to make it happen. Royal laws for protection of the Indians did not prevent their abuse but did provide defenders such as Las Casas with a valid standpoint from which to challenge the abuse and gain some amelioration of conditions. The constitution, like the laws of the Indies, is not intended so much as a literal control on behavior as a definition of what behavior shall be considered legitimate.

The new constitutions of Brazil and Colombia both recognize indigenous peoples in a corporatist manner, giving them by name not only full rights of citizenship (which they had as individuals already) but also corporate rights to defend their own cultures and traditions. These provisions will not by themselves stop abuse of Amazonian tribes and other indigenous peoples, but by committing the state to respecting and defending them, the new constitutions strengthen the moral and legal resources of indigenous peoples and their defenders.

POPULAR RESISTANCE AND THE ROOTS OF DEMOCRACY

In this section we will focus on the Latin American tradition of popular resistance to oppressive authority. Since Latin America was built on the conquest and exploitation of native Americans and relied heavily on the labor of African slaves, revolts by either of these two groups would be the most obvious place to look for popular resistance. There are numerous examples of both. The indigenous rebellion led by Tupac Amaru in Peru in the 1780s nearly succeeded in taking Cuzco.[31] There were many other cases of indigenous uprisings, though none so close to success. On the margins of the empires, especially in southern Chile and Patagonia, northern Mexico, and the Amazon Basin, some indigenous peoples avoided subjugation, partially by flight and partially by armed resistance, well into the era of independence. Respect for such indigenous resistance became a tradition, institutionalized most fully by the indigenist mythology of the Mexican Revolution (see later discussion). The idea of a conquered people rising up against its exploiters is essentially democratic, in that such an uprising implicitly or explicitly entails a demand for self-determination. In addition to Mexico, several contemporary Latin American nation-states have appropriated such a tradition to bolster their own legitimacy.[32]

In Brazil and the Caribbean, where plantation agriculture employed large numbers of African slaves, rebellions were frequent, as were autonomous republics of escaped slaves. Of course, the most successful occurred in Haiti, where a slave revolt became a true social revolution, the first in the hemisphere. And the revolution in Haiti drew a strong, democratic inspiration from the French Revolution, whatever the subsequent failings of many of its leaders and whatever the long litany of betrayal and subversion of Haiti by outsiders. Some of the Brazilian escaped slave societies, or *quilombos,* survived for decades, and in the Guianas descendants of escaped slaves still maintain organized societies in the bush.[33]

All these instances of indigenous and African resistance represent something quite different from the types of elite resistance described in the previous section. These people were fighting for liberation from oppression at the hands of their conquerors and masters. To the extent that they succeeded, they established new social orders in which the old rulers were deprived of their privileges. They showed little or no interest in either the ancient Iberian tradition of *fueros* or in the more modern liberal emphasis on limitations on government authority. Rather, these instances of popular resistance demanded independence or self-determination for a particular people. In short, although aspects of elite resistance to authority have tended to provide underpinnings for constitutionalism, indigenous and African resistance movements have provided reference points for radically egalitarian democratic impulses.

Such resistance typically appealed little and posed considerable threat to the mass of Spanish- or Portuguese-speaking people (whether mestizos, mulattoes, or creoles) without property or office but with the status that came from being part of the dominant linguistic-ethnic community. The colonial social hierarchy (little changed by independence except at the top) typically had blacks at the bottom, then indigenous people (defined by their linguistic distinctiveness and semiautonomous social organization), then the mass of poor mestizos or mulattoes and propertyless whites. At the top were merchants, landowners, and, of course, royal officials. The poor mestizos, mulattoes, and whites would typically support the elites in the face of indigenous or slave rebellions, but they were themselves subject to intense exploitation, and there were many instances of popular resistance emerging from the poor masses. The best example from the colonial era was the *Comunero* revolt in Nueva Granada (now Colombia) in 1783.[34] The same Bourbon economic reforms that had touched off the contemporaneous Tupac Amaru revolt in Peru provoked mestizo resistance in Nueva Granada, where the indigenous presence was much weaker. In the latter case, craftspeople and small merchants who were disadvantaged by a combination of economic liberalization (loss of subsidies and protection from international competition) and tax increases rose against the viceroyal government and came very close to capturing Bogotá itself. The city was saved by a settlement negotiated between the rebel leadership and the authorities; once the rebel army was disbanded, the settlement was abrogated and the leaders were executed.

The *Comunero* revolt and others like it were characterized by professed devotion to the king even as the rebels resisted the authority of the king's officials. Almost universally, the allegation was made that the officials were exceeding their proper authority and trampling on rights previously granted by the Crown. Unlike the indigenous and black revolts, these rebellions did not directly challenge the legitimacy of the whole colonial order, but they were threatening enough to the creole elites that the latter stratum uniformly supported the royal authorities against the rebellions.

The struggles for independence in South America (Bethell, 1987c) were partially grounded in the same tradition of royalist legalism exemplified by the *Comuneros,* as local elites in Buenos Aires, Caracas, and Bogotá acted initially, in 1810, to defend legitimate royal authority in the face of Napoleonic usurpation of the Spanish throne. They also harbored grievances, however, against the officials of the king whose legitimacy they defended. Finally, the independence struggles came increasingly to draw on the radically democratic themes of the French Revolution itself.

In the struggle for independence in Mexico, a variation on this pattern blended popular and indigenous rebellions.[35] As the creole elites were taking control of the movement in northern and southern South America in 1810, in the old viceroyal capitals of Mexico and Peru equivalent elites clung to the Crown. In Mexico, however, a popular revolutionary movement emerged, calling not only for political independence but also for egalitarian social and economic reforms. The movement included both indigenous people and poor mestizos and whites. Under the leadership of Father Miguel Hidalgo and subsequently Father José María Morelos, the movement constituted a mortal threat to both the colonial regime and the

Mexican class structure. Only after first Hidalgo and then Morelos were captured and executed was it possible to suppress the rebellion in 1814. Then, only after 1820, when liberals gained power in Spain and posed a new threat to the Mexican status quo, did the local elite support independence under the ephemeral imperial rule of Spanish general Agustín de Iturbide.

After independence, many caudillos arose out of similar popular rebellions, protests against injustices, and defiance of tyrannies. In such a context, a dynamic leader like Rafael Carrera, José Antonio Páez, or Juan Manuel Rosas would be precisely what a spontaneous popular insurgency would need in order to confront an entrenched regime successfully. Thus caudillismo, central to politics in the nineteenth century, is inextricably linked to popular revolt and resistance. Tragically, though, caudillos also transmuted the popular impulse for justice into a clientelistic pursuit of office and favors.

Carrera illustrates the point.[36] He was a caudillo who came to prominence in opposing the Central American Federation, which broke up in 1838. By 1844, General Carrera was elected president with strong support from the church, conservative landowners, and the peasantry. A militant opponent of liberal secularization, he was able to hold the liberals at bay until his death in 1865, primarily because of his devoted popular support. He used this support to bolster conservative economic interests, which included promoting infrastructure development. He did not provide much in the way of real benefits to the majority of his devoted followers.

Robert Gilmore, in his study of caudillismo in Venezuela (1965), argued that Juan Vicente Gómez (in power from 1908 to 1935) was the last Venezuelan caudillo because he was uniquely successful in eliminating the social foundations for the emergence of rivals who might challenge him for power. Beginning as a general in the Andean army that seized power in 1899, Gómez shaped the perfect clientelist regime, effectively insulated against external opposition. What began as a movement against corruption and for renovation had deteriorated (even before Gómez muscled aside his chief, Cipriano Castro, in 1908) into a government in the hands of a self-serving dictator and his clique.

The Mexican Revolution that began in 1910 and occupied an entire generation in the world's most populous Spanish-speaking country was the apotheosis of all these strands of democratic impulses in Latin America; as such, it embodies their contradictions.[37] The initial spark was the liberal reformist campaign led by Francisco Madero against the rickety dictatorship of Porfirio Díaz, under the slogan, "Effective Suffrage, No Reelection" (which had been Díaz's own slogan when he was first elected in 1876). After fraud gave the election to Díaz, a popular insurrection forced him to leave the country, giving way to Madero. A conservative coup three years later resulted in the death of Madero and provoked insurrections by several independent groups, which were to struggle for supremacy over the next several years. All the insurrections shared a general sense of struggling against injustice and for the common people, but no systematic ideology ever became dominant. Each major insurgent group produced a revolutionary caudillo around whom military and political action centered. Most prominent among them were Emiliano Zapata, Venustiano Carranza, and Pancho Villa. By 1917, Carranza had achieved national dominance, and in short order both Zapata and Villa had been assassinated.

Under Carranza's leadership the constitution of 1917 was framed. It articulated the populist, reformist, and democratic aspirations of the revolution, mandating, for example, agrarian reform and state ownership of mineral resources. However, just as the Latin American tradition might lead one to expect, few of these reformist commitments were fully implemented. Similarly, reflecting the rallying cry of Madero, the president was prohibited from reelection. Again, the emerging revolutionary establishment acted as one would expect Latin American elites to act: they subscribed to the constitution while developing a political machine that would allow the top leaders to control elections and thus evade the substance of the prohibition. Two successors to Carranza, Generals Alvaro Obregón and Plutarco Elías Calles, set up an alternation in the presidency during the 1920s, but the plan was foiled when Obregón was assassinated just as he was about to assume office for the second time. Calles, whose term was ending, sought to maintain his power without openly continuing in office; his means to that end was the official Institutional Revolutionary Party (PRI). Maintaining personal control over the party, Calles was able to rule through a series of client presidents for six years. But his last client, General Lázaro Cárdenas, turned on him and forced him to leave the country. During his term (1934–1940), Cárdenas furthered the development of the PRI in three ways. First, he cemented popular loyalty to the revolution by pushing through major reform measures such as an extensive agrarian reform, labor reforms, social welfare measures, and the nationalization of foreign-owned petroleum companies. Second, he organized the official party to incorporate its constituents into sectoral organizations based on occupation (i.e., peasant, labor, "popular," or state employee, and military groups; the last category was useful initially in absorbing revolutionary caudillos into the party but was subsequently abandoned). Third, by his own behavior after leaving office, he established the norm that past presidents do not continue to rule behind the scenes.

Cárdenas's decisive actions during his presidency reconstituted the most basic structures of Mexican politics. After he left office in 1940, the greatest popular uprising in the history of Latin America had been transformed into a near-perfect political machine. Most particularly, the old vice of caudillismo, the incessant and usually violent struggle for power, was transmuted into a ritual succession of constitutional dictators every six years without fail. The political action of peasants and workers was channeled into official organizations under party control. The political leadership takes care to maintain its rhetorical commitment to the goals of the revolution while in practice moving ever further from them.

The hegemony of the PRI has been eroding in recent years, but it still exemplifies the complex and equivocal place of democratic currents in Latin American politics. Rooted squarely in the traditions of the revolution, the PRI's historic role has been to mystify and mitigate the democratic impulses of that revolution.

CONCLUSION

I have tried to show in this chapter that there are structural elements in the Latin American political tradition that are useful to those seeking to foster democracy in the region. This is not to say, of course, that the tradition is predominantly democratic, but neither is it true that democracy is wholly alien to the tradition. Rather, democratic elements are regularly appropriated by political actors to legitimate their demands. In any country, those acting to resist abusive authority have instances of similar struggles from their own histories. Whether the struggle at hand is liberal and constitutionalist or radical and revolutionary, the tradition provides inspiration that is just as deeply rooted as authoritarianism itself.

NOTES

1. See especially Véliz (1980), and essays by Dealy, Véliz, and Wiarda, in Wiarda (1992).
2. On this tradition, see Morse, in Wiarda (1992); Lockhart and Schwartz (1983), p. 361; Keen and Wasserman (1988), p. 126.
3. The tradition of *fueros* may be reflected in contemporary controversies over amnesty for military personnel accused of violating human rights during the dictatorships of the 1970s and 1980s in South and Central America.
4. Lockhart and Schwartz (1983), p. 103.
5. Ibid., pp. 267–268.
6. Monge Alfaro (1980), chap. 4–7.
7. It would be a mistake to make too much of this rather self-serving national myth, but Costa Rica really was poor and isolated and seems to have suffered remarkably little interference even from Guatemala, much less points more distant. Costa Rica is discussed in detail in Chapters 2 and 3.
8. See Las Casas (1992). On the Jesuits, see Reiter (1995). On Claver, see Bushnell (1993), p. 20.
9. On the independence period, see Williamson (1992), chap. 6; Bethell (1987c). On the Brazilian empire, see Burns (1993).
10. Caudillismo is the pattern of political dominance asserted by self-made men on the principal basis of military prowess, in an era of political instability and decay during the decades immediately after independence. See Gilmore (1965).

11. Nevertheless, Gilmore (1965) argued that Juan Vicente Gómez did precisely that and consequently was Venezuela's last caudillo.

12. Boves was killed in battle during the War for Independence.

13. On Sarmiento and this theme generally, see Rock (1987), chap. 3 and 4; Williamson (1992), chap. 8.

14. See Burns (1993).

15. See Halperín Donghi (1993), chap. 4; Burns (1980); Bushnell and Macaulay (1994), chaps. 9–11.

16. On Juárez, see Bushnell and Macaulay (1994), chap. 9; Meyer and Sherman (1991), pt. 6.

17. See Gudmundson and Lindo-Fuentes (1995).

18. On Barrios, see Torres Rivas (1993), chap. 2; Pérez Brignoli (1987), chap. 3.

19. Gudmundson and Lindo-Fuentes (1995) have argued that many of the developmentalist policies traditionally associated with late nineteenth-century liberalism were in fact prefigured by earlier conservative governments in Central America.

20. In Argentina, Chile, and Colombia, for example, late nineteenth-century elitist constitutionalism, generally comparable to the Costa Rican example cited previously, took place under conservative rule. See Rock (1987), chaps. 4–5; Blakemore (1993); Bushnell (1993), chap. 6.

21. Useful sources on constitutionalism in Latin American history include Loveman (1993); Baracho (1985); Wahl (1986); Pimenta (1989–1990); Bethell (1987a, 1987b, 1987c, 1987d, 1993); Vélez Rodríguez (1987).

22. I exclude here Aristotle's usage of "constitution" as a description of how a polis is *constituted* and how it works. See "The Constitution of Athens." The usage here implies explicit legal norms that, if followed, confer legitimacy on the acts of magistrates or rulers. See Finley (1983); Hill (1970); Wilkinson (1972); Balladares (1987).

23. In the late Middle Ages, the church taught that natural law is the universally valid dictates of reason as informed by divine revelation. See especially the works of Thomas Aquinas.

24. On Spanish and Portuguese history, see Payne (1973).

25. The Brazilian case is clearly distinct from Spanish America on this point. The Brazilian imperial regime was a less distinct break from the old regime; although it did use contractarian conventions in its constitutionalism, it relied heavily on the older traditions as well. See Burns (1993).

26. The ubiquity of constitutions is also partially attributable to changes on the international level, notably the rising power of Britain and the United States. Liberalism and constitutionalism were prevalent in those countries, so it was useful for Latin American elites to adopt those ideologies. The visible symbol of a constitution was a powerful tool in the search for international respectability.

27. See note 3 for a comparison with the *fuero* tradition.

28. On this general cultural trait, see Williamson (1992), chaps. 4–5; Wiarda (1992), chaps. 1–5; Rouquié (1990), pts. 1–2; Davis (1972), chaps. 1–2; Jorrín and Martz (1970), chap. 1.

29. Contrast this pattern with Anglo-American pluralism, a version of liberalism that construes groups, rather than individuals, to be the primary political actors. Under the classic formulation of pluralism, central authority simply responds to pressure from groups; it does not decide which groups are legitimate participants. See Dahl (1989); Truman (1951).

30. Nothing in the preceding argument should be construed as setting up a

black/white distinction between Anglo-American and Latin American constitution-alism. If there is one thing all political scientists can agree on, everywhere, it is that constitutions are never a perfect reflection of the realities of political power and political practice.

31. On Tupac Amaru, see Fisher (1966); Williamson (1992), pp. 200–202.

32. In addition to Mexico, these would certainly include Peru, Bolivia, Chile, and Paraguay.

33. On slavery, slave rebellions, and the Haitian Revolution, see Burns (1986); Williams (1984).

34. On the *Comuneros* of Nueva Granada and other revolts of the 1780s, see Phelan (1978); Williamson (1992), pp. 200–202.

35. On the Mexican independence struggle, see Meyer and Sherman (1991), pt. 4; Burns (1986), pp. 82–84.

36. On Rafael Carrera, see Woodward (1993); Gudmundson and Lindo-Fuentes (1995); Calvert (1985), pp. 64–65.

37. On Mexico, and the Mexican Revolution in particular, see Meyer and Sherman (1991), pts. 8–9; Knight (1986); Hellman (1983), chap. 1.

2

Early Democracies:
Managing Participation

Five countries stand out in Latin America for the length and stability of their democratic experiences and because they started those experiences while democracy was still an exotic and fragile flower in Latin America. Chile and Uruguay began democratic regimes well before World War II, Costa Rica during and after the war, and Colombia (by some criteria) and Venezuela in the late 1950s. Each of the five countries built democracy on the structure created by its own history of political conflict and caudillismo, and each had failures and false starts. What distinguished these early democracies from their neighbors was that competing elites in each case ultimately found ways to act cooperatively in managing expanding popular participation while establishing and maintaining liberal, competitive political systems. The result in each case was liberal democracy. In Chile and Uruguay, the regimes broke down in 1973 and had to be reestablished (see Chapter 3). In Colombia, the achievement of a full liberal democracy has been slow in coming and beset by crises. In Venezuela, structural economic crisis in the 1980s and 1990s has brought the democratic regime to the edge of breakdown. Of the five cases, only Costa Rica has survived without a breakdown or a regime-threatening crisis.

ESTABLISHING DEMOCRACY

Liberal democratic regimes were established in Chile and Uruguay between World Wars I and II, and Costa Rica established its regime in the immediate aftermath of World War II. Colombia and Venezuela saw abortive attempts to establish democracy in the late 1940s and then saw successful establishment a decade later, in the late 1950s. In each case, establishment of the regime reflected both internal conditions and the international conjuncture of the time. In particular, liberal democracies were successfully established when competing elites could agree on modes of absorbing the expansion of political participation. In other cases, notably Argentina, such agreement was never achieved, and democracy was not successfully established.

It is useful in each case to review the nineteenth-century roots of the twentieth-century regimes. Elections were a regular part of the political process in all five countries, but it is important to emphasize that elections were not the principal means of changing governments; rather, they typically served to legitimate an incumbent government or its chosen successor. Once individuals (in Venezuela or Costa Rica) or parties (in Colombia, Chile, or Uruguay) established hegemony, often by force of arms, they would utilize the government apparatus to control elections, thus perpetuating themselves in power. Opposition groups could normally capture the government either by force of arms or occasionally by coalescing with government dissidents to win an election in spite of the powers of incumbency.

Chile

The principal distinction of Chile in nineteenth-century Latin America was the relative political stability that prevailed from the early 1830s, precisely during the era when most other Latin American countries were suffering prolonged political turmoil.[1] In Latin America, only Brazil under the Emperor Pedro II matched Chile's political stability during this era. Conflict did occur and became violent on occasion, notably insurrections in 1851 and 1859 and the civil war of 1891 (Zeitlin, 1984). These three armed conflicts may be interpreted as unsuccessful attempts to overcome the economic and political dominance of a strong agroexport oligarchy based on the productive estates of the Central Valley and allied commercial houses of Valparaíso and Santiago (Zeitlin and Ratcliff, 1988). Diego Portales, the hegemonic political figure from about 1830 to his assassination in an abortive coup in 1837, exemplified those interests and indeed may have become involved in politics as a means of protecting his own commercial interests. Although Portales himself never held the presidency, his was the key impetus behind the establishment of lasting, strong state institutions that constrained the struggle for political power within legal channels for the better part of the century (Nunn, 1976, chap. 3). The great landowners exercised tight control over the tenants and workers on their land, and suffrage restrictions based on property, education, and gender restricted voting to a small percentage of the population. The restricted franchise facilitated the control of elections by the national executive in alliance with local notables. Thus, under Portales and the series of ten-year presidents who held office after his death, the hegemonic leader was able to control the elections of several successive presidents through his control of the national executive.

The Chilean regime also benefited after 1830 from consistent support from British investors and the British government, at a time when Britain was the undisputed dominant world power. British merchants and bankers were active collaborators with the Chilean ruling class in both agriculture and commerce (Loveman, 1988, chap. 5). Moreover, British capital was deeply involved in the Chilean penetration of the nitrate fields of Peru and

Bolivia, a development that led eventually to the War of the Pacific (1879–1883), in which Chile defeated Peru and Bolivia and took from those countries the provinces of Arica, Tarapacá, and Antofagasta (Kinsbruner, 1973, chap. 6; Loveman, 1988, chap. 6).

The ruling elite began to fragment about midcentury, divided over the power and privileges of the church as well as conflicting economic interests. Copper miners, manufacturers, and small landowners all had reasons to oppose the dominant coalition, as did the emerging middle and working classes in the cities and mines (Zeitlin, 1984). By about 1860, the first clearly defined political parties (conservatives and liberals) emerged, quickly followed by the radicals (Scully, 1992, chap. 2; Remmer, 1984, chap. 1; Collier, 1993). With this development, a tripolar party system crystallized in Chile for the first time. The tripartite pattern would persist through partisan realignments and even through the Augusto Pinochet dictatorship, reemerging with the opposition to Pinochet in the 1980s. In such a party system, the center party would tend to play a moderating role, occupying the presidency the majority of the time. According to Timothy Scully (1992; see also Gil, 1966), the Liberal Party played that role until 1912 and the Radical Party from about 1920 to 1952; the Christian Democrats were the dominant center party from 1958 to 1973 (and resumed that position as the opposition to the dictatorship reemerged in the 1980s).

Timothy Scully (1992, 1995) showed that the principal cleavage underlying the party system prior to 1912 was the clerical-anticlerical issue, but with the political emergence of the middle and working classes in the late nineteenth century, the importance of class increased as the focus of conflict. Throughout the twentieth century, class conflict has been nakedly reflected in the Chilean party system to a degree unprecedented in Latin America (see also Petras, 1969). Broadly, conservative-liberal dominance up to 1920 may be seen as reflecting the hegemony of the traditional agroexport ruling class, a hegemony increasingly under challenge after 1900.[2] After 1920, the old ruling class only regained hegemony by military force from 1973 until the early 1980s. During the long era of Chile's democracy (1920–1973) and especially after the consolidation of that democracy during the 1930s, the old ruling class protected its interests not by brute power but rather by maneuvering within the tripolar party system and by astutely using the checks and balances of Chile's democratic constitution of 1925.

The institutional balance between executive and legislative branches underwent important changes between 1890 and 1925. When the landowners who dominated Congress prevailed in the civil war of 1891, they imposed a parliamentary system that persisted until the election of Arturo Alessandri in 1920. The era of parliamentary government coincided with, and rested upon, control of elections by local notables rather than the executive control that prevailed earlier. Alessandri presided over the drafting of the new constitution of 1925, with a stronger presidency but also numerous checks and balances vested in the two houses of Congress (elected for staggered terms different from that of the president) and the courts (relatively insulated from political pressure).

The new constitution was not actually implemented until 1932, after seven years of military intervention that included the dictatorship of Carlos Ibáñez and several other, short-lived military governments (Nunn, 1976; Ramírez Necochea, 1985; Drake, 1993). After 1932, the Chilean democracy was maintained unbroken until its overthrow in 1973. It was characterized by a multiparty system with a broad ideological range, durable and well-institutionalized parties and interest groups, and moderate levels of mass participation. Women were enfranchised in the late 1940s, but illiterates were permitted to vote only in 1970. The electorate was consistently divided into three roughly equal camps, Right, Center, and Left; none could capture a national majority alone, but each could win enough votes and congressional seats to protect its interests.

The Right, composed of the Liberal and Conservative Parties, was based largely in the countryside, where clientelistic control over peasants continued to provide a mass base to enable the upper-class leadership of these parties to compete in democratic electoral politics. Thus a core economic and political interest of the Right was to avoid policies that would erode that control, policies such as agrarian reform or peasant unionization. The liberals and conservatives, normally allies since 1912, formally merged to form the National Party in the 1960s. The Center, dominated before 1960 by the radicals and subsequently by the Christian Democrats, was based on the urban middle class and working class. The interests of these two growing classes centered on the promotion of industrialization and a rising living standard, including expansion of government services. The Left, consisting largely of communists and socialists, had a mass base among urban and mining workers and some members of the middle class. The ultimate objective of the Left was the socialist transformation of society, but in a more immediate sense its core interests included maintaining and expanding space for labor organization and expanding government services.[3]

This tripartite balance shaped the policy characteristics of the democratic period in Chile. The center-left Popular Front governments of the late 1930s and early 1940s promoted labor union organization and worker rights and established an extensive social welfare system. But neither these governments nor those of the 1950s seriously attacked the vital interests of the Right. Specifically, no action was taken to enfranchise rural workers or to redistribute rural property. This moderation was a result of recurrent bargaining among political and economic forces, whereby the traditional landowners, backed by the liberals and conservatives, repeatedly demanded and got the cooperation of successive reformist governments in obstructing the organization of rural workers (Loveman, 1988, chap. 8). The resulting political order ensured each of the major political forces enough power to block hostile initiatives while denying any sector the possibility of centralizing power. Presidential terms were six years, with no immediate reelection. The entire Chamber of Deputies was elected every four years. One-third of the Senate was elected every two years, for six-year terms. Congress was chosen on the basis of proportional representation, whereas presidential elections were by majority, with the proviso that Congress elect the president from the two leading candidates if no one received an absolute majority. Judges were effectively insulated from direct political control. Thus the formal constitutional structure served to stabilize the democratic regime by virtually blocking any actor from amassing enough power to push through major policy changes (cf. Gil, 1966).

Uruguay

The political history of Uruguay[4] during the nineteenth century was a notable contrast to the authoritarian stability of Chile, though the two polities did share a commitment to creating export economies. Uruguay's economy was pastoral, whereas Chile's was oriented to agriculture and mining. Uruguay's ruling class came to be more politically divided by economic interests than was the case in Chile. Pastoralists tended to gravitate to the Blancos, but mercantile interests were attracted to the Colorados. Uruguay had some modest foreign investment, principally British, but it was not nearly so attractive to investors as Chile. Uruguay was highly attractive to immigrants from southern Europe in the late nineteenth century, and their population swelled Montevideo (Finch, 1981).

The two traditional parties—Blancos and Colorados—that still dominate Uruguayan politics crystallized during the 1840s, the former basically conservative and based in the pastoral countryside, the latter liberal and rooted in Montevideo. The Colorados have been dominant on the national level almost from the beginning but never destroyed the local bases of the Blancos. Thus, when elections were held, they were routinely controlled by local notables linked to one of the national parties and ultimately by the sitting president acting in concert with the ruling party. In this respect, nineteenth-century Uruguayan and Chilean politics were alike. But in contrast with Chile (where clientelistic control was exercised most of the time without major civil strife), in Uruguay there were frequent civil wars, culminating in the war of 1903–1904, the last attempt by one of the traditional parties to seize power by force.

Thus, whereas competing coalitions in nineteenth-century Chile almost always resolved their disputes over power without resort to arms, in Uruguay civil war was frequent. The Uruguayans early developed the practice of the elite pact as a means of putting an end to armed conflict. That is, the winning side (usually the Colorados) would agree to share the perquisites of office with the losers (typically the Blancos) on both national and local levels. Nationally, this entailed offering some ministries to the Blancos; locally, it meant that the national executive would forgo any attempt by the state to control the Blanco strongholds in the interior.

The structure of politics in Uruguay thus evolved in a manner quite distinct from that in Chile. The two-party system contrasted markedly with the tripolar system of Chile. Instead of having a center party able to use its strategic position to moderate the system, the Uruguayans developed power-sharing pacts as a means of maintaining or restoring political stability. The clerical-anticlerical split that dominated Chilean politics in the past century also helped to define the two traditional parties in Uruguay. But whereas class conflict came to be directly reflected in the twentieth-century Chilean party system, in Uruguay the traditional parties maintained their dominance, concealing and transmuting class conflict.

The last of the great partisan civil wars in Uruguay ended in 1903 with a Colorado victory. This time, though, the Colorado caudillo who became president, José Batlle y Ordóñez, refused to offer the Blancos participation in his government.[5] Instead, he pushed through reforms that created a modern, activist state committed to providing material welfare to all citizens and to providing leadership and material support for the country's economic development. Batlle was among the most innovative, original political leaders in twentieth-century Latin America, and the changes wrought during his two presidencies (1903–1907, 1911–1915) would decisively shape modern Uruguay. Batlle sought to use the benefits from these policies to build durable political support for the Colorados. This clearly held considerable danger for the Blancos, but the Uruguayan outcome was not a slide into renewed civil war.

One important reason for this relatively peaceful resolution lies in the other set of changes brought about by Batlle, changes in the organization of the national government and the party system. In 1913, with his social and economic program in place, Batlle proposed to replace the president by a collegial executive. Influenced by the Swiss practice of a plural executive that avoided the excessive concentration of power in the hands of one man, Batlle proposed a similar structure for Uruguay. His motives have never been satisfactorily explained, but he may have thought that, at best, his own faction would predominate while his opponents would gain sufficient access to patronage to mute their opposition. At worst, he may have thought, a collegial executive would safeguard his reforms by its very immobility. He initially imagined such an executive as drawn entirely from the governing party, but his conservative opponents in both parties transformed the proposal to mandate representation of both major parties in the executive (i.e., co-participation). The executive would be headed by a president and a national council of administration. The president, elected every four years, would control foreign relations and security, and the council would supervise all other activities of the state. One-third of the council's nine members would be of the minority party, and one-third of the members would be elected every two years. The adoption of this constitution, in 1917, supplemented by another pact of 1931 that provided for the distribution of public sector jobs to both parties, effectively established a grand coalition style of government before partisan conflict reached the point of threatening stability.

Another highly distinctive aspect of Uruguayan democracy originated during this period: the electoral system of the "double simultaneous vote," also known as the "Ley de Lemas," the law that regulates the participation of party factions in elections. From its origins each party has been an alliance of clientelistic factions; the electoral law not only recognizes but reinforces this feature. Any faction within a party may run its own list of candidates in a general election; representation in Congress and local government is allocated to factions on the basis of proportional representation. The votes for all lists within a party are counted toward the total of the party in both legislative and presidential races; the leading candidate of the party receiving the most votes wins the presidency. This occasionally (e.g., in 1971 and 1984) has had the effect of electing a president who did not personally receive the most votes, but it has also effectively maintained the electoral hegemony of the two factionalized parties.[6]

If most of Batlle's institutional reforms were left intact in subsequent decades, their nationalistic, social democratic spirit and intellectual integrity were lost. Batlle had been convinced that Uruguay must and could industrialize using its own capital resources and that it was proper for the government, with a concern for the common interest, to lead that development. However, subsequent governments tended to see the reforms largely as a source of jobs; the bureaucracy tended inexorably to expand, with remarkably little concern with or effort toward paying the costs of these programs. Batlle sought to move the country toward self-sustaining industrial growth, but little progress was made to that end after 1916. The country remained totally dependent on the exports of an agricultural economy that was permitted to sink slowly into decrepitude.

A political system premised on shared power for all established interests and on patronage rather than policy coherence could discuss these issues at great length but was not equipped to resolve them. Instead, when the nation's problems periodically reached crisis proportions, the usual response was to release pressure by changing the organization of the government, from collegial to presidential and back. Thus in the context of the world economic crisis of the 1930s, President Gabriel Terra, a Colorado (indeed, a Batllista), collaborated with sectors of the Blancos to reestablish a presidential constitution. Terra was a dictator for ten years, but the presidential constitution persisted for another decade. In 1951, a resurgence of radical Batllismo led by Luis Batlle Berres (a nephew of the older Batlle) induced more conservative sectors of the Colorados (including the sons of Batlle y Ordóñez) to cooperate with the Blancos in pushing through a reestablishment of a form of plural executive, probably as a means of keeping Batlle Berres in check.

Costa Rica

In both colonial times and the nineteenth century, Costa Rica presents an interesting comparison with the other four countries.[7] In colonial times, Chile, Colombia, and Venezuela were rich and important; Costa Rica, like Uruguay, was poor and ignored.[8] Costa Rica did not suffer damage from the wars for independence; Colombia and Venezuela suffered severe destruction, and Chile and Uruguay saw considerable damage. After independence, Costa Rica was less subject to turmoil and civil war than Uruguay but slower to establish political stability than Chile. Costa Rica was among the first Latin American countries to commit itself to exporting coffee, and by 1850 that crop had become the mainstay of what had previously been the weakest economy in Central America. After 1850, coffee enabled a rather evident (Stone, 1975), if weak, ruling class to consolidate its power and to stabilize the state well in advance of the other Central American countries (Gudmundson and Lindo-Fuentes, 1995, chap. 1).

Costa Rica was slower than the other four countries to develop clearly defined, durable political parties, even in the minimal sense of the relatively stable elite factions of liberals and conservatives that came to dominate politics elsewhere in Central America. The great liberal-conservative cleavage did affect Costa Rica, but those of liberal persuasion prevailed in the 1880s without ever needing to institutionalize a durable party. The church, linchpin of conservative thinking in the past century, was relatively weak in Costa Rica,[9] and a self-conscious Conservative Party never formed. Instead, within the basic political economy of dominance by an agroexporting capitalist class, the political process consisted of a series of conflicts between identifiable factions within that class. These factions struggled for control of the state in a clearly defined cycle of personal hegemonies punctuated by unstable interregnums, a cycle that lasted until 1948 (Peeler, 1985, chap. 2). These hegemonies were maintained principally through the personalistic links of family and clientele. By the early twentieth century, the use of force tended to decrease, whereas elite bargaining and clientelism became relatively more important in the twentieth century. Still, incumbent presidents could assure the victory of their chosen successors most of the time until 1948. Politics gradually became less elitist in the first third of the twentieth century, with the implementation of direct elections, rising literacy, and the emergence of local *gamonales,* or political chiefs, who typically were not drawn from the national economic and social elite (Stone, 1975, pp. 223–226).

The 1930s, in Costa Rica as elsewhere, were a time of economic and political crisis. Signs of political change were evident as early as 1932, with the organization of the Communist Party and its leadership of an important strike of banana workers, an initiative that earned the party the lasting loyalty of that sector of the working class. But the crisis did not become acute until after the inauguration of President Rafael Angel Calderón Guardia, in 1940. Calderón had been an establishment politician, working his way up through loyal service to his predecessors and patrons. But once in power, Calderón proved a highly innovative leader and emerged as the new republican caudillo.

In his search for a way to consolidate his power over the opposition of his old comrades, Calderón sought to gain the loyalty of the working class. In this he was strongly influenced by his close friend, Archbishop Víctor Sanabria, and by Catholic social doctrine. He formed an alliance with the Communist Party, whose highly organized membership and cadres provided a ready political apparatus. Using the republican majority in the Assembly, he pushed through several innovative laws, most notably an advanced social security system and a new labor code very favorable to unions. In classic clientelist style, he then sought to use the new government programs and benefits to cement political support for himself.

Calderón's clear intent to perpetuate himself as a political boss, as well as his alliance with the communists, made his conservative opponents led by his predecessor, León Cortés Castro, all the more militant and desperate. Opposition also emerged from a different quarter: the moderate Left. The newly emerging Social Democratic Party, led by José Figueres, objected to the political abuse of Calderón's reforms, though they supported the reforms in principle. More broadly, they condemned the increasingly open corruption of the Calderonista regime. Finally, they rejected Calderón's alliance with the communists, with whom the social democrats were competing for control of organized labor.

The elections of 1944, marred by serious charges of fraud against the Calderón government, were won by a Calderón loyalist, Teodoro Picado. After the midterm elections of 1946, the opposition successfully demanded effective control of the electoral tribunal as a condition for participation in the 1948 presidential elections. Calderón was seeking to return to the presidency against a unified opposition behind the candidacy of conservative newspaper publisher Otilio Ulate. When the election results showed Ulate with the victory, the Calderonista majority in the Assembly voted to annul the election on grounds of fraud. Figueres, meanwhile, had been building an armed force at his farm in southern Costa Rica; he marched on San José demanding the resignation of the government and the recognition of Ulate as constitutional president. After a short, bloody war, Calderón, Picado, and the communist leadership negotiated a surrender and were allowed to leave the country. José Figueres and the Army of National Liberation were masters of the scene.

The negotiations that led to the establishment of liberal democracy are best seen as beginning in the crisis of 1948.[10] As it became clear that Figueres had the upper hand in the civil war, several interests pushed for a settlement. The Calderonistas wanted to avoid the destruction of their reforms and their political position. The communists wanted to retain legal status and their foothold in organized labor. Figueres's conservative and business allies, backers of Ulate, wanted the latter declared president without having to depend on the bayonets of Figueres. The social democrats wanted the way cleared for creation of the new social democratic order envisioned in their program. Figueres himself, in addition to these programmatic concerns, seemed intent on a total military victory that would leave him free to act.[11]

On 1 May 1948, having entered the city with his army a week earlier, Figueres signed a pact with Otilio Ulate, providing that the latter would assume office within eighteen months and that the country would be ruled by a provisional junta in the meantime. The junta would be responsible for holding an election for a Constituent Assembly to draft a new constitution and would have authority to rule by decree during its tenure. Figueres, as president of the junta, thus received extensive provisional powers, which were used, for example, to abolish the army, to nationalize banking, and to endow the state with the authority to guide the economy. These and other measures were intended to lay the groundwork for the social democratic program of restructuring society. This plan was frustrated when the social democrats' neglect of popular organization led to their defeat in elections for the Constituent Assembly, which instead had a strong majority for Ulate's conservative Unión Nacional. The innovative draft constitution proposed by the junta was rejected in favor of amendments to the existing document, including the enfranchisement of women. Most of the innovations decreed by the junta were ratified, but the social democrats nevertheless fell short of leading a thorough transformation of Costa Rica.

The pact with Ulate was not strictly necessary, for Figueres and the Army of National Liberation had a complete monopoly of military force; moreover, the United States was not inclined to intervene. That he undertook and honored the pact seems to reflect a commitment by Figueres to the principles of procedural democracy, independent of his commitment to the substantive program of the social democrats. The Figueres-Ulate Pact of 1948 was an agreement that served to regulate competition, within a liberal democratic framework, between the two major sectors of the victorious opposition. From 1948 until the mid-1950s, Calderón and his supporters were outside the political process, twice trying to overthrow the government through invasions from Nicaragua. Only with the election of 1958 did Calderón reintegrate himself into the political process, accepting the institutional framework and party system that had taken shape. Calderón joined the loose conservative coalition that was evolving to oppose the National

Liberation Party (PLN), which had been built up by Figueres after the junta left office in 1949 and which led Figueres to victory in the 1953 elections. As of 1958, then, the transformation begun in 1948 was extended to include the principal loser of the civil war. There was no explicit pact defining the terms of Calderón's reintegration, but the commitments made during 1948–1949 facilitated the later incorporation of Calderón, in that his key institutional innovations (social security in particular) were left intact. Calderón was always able to gain political credit among potential voters for his establishment of social security. The decisions of 1948–1949 thus laid the foundation for civil political competition by minimally satisfying not only the victors but also the most important vanquished, Calderón.[12]

The liberal democratic regime in Costa Rica since 1949 has displayed a high level of stability based on the interaction of a strongly presidential political system with proportional representation in congressional elections. Unrestrained but civil competition between the PLN and its opponents has been the rule. Co-participation in the government by the opposition has not been characteristic. Control of the presidency has tended to alternate between the center-left PLN and a gradually consolidated anti-PLN coalition of the Center-Right, now called the Party of Social Christian Unity (PUSC). Seven presidents since 1949 have been PLN members, and five have been from the anti-PLN sector. The PLN has normally held at least a simple majority in the Legislative Assembly, but the PUSC did achieve an absolute majority under President Rafael Angel Calderón Fournier (1990–1994). Parties of the Left have not exceeded 5 percent of the vote since 1949 (Chalker, 1995; Yashar, 1995).[13]

Colombia

Nueva Granada (now Colombia) was an important colonial center: in the eighteenth century Bogotá became the capital of a viceroyalty that included not only present-day Colombia but Panama and the largely autonomous provinces of Quito (Ecuador) and Venezuela.[14] The highlands of Nueva Granada were important sources of gold for the Crown, and the great Caribbean port of Cartagena was a principal transportation link for Spanish fleets to and from western South America. Nueva Granada, in short, was one of the principal centers of the Spanish empire in America. Correspondingly, it developed a very strong, self-conscious, and self-confident creole upper class that was among the earliest collaborators with Simón Bolívar in the struggle for independence.

The independence struggle weakened the Nueva Granada elite, but the people who gained power after independence were predominantly from the old upper class. Political discourse came to be couched in the confrontation between liberals and conservatives that was virtually universal in Latin America at the time. In Colombia, organized Liberal and Conservative

Parties actually became the central organizing reality of the political process, which was perhaps a reflection of the surviving strength of the colonial ruling class: it remained possible for members of the colonial elite to bring together enough resources—using property and clientelistic ties—to control the government, without having to put themselves in the hands of rough caudillos of the type who came to dominate Venezuela. The elite simply divided into liberal and conservative factions, cemented by both clientelism and ideology. The political process became a struggle for hegemony, punctuated by periods of indeterminacy. However, the periods of hegemony in the Colombian case were more partisan than personal. As in Uruguay, a distinctive feature of Colombian politics emerged from this primitive party system: the practice of bipartisan coalitions as a means to end periods of turmoil or to facilitate change of party hegemony.

Colombia, synonymous with good coffee today, was a latecomer to the crop, becoming a large-scale producer only in the 1880s. As in Venezuela, the coffee boom served to strengthen a particular region, in this case Antioquia. In the twentieth century, the profits from coffee would provide the foundation for the first major wave of Colombian industrialization, centered in the *antioqueño* capital of Medellín. However, the regional elites who benefited from coffee were, for the most part, already well-established members of the national elite.

The needs of the emerging Colombian coffee industry had a great deal to do with the settlement presided over by Rafael Núñez after 1886, after thirty years of inconclusive civil strife between liberals and conservatives. The constitution of 1886 reflected a consensus among "people of substance" (especially the ambitious coffee interests) in favor of "order and progress,"[15] which would be achieved by (1) establishing a strong, centralized state (negating extreme liberalism); (2) establishing the Catholic Church while reaffirming religious liberty (protecting the basic Catholicism of society but negating doctrinaire conservatism); and (3) enshrining liberal concepts of enterprise and property (essential to promoting economic growth).

By the second decade of the twentieth century, Colombia was under the rule of a succession of elected conservative governments in a context of restricted suffrage and clientelistically controlled elections. The stage was set for years of economic crisis and world war, with attendant social and political upheaval. The conservative hegemony that had lasted since 1886 collapsed in 1930, when a split in the party allowed the liberals to win national elections, in coalition with dissident conservatives, to win national elections. Four years later, the more partisan liberal government of Alfonso López Pumarejo initiated a program of modernizing and democratizing reforms that included universal male suffrage, labor law reform, and welfare state measures. The liberals, like their predecessors, sought to use the vast powers of the central government to cement their hold on power.

Expansion of suffrage and the innovative legislation they promised enabled them to gain a virtually permanent lock on power by gaining the loyalty of the bulk of the new voters, especially with the emergence of the dynamic liberal populist Jorge Eliecer Gaitán. Gaitán was not part of the old ruling class, and he indeed called for an end to the old elitist political and economic order (see Sharpless, 1978).

The conservatives' defensive response was led by Laureano Gómez, who sought to mobilize a mass base for his party, not only by appeals to traditional Catholic values but also by inflammatory condemnations of liberals as subversive or even diabolical. Politics in the late 1930s and 1940s were thus increasingly polarized. When the liberals split between Gaitanistas and regulars in 1946, the conservatives were able to win the presidential election with a minority in favor of Mariano Ospina Pérez. With Gómez in charge of the party machinery, they attempted to expel liberals from all centers of political power and entrench conservatives, using violence extensively. Liberals increasingly responded in kind. After Gaitán was assassinated on the streets of Bogotá in 1948, massive riots threatened to bring down the government and initiate a popular revolution; in response, key liberal leaders joined the conservative government in an effort to maintain order. But official and conservative violence against liberals continued, leading ultimately to a liberal boycott of presidential elections in 1949 and the election of Laureano Gómez. Thereafter, the violence increasingly took on its own dynamic, as local and personal agendas such as revenge, plunder, or revolution made it steadily less possible for party leaders to control the violence for their own purposes.

By 1953, all factions of both parties, except the backers of the incumbent Laureano Gómez, supported the seizure of power by the commander in chief of the army, General Gustavo Rojas Pinilla, with the objective of enforcing an end to the violence. By 1957, however, Rojas had shown himself inclined to remain in power and build his own popularly based political movement in an effort to permanently supplant the traditional parties by taking away their mass support. The response of the traditional elites was to unify in a successful movement for his ouster.

Colombia thus experienced a movement in the 1940s that sought the establishment of a liberal democratic regime. Unlike Costa Rica, this attempt failed as intense political rivalries were exacerbated by growing mass political mobilization, for which the existing political parties were unprepared. Costa Rica was able to surmount its crisis in the 1940s and to establish a liberal democracy whose initial narrow base would subsequently expand. In Colombia, the ensuing authoritarian regime helped to crystallize a determination among rival elites to break with authoritarian rule and establish a partially democratic regime. Willingness to compromise and accommodate, in short supply in the late 1940s, was key to the breakthrough of the late 1950s.

Confronting a military government that showed signs of building an independent popular base and perpetuating itself in power, Colombia's fractured traditional elites began to come together in 1956, and a series of pacts among the major liberal and conservative leaders led to a popular referendum on constitutional amendments and the establishment of the National Front.

As finally implemented through a constitutional amendment, the National Front called for the two traditional parties to alternate in the presidency over four terms of four years each. The two parties would share equally all seats in the Chamber of Deputies, the Senate, and lower-level elective bodies. All appointive posts would also be equally shared. Thus the partisan balance was completely insulated from elections. Elections did matter, however, in determining the fate of individual leaders and factions within the parties. Moreover, other political parties were excluded from independent competition in elections: they could only compete by offering candidates and lists within the Liberal or Conservative Party.

The National Front was a direct response by the traditional political elites to a dual threat. On the one hand, their competitive mobilization of mass followings had escaped their control and taken the form of rampant violence. On the other hand, the military government had sought to displace the parties entirely as the dominant leadership of the nation. The party leaders saw the need to cooperate in the political demobilization of the populace, the better to maintain control through tested clientelistic mechanisms.

This conservative pact of political demobilization in fact lasted its allotted sixteen years, in spite of serious challenges. During the 1960s, chronic violence in many parts of the countryside gradually resolved itself into several durable revolutionary guerrilla movements, none of which were able to threaten the government's survival. There were two major challenges to the National Front from within the constitutional system, but both fell short. During the National Front, voting turnout fell to very low levels (below even those of the United States) and has risen only slightly since the resumption of competitive elections in 1974. Other forms of political participation were also at low levels during the National Front. In short, the National Front accomplished the objectives set for it by the traditional party elites who negotiated it.

Venezuela

Caracas was the capital of the Captaincy General of Venezuela, created in the eighteenth century like the Viceroyalty of Nueva Granada to which it was nominally subordinate. Venezuela's economic importance derived from its status as the empire's principal supplier of cacao, mostly grown on large, slave-based plantations near Caracas. The planter class, from which sprang Bolívar and most of the other leaders of the Venezuelan independence movement, matched the upper class of Nueva Granada in its self-confidence and assertiveness, and it was elements of these two classes together who led the long and ultimately successful struggle for independence in northern South America.

The independence struggle weakened the Nueva Granada elite, but it destroyed that of Venezuela. In Venezuela, the remnants of the old elite after independence were reduced to pacts with plebeian caudillos from the interior, who used clientelism to forge popular bases and mobilize armies. The caudillos typically became president; the Caracas elites served as ministers and financiers. Venezuelan politics evolved increasingly as a struggle for hegemony among caudillos, each with a clientelistic local power base that enabled him to raise an army and with ties to moneyed interests in Caracas that enabled him to buy arms and maintain his troops. The basic political cycle in Venezuela was from personal hegemony to indeterminacy to a new personal hegemony. Some caudillos were liberals and others conservatives, but party was not a powerful factor in Venezuela. It ceased being a factor at all after the definitive defeat of the conservatives in the civil wars of the 1860s. (For a full analysis of this era in Venezuela, consult Gilmore, 1965).

Venezuela was (like Costa Rica) among the earliest countries to enter coffee production on a large scale, in the 1840s. Indeed, for much of the century Venezuela was the world's leading producer. Coffee cultivation gave added political weight to Venezuela's Andean region, and the successful insurrection of 1899 inaugurated an Andean hegemony that would last unbroken until 1945. In the hands of Juan Vicente Gómez (1908–1935), the logic of caudillismo was developed so fully, according to Gilmore (1965), that Juan Vicente Gómez was necessarily the last caudillo, for he systematically destroyed his rivals and used the windfall from petroleum sales to build up the state to the point that caudillismo was no longer possible after his death in 1935. The political order was virtually coterminous with the clientele of the dictator and effectively became the state after his death. His two successors, Eleazar López Contreras and Elás Medina Angarita, were transitional figures rather than true caudillos.

The death of Juan Vicente Gómez in 1935 opened the way for a political struggle that had already begun in the shadows, between the military and civilian elites who were the heirs presumptive of the tyrant and new mass-based political movements (communist and noncommunist). In the ten years after the death of Gómez, two successors (López Contreras and Medina Angarita) sought to bring about liberalization without loss of control. This effort failed in 1945 when Democratic Action (AD) collaborated with midranking army officers to overthrow the government of Medina

Angarita. The ensuing reformist government lasted three years (hence its name, the Trienio). AD sought to bring about a rapid democratic revolution, including the full establishment of a liberal democracy, a major increase in the state's royalties on petroleum products, labor laws favorable to unions, secular educational reform, and important elements of a welfare state. AD was the only political organization with a popular base at that time, and thus in three elections during the period it completely dominated its competitors, in spite of the formal honesty and openness of the process. Venezuelan economic elites, foreign petroleum companies, and rival political party elites thus all had reasons for wanting AD's overthrow, which occurred in 1948, followed by the dictatorship of Marcos Pérez Jiménez. By 1957, most of those who had supported the coup were working actively for his overthrow, including a large popular underground under the leadership of communist and AD cadres.

Thus Venezuela, like Colombia, underwent an abortive attempt to install liberal democracy in the late 1940s, while Costa Rica was successfully making that transition. Like their Colombian counterparts, the Venezuelan elites learned the importance of accommodating one another's interests and the need above all to avoid dictatorship. The Venezuelans went much further than the Colombians, establishing a full liberal democracy.

There were more actors, and more diverse actors, centrally involved in the Venezuelan transition process than in Colombia.[16] Pérez Jiménez had alienated a steadily broadening circle of Venezuelans, elite and mass. By 1957, there were active consultations and cooperation taking place among the various sectors opposed to the dictator. Many of the younger cadres of AD were working underground in close alliance with their counterparts in the Communist Party, seeking not only to oust the dictator but to create the conditions for a revolutionary transformation of Venezuela. The existence of this working revolutionary pact set the terms for the other consultations and negotiations during this era.

The other major actors included: (1) top party elites: AD, center-left; Committee for Political Organization and Independent Election (COPEI), social-Christian, center-right; Democratic Republican Union (URD), center-left; and Communist Party of Venezuela (PCV), left; (2) the military elite not allied with Pérez Jiménez; (3) the business elite; and (4) the labor elite. Bitter rivals during the Trienio, AD, URD, and PCV collaborated against the Pérez Jiménez government after 1953. By 1956, COPEI, too, had been driven into opposition. Communication and consultation increased, and these consultations bore fruit when the dictator was overthrown on 23 January 1958. A provisional junta was established that included three military officers and two leading businessmen. This arrangement had the tacit approval of the party leaders.

During 1958, several pacts laid the foundations of the new democratic order (López Maya and Gómez Calcaño, 1989, pp. 68–76; for texts of agreements, see pp. 109–123). The Pact of Punto Fijo was signed on 31 October 1958 by the top leadership of URD, COPEI, and AD as the campaign for the first election was about to enter its last month. The party leaders agreed to defend constitutional government against any possible coup d'état, agreed to form a government of national unity (to guard against a systematic opposition that would weaken the democratic movement), and agreed to formulate a minimum common program to be enacted regardless of which party won the December elections.

Margarita López Maya and Luis Gómez Calcaño point out (1989, pp. 74–75) that the centrist leaders devoted much effort in the early years of the regime to forging an understanding with the armed forces that would lead the latter to accept the apolitical, nondeliberative role assigned to them. The main thrust of these efforts concerned improving the socioeconomic conditions of military personnel and ensuring them both full participation in decisionmaking and autonomy of action in all directly military affairs. These authors also consider the concordat with the Vatican (signed in 1964) as an additional pact important to the overall settlement in Venezuela. The hostile relations between the church and AD during the Trienio were thus transformed, and a major point of potential conflict between AD and COPEI was eliminated.

The communists and leftists sectors of AD and URD were largely left out of these complex negotiations and the resultant settlement. It is difficult to see how the settlement could have successfully included all the major centrist parties, as well as the business and church elites and the armed forces, if an effort had been made to respond to the demands of the Left for radical social transformations. The centrist elites chose, in effect, to build a winning coalition around procedural democracy and mild reform and to risk the opposition of the Left. In reaction, and inspired by the recent success of Fidel Castro in Cuba, the communists and the left wings of AD and URD raised the banner of socialist revolution in 1961. By the late 1960s, the movement had been defeated, and many of the former guerrillas accepted amnesty and integrated themselves into political life as members of peaceful political parties of the Left (most notably the Movement Toward Socialism [MAS], and the Revolutionary Left Movement [MIR]). There is clear evidence that the established elites intended to incorporate the Left into the political system at this time, and that the Left intended to accept the legitimacy of the liberal democratic system (see especially López Maya and Gómez Calcaño, 1989; Myers, 1986).

Venezuela has had an unbroken series of honest and competitive elections every five years since 1958.[17] Opposition candidates won the presidency in 1968, 1973, 1978, 1983, and 1993. The party system evolved through a period of extreme fragmentation in the late 1960s to a strongly bipolar system dominated by AD and COPEI, with the Left (MAS and

MIR) as a stable minority presence garnering about 10 percent of the vote. Voter turnout remained consistently very high until the late 1980s and other forms of political participation respectably high. There is an active and diverse organizational life, and interest groups (especially business, labor, and peasant groups) are actively involved in the political process.

The ability to absorb the Left without undermining stability has been enhanced in Costa Rica as well as Venezuela by the interaction of strongly presidential political systems with proportional representation in congressional elections. A strong presidency tends to promote centrist, bipolar party systems, with the Left usually marginalized in presidential elections. At the same time, proportional representation provides leftist elites an institutional base in the Congress, a platform for disseminating their views. Thus centrist elites can permit legalization of the Left in the assurance that the risk of their winning a presidential election is minimal. Leftist elites can accept the liberal democratic constitutional order in the confidence that they will not be excluded from public forums.[18] This same mechanism could also work in Colombia, if the government had enough control over security forces and death squads to prevent assassination and other harassment of leftist political elites (see the next section).

CRISIS, BREAKDOWN, AND REGIME MAINTENANCE

Chile and Uruguay

The balance of the Chilean and Uruguayan regimes began to break down in the 1960s. In Chile, the Christian Democratic (DC) government of Eduardo Frei, elected in 1964 with the support of the Right (and of a U.S. government preoccupied with preventing another Left victory in the wake of the Cuban Revolution),[19] was more narrowly and exclusively partisan than its predecessors, making little attempt to negotiate with its right and left rivals. Christian Democratic self-assurance was reinforced by Frei's unprecedented absolute majority, which was followed by capturing a majority of the Chamber of Deputies in 1965. The Christian Democrats tended to ignore the importance of the Right's support in these two victories, using the power base thus obtained to push through their program aimed at taking electoral support from the Left while undermining the electoral base of the Right. The program included an extensive agrarian reform law (encouraged by the U.S. Alliance for Progress); moreover, the Christian Democrats and the parties of the Left began for the first time to actively organize the rural workforce. These two initiatives directly challenged the interests of the Right to an unprecedented extent, even as the Christian Democrats aimed directly at weakening the Left. Not surprisingly, both Left and Right responded with hostility to this Christian Democratic attempt to establish a lasting electoral dominance.

By 1969, the Christian Democratic gambit had failed. Without rightist support, the DC lost its majority in the Chamber. In spite of growing support for Salvador Allende and his Popular Unity (UP) coalition on the Left, another center-right alliance proved impossible to achieve. In 1970, Allende won the presidency in a narrow victory in a three-way contest. His government, like Frei's, was committed to the constitution but it was also committed to bringing about major changes in the social and economic structure. Pressed for radical action by his more leftist supporters, and consistently obstructed by centrist and right-wing forces occupying positions of power in Congress and the courts, Allende had an ever-narrower constitutional ground on which to stand. However, when Popular Unity actually increased its share of the vote in the congressional elections of 1973, his opponents realized that they had no hope of removing him constitutionally. It was then that key Christian Democrats joined the Right in supporting a military coup. The procedural democracy that had for so long preserved a policy impasse could not survive the breakdown of that impasse.

In Uruguay, economic stresses made themselves unmistakably evident by the mid-1960s. Export production was stagnating, the state was growing but without adequate means to finance that growth, and standards of living were declining. In the face of these difficulties, both the Right and Left gained strength, creating a steadily increasing likelihood of political crisis. A presidential constitution was reestablished in 1966. The two-party system was not working particularly well. A right-wing Colorado vice president (Jorge Pacheco Areco) succeeded to the presidency in 1967, and the fragmentation of the two major parties combined with the electoral system to produce, in 1971, a right-wing Colorado successor (Juan María Bordaberry), who represented a small minority of the electorate. With strong commitments to impose order and discipline on the society, both Pacheco and Bordaberry tended to compensate for their lack of a popular mandate by an increasingly authoritarian exercise of their powers. At the same time, in addition to serious economic stagnation and a fiscal crisis of the state, there was a paucity of new ideas and a surplus of temporizing and buckpassing. Popular frustration at the evident inability of the government to confront these problems was manifested generally in an increase in strikes and agitation and in the emergence of two major political movements.

The Tupamaro urban guerrilla movement of the late 1960s and early 1970s[20] sought to adapt the experience of the successful Cuban Revolution to the unique urban setting of Uruguay, where there is no Sierra Maestra in which to take refuge and oppressed peasants and rural workers are a small part of the population. The thinking was that the city itself and its workers would shield and support the guerrillas. The Tupamaros rejected the legitimacy of Uruguay's liberal democracy, following the marxist revolutionary analysis that it was a fraud and a distraction for the working class and that only a violent seizure of power could permit a true revolution and hence the ultimate establishment of a genuinely democratic regime. The Tupamaros proved uncommonly adept at covert organization and at carrying out propagandistic attacks embarrassing to the regime. But the Tupamaros alone never came close to the mass support that the Left had during the same period in Chile. They are more similar to the Chilean MIR (Movement of the Revolutionary Left), that is, primarily a cadre of underground combatants with a network of covert supporters.

Alongside the Tupamaros emerged a mass-based leftist movement, the Broad Front (FA) challenging the traditional parties in the electoral arena. The FA grouped together diverse social democratic, socialist, and communist parties and factions, around a very general program of criticism of the status quo and a commitment to move toward socialism. It was thus quite similar to the Chilean Popular Unity in its basic orientation and composition. But whereas in Chile the communists and socialists were mass-based parties with long histories that had coalesced often for electoral purposes, their counterparts in Uruguay had never before attracted a mass base. Thus, when the FA gained 18 percent of the vote in the 1971 elections, this was utterly without precedent.[21] The stability of the two-party system in Uruguay was severely threatened.

Under these conditions of a paralytic regime confronted by increasingly insistent demands for radical change, the armed forces were drawn ever more into the political arena. Influenced by the new doctrine of national security that had become current in Latin America since the Cuban Revolution, many officers were losing patience with the seeming inability of the democratic regime to cope with what they saw as serious threats to national security. In February 1973, faced with a series of military mutinies demanding economic and social reforms as well as the suppression of the Tupamaro insurgency and finding himself unable to mobilize civilian support for the democratic regime, Bordaberry accepted the establishment of a military National Security Council that would, in effect, supervise his exercise of the presidency. The slow-motion coup culminated five months later when Bordaberry closed the Congress after it refused to lift the immunity of a member accused by the armed forces of complicity with the Tupamaros.

One of the great issues of democratic theory is how to combine political equality with economic equality in order to approach true equality of power. And if democracy is indeed to be liberal, it must do this without sacrificing individual liberty. During its first democratic era, Uruguay came closer than any other Latin American country to achieving all three ends: political equality, economic equality, and liberty. Yet Uruguay never really left behind the clientelist politics of the nineteenth century, and clientelism came to permeate the liberal and democratic structure of the modern polity.

Batlle's nationalist vision became a ritual and the nation a cow to be milked.

The pathology of democracy in Uruguay was thus markedly different than in Chile. While democracy in Chile was an arena for open class struggle, the traditional parties in Uruguay blurred class conflict by establishing clientelistic political ties. They were unable to adapt to liberal democracy by opening themselves and the system to new ideas and visions. The parties and the polity they created became so fragmented and immobilized that an effective response to crisis was impossible. Yet it was ironic that these same ties of clientelism and habitual loyalty enabled the traditional parties to reemerge as dominant political actors in the transition of the 1980s (see Chapter 4).

Costa Rica

For Costa Rica, the 1960s and early 1970s were not a time of crisis like those that led to regime breakdown in Chile and Uruguay. However, the twin crises of the 1980s (the Third World debt crisis and the Central American revolutions), though different in character, were similar in intensity to the crises that destroyed democracies in Chile and Uruguay. That Costa Rica's democracy survived is thus worthy of attention in this comparative analysis. The debt crisis increased Costa Rica's dependence on U.S. aid and vulnerability to U.S. pressure, as the country, like many others, found itself unable to service its debt.[22] At the same time, the escalation of the U.S. confrontation with the Sandinistas made Washington pay more attention to the region and rendered Costa Rica, as Nicaragua's southern neighbor, strategically important. The result was that Costa Rica got more aid than it might otherwise have gotten, cushioning the effects of the debt crisis. However, successive governments were under much more U.S. pressure on several issues than was customary, with demands for covert contra bases in Costa Rica and the expansion and militarization of the Civil and Rural Guards (the lightly armed forces Costa Rica maintains in lieu of an army). The government of Luis Alberto Monge (PLN, 1982–1986) proved highly amenable to these pressures, but Monge's successor, Oscar Arias Sánchez (PLN, 1986–1990) was more resistant.[23]

Costa Rica also found itself under substantial pressure regarding its economic and fiscal policies as a result of its inability to pay its foreign debts. The major source of credit in such emergencies is the International Monetary Fund (IMF), which, as always, insisted upon steps to increase government revenues, reduce expenditures, and lower barriers to trade. The implications for Costa Rica's welfare state and government-directed economy were serious. The pressure was intense to privatize banking and insurance; open the medical system further to private practice; and reduce budgets for health, social security, and education. In general, over the decade,

Costa Rican elites have had to accept a substantial reduction in social services and a significant shrinkage of the government role in the economy because the state simply lacked the necessary resources and could not borrow what it needed abroad to maintain them. Nevertheless, it is striking that the social democratic state still exists in recognizable form in spite of over a decade of neoliberal pressure. In economic policy, as in strategic policy, the Costa Rican elites have had substantial success with a strategy of bending to pressure in order to avoid being broken.

Costa Rica continues to display a propensity to political pacts and negotiation between the major parties. In June 1995, President José María Figueres (PLN, son of former president José Figueres) signed a political pact with his predecessor, Rafael Angel Calderón Fournier (PUSC, son of former President Rafael Angel Calderón Guardia) to assure parliamentary support for an array of economic policy initiatives, which would in general continue the neoliberal policy direction of the Calderón government (1990–1994). The pact was advantageous to Figueres because the PLN was one vote short of an absolute majority in the Legislative Assembly. Nevertheless, he was widely criticized by his own partisans for accepting the neoliberal approach of the PUSC.[24]

Venezuela

The major challenges confronting Venezuela in the past decade have been centered around the consequences of the worldwide stagnation and decline of petroleum prices.[25] Successive governments since Gómez have used petroleum revenues to enhance the capabilities of the state to deal with problems of Venezuelan society. The government's share of oil profits expanded gradually over the years as new contracts were negotiated. Careful management of this resource meant that the Venezuelan government was traditionally one of the most solvent in the Third World.

When the world oil crisis of 1973–1974 sent prices skyrocketing, it was thus natural that newly elected President Carlos Andrés Pérez should react in a highly self-confident manner. First iron and steel and later petroleum itself were nationalized, and government social programs were rapidly expanded. Rising government expenditures were financed with international loans based on the assumption of continuing increases in oil prices. But when prices in fact leveled off, the government failed to adjust, and the external debt began to be a major problem. The difficulties were compounded by the inability of the succeeding administration of Luis Herrera Campins to carry out an austerity program. By 1983, Venezuela found itself alongside Mexico and Nigeria as an oil-rich country in deep economic trouble. Little progress was made during the administration of Jaime Lusinchi, so that when Pérez returned to the presidency in early 1989, he had little alternative but to impose an orthodox austerity program, even though he had campaigned as a populist. The resultant riots and repression profoundly undermined the confidence of the people. In 1992, two abortive military coups further shook the country. Pérez was forced out of office by impeachment in 1993, and Rafael Caldera was elected president later that year on a vaguely populist program opposed to neoliberal reforms. However, Caldera has been consistently unable to right the economy. Disillusionment and anger are still widespread.[26]

Colombia

The evolution of Colombia since the establishment of a liberal democracy after the end of the National Front in 1974 cannot be characterized as a consolidation of the regime. If anything, we are witnessing a process of deconsolidation, of slow-motion breakdown.[27] The major problems were an inability to either defeat or reach a settlement with several major guerrilla groups, the growing power and impact of drug trafficking, and the persistence and growth of social violence on all levels. Despite these formidable problems, the formal aspects of the political order have remained remarkably stable. Full electoral competition has been unbroken since 1974, with the opposition winning the presidency in 1982 and 1986. Left parties and coalitions have competed in elections throughout the period, generally receiving less than 5 percent of the vote. Voter turnout and other forms of political participation have increased since the end of the National Front but remain at rather low levels as compared with Venezuela and Costa Rica. There has been some fragmentation of the party system; parties of the Left (notably M-19) have gained, while the Conservative Party has been weakened by serious defections, including that of senior statesman Alvaro Gómez.

Elections held in 1990 may have indicated the early stages of fundamental shifts. The first of the guerrilla groups to reintegrate itself into civil political life, M-19, after a poor performance in congressional elections, finished third in the presidential race (12.5 percent, more than the official candidate of the conservatives). The Conservative Party split, with Alvaro Gómez leading his National Salvation Movement to a second-place showing. The Liberal Party easily led both congressional and presidential votes, and César Gaviria Trujillo was elected president. The voters also approved a referendum to call a constitutional convention, elections for which were held in December 1990. The meteoric rise of M-19 continued, as it received about 35 percent of the vote, against 26 percent for Gómez's National Salvation Movement. The governing liberals were in third place; the official conservatives fourth. However, the national elections of 1994 showed the liberals and conservatives still very much in control: together, they received 90 percent of the presidential vote.[28]

It is at less formal levels that the crisis of the regime becomes more apparent. The effort to deal with the guerrilla movements that have been active since the 1960s has been schizophrenic, alternately emphasizing repression and the search for a negotiated political settlement that would permit the integration of these movements into national political life. The only clear success has been the integration of M-19 into political life after it agreed to forswear violence. Even so, M-19 and other groups on the Left have suffered severely from political assassinations at the hand of right-wing death squads. The other major guerrilla movements remain in the field, although negotiations continue. The government has been progressively less able to concentrate its attention on the insurgencies because of the growing size and power of the underground drug economy. Colombia has for many years been a major supplier of marijuana to North America, but in the last twenty years it has also become the nerve center of the rapidly growing cocaine industry. From a Colombian point of view, the positive side of this phenomenon is the uncounted dollars that the drug trade pumps into Colombia.[29] But this is heavily outweighed by the negative consequences, notably for the Colombian political elite and political system. The Colombian state lacks control over the country's largest industry and the most general threat to social order.

Confronting these threats, the political elites and the state have shown themselves remarkably incapable of meaningful innovation. Both the major parties and the military have been unreceptive and often hostile toward efforts to promote new approaches that might cause significant changes in Colombian social structure. Their response has basically been a reaffirmation of two strategies that have worked in the past: repression and negotiation. But because the elite capacity for action is weak and dispersed, the two strategies have frequently canceled each other out, as happened with Belisario Betancur's attempt to open the political system to the leftist insurgencies, which was frustrated in November 1985 by the seizure of the Palace of Justice by the M-19 and the assault on the palace by the army (Carrigan, 1993). More fundamentally, in twenty-five years of counterinsurgency and ten years of a war on drugs, the Colombian state has shown itself incapable of prevailing in either struggle by repressive means, and the strategy of negotiation has not worked because the established elites have been unwilling to make the concessions that a new settlement would involve. Instead, they resorted to tinkering with institutions, most notably in the new constitution of 1991, which contains numerous provisions that further democratization in theory but do little in practice to change the basic power structure of society.

President Ernesto Samper (Liberal Party), elected in 1994 under a cloud of allegations of having received campaign contributions from the Cali drug cartel, clung to power in spite of mounting evidence against him, including the conviction and imprisonment of key campaign officials. Nevertheless, Samper's solid liberal majority in Congress refused, in June

1996, to accept the prosecutor's recommendation that he be impeached, voting instead to exonerate the president on the grounds that any violations occurred without his knowledge. There was also much speculation that drug money had already so penetrated the political class as to render a majority of members of Congress unwilling to expose themselves to similar investigations, which might follow if Samper were convicted.

CONCLUSION

Liberal democracy evolved in each of these cases out of a civil oligarchy in which political elites developed customs of political contestation, a political grammar, as it were. This is in accord with Robert Dahl's (1971, 1989) argument that democracy is more likely to be stable if methods of contestation are established before inclusion. Liberal democracies emerged when the regimes proved able to absorb and co-opt substantial expansions of suffrage and other forms of political participation without so altering the balance of political power as to provoke rebellion by major interests. This expansion of the polity took place only after a prolonged crisis in which conservative sectors resisted the expansion of participation. When parties and leaders emerged that were able to manage this expanded participation without threatening fundamental conservative interests, the crises were surmounted and liberal democracy was stabilized. In Chile, the crisis began with the election of Alessandri in 1920 and ended with his return to the presidency under a new constitutional and political order, in 1932.[30] The authoritarian regime of Terra in Uruguay (1933–1942) was a conservative attempt to impose order in the wake of Batlle's reforms. The crisis of 1940–1949 in Costa Rica was directly provoked by Calderón's populist attempt to incorporate the working class.[31] In Colombia, the crisis began with the reformist presidency of López Pumarejo in 1934; its end might be marked by the implementation of the National Front in 1958, but continuation of large-scale political violence suggests that the crisis has not yet been resolved. Finally, in Venezuela the crisis began with the death of Gómez in 1935 and ended with the consolidation of AD-COPEI dominance in the elections of 1973.

All of these regimes represented decisive steps forward for their peoples, yet each was constituted to privilege order over justice. Had it been otherwise, they would not have lasted so long. All remained *politically* stable for decades because each was structured to maintain *social and economic stability*. These regulating structures varied according to the historical specificity of the cases, but all contrived to protect the basic distribution of resources under which the regime had arisen. Each system had a *centrist bias,* a proclivity to avoid radical departures. The Left was co-opted or marginalized in each case, part of mainstream politics, but unable to implement its policy agenda without endangering the stability of the democratic regime. Conversely, the Right, although stronger than the Left in each case, had lost its political dominance with the establishment of liberal democracy and could only regain that dominance by terminating the democratic regime itself (as in Chile and Uruguay in 1973).

The centrist bias resulted from compromises among competing elites that reflected a particular balance of forces in the society as a whole. Such compromises functioned to reduce to tolerable levels the uncertainty inherent in democracy (Przeworski 1991, pp. 36–37). The major elite protagonists and their constituencies had assurance of sufficient electoral success to be able to block assaults on their most basic interests, and none could expect to impose their will without compromise.

The prominence of equilibrium and compromise in these cases was aided by the relative weakness of ideological cleavages, as distinct from conflicts of interest and competition for power and office. Even in the Chilean case, where a clear and broad ideological spectrum existed, prior to the Allende period the principal actors on both Right and Left showed themselves more concerned with the pursuit of office and the give and take of the political process, than with ideological consistency.

From 1900 to 1975, most Latin American countries dealt with expanding political participation in one or more of three ways: (1) through populist authoritarianism and electoral manipulation (e.g., Getulio Vargas in Brazil or Juan Domingo Perón in Argentina); (2) through repression (e.g., overthrows of Perón and Vargas); (3) through revolution (e.g., Bolivia, Cuba, and Nicaragua). None of these routes led to stable democracy, though often they led through unstable democracy.

The five countries that are the subjects of this chapter, however, distinguished themselves by confronting the expansion of participation in ways that allowed the establishment and prolonged maintenance of liberal democratic regimes. The modes of establishing the regimes varied considerably according to the particular historical conjunctures that surrounded and conditioned the process. Rival political elites played central roles in each case but were impelled to political innovation by the growing political assertiveness of nonelites. In Uruguay and Chile, in the second, third, and fourth decades of the century, elites moved haltingly toward liberal democracy without an overarching elite settlement along the lines set out by John Higley and Richard Gunther (1992). In Uruguay there was frequent use of pacts by the Colorados and Blancos, but none had the status and durability of a true elite settlement. In Chile there was recurrent bargaining to arrive at and maintain a delicate political and social balance, but there were no comprehensive pacts between rival elites. In both of these early cases, the evolution of liberal democratic practice resembles more the Higley-Gunther concept of convergence. There was no explicit settlement because at the time there was no widespread consciousness that a radically new regime was being established. That became clear only after the fact.[32]

In the post–World War II epoch, however, establishment of democracy became much more explicitly part of the agenda of the times. Thus, Costa Rica's democracy was based on a pact that guaranteed fair electoral competition between the two main winning factions in the civil war of 1948. The terms of that pact later accommodated the return of Calderón to the political arena and the acceptance of a legal role for the communists in the 1970s; both shifts may be construed as elite convergence within the context of the founding elite settlement. Attempts to establish democratic regimes in Colombia and Venezuela in the same period (late 1940s) failed, in considerable part because there was no successful elite settlement to control political competition. By the late 1950s, elite settlements were forged in both countries, which permitted the establishment of the National Front in Colombia and of a liberal democracy in Venezuela.

All five countries could establish and maintain liberal democratic regimes for decades because of the evolution of highly institutionalized party systems.[33] The characteristics of these party systems varied enormously, but all showed a substantial centripetal tendency, that is, a tendency to encourage voters to support relatively moderate, rather than extreme, parties and candidates. The unavoidable winner-take-all character of presidential constitutions also encouraged moderation in candidates and voters for the purpose of maximizing votes in presidential elections, where there can be only one winner. The interaction of these two forces produced two-party, or bipolar, party systems in every case but Chile, whose tripolar system orbited around a centrist party, thereby achieving moderation via a distinct mechanism.

A long history did not render any of these regimes immune from breakdown. Both the Chilean and the Uruguayan democracies broke down in 1973, when this chapter's narrative stops. In both cases, a breakdown of elite consensus was rendered acute by a relatively sudden political mobilization of the Left that was seen to threaten the basic interests of other elite sectors. Thus, these two oldest democracies, which arose to manage expanded participation, ultimately could not do so and fell. In contrast, Venezuela, Colombia, and Costa Rica confronted crises in the 1980s that had less to do with managing expanded participation and more with managing an increasingly complex, globalized economy. Although neither the Colombian nor the Venezuelan regime has broken down at this writing, both are clearly in crisis, while Costa Rica, also confronting serious challenges, is troubled but scarcely in crisis.

Why has the Costa Rican democratic regime been so much more successful than the other four cases in coping with regime-threatening crises? Part of the explanation certainly lies in the seriousness of the challenges.

Costa Rica has not had to deal with large-scale insurgencies and major drug cartels like Colombia, nor has it had as far to fall economically as Venezuela. As noted previously, Costa Rica received substantial external aid during the 1980s, far more on a per capita basis than Venezuela or Colombia. An additional explanation could be its intelligently formed political institutions, embodied in the constitution of 1949, such as the relatively even balance between president and legislature and the abolition of the army.[34] Finally, the Costa Rican political elite has long displayed an uncommon level of political wisdom and sophistication, as compared with their counterparts elsewhere in Central America (Peeler, 1995b).

In confronting the challenges of the 1980s, then, these five older democracies had a great deal in common with the newer democracies around them, to which we now turn.

NOTES

1. Principal sources on Chilean political history and political economy include Bethell (1993); Loveman (1988); Remmer (1984); Petras (1969); Gil (1966); Kinsbruner (1973); Scully (1992, 1995); Zeitlin (1984); Zeitlin and Ratcliff (1988); Osorio (1990); Ramírez Necochea (1985); Nunn (1976); Valenzuela (1978, 1989); Oppenheim (1993); Nef and Galleguillos (1995).

2. By some interpretations, as early as the doomed presidency of José Manuel Balmaceda, 1888–1891. See Zeitlin (1984); cf. Blakemore (1993); Drake (1993).

3. Collier and Collier (1991), in their massive comparative study, have argued that Chile dealt with the problem of incorporating labor into the political system by depoliticization and control of the labor movement, while in Uruguay that movement was mobilized by one of the traditional ruling parties, the Colorados.

4. Principal sources on Uruguayan political history and political economy include Weinstein (1988, 1995); Gillespie (1991); Gillespie and González (1989); González (1991, 1995); Kaufman (1979); Vanger (1980); Finch (1981); Rottenberg, ed. (1993); Panizza (1990).

5. Vanger (1980) provides the most detailed narrative of the Batlle era.

6. The Uruguayan electoral system is often cited as unique; it has been little noted that Honduras adopted essentially the same system for the 1986 elections, with similar results: the president elected had not received the most votes, but he was the leading candidate of the leading party. See Rosenberg (1989). Several Argentine provinces have also recently experimented with the system.

7. Principal sources on Costa Rican political history and political economy include Monge Alfaro (1980); Ameringer (1982); Yashar (1995, 1997); Longley (1997); Chalker (1995); Stone (1975); Cerdas Cruz (1985); Vega Carballo (1982); Muñoz Guillén (1990); Rovira Mas (1988); Oconitrillo (1982); Gudmundson and Lindo-Fuentes (1995); Peeler (1985, 1992).

8. It is a commonplace of Costa Rica's national mythology that this historic poverty and equality laid the foundation for the country's later development of democracy. However, contemporary historians now see this as overstated.

9. A diocese was not even created until 1850, and church-state relations

thereafter were consistently difficult, culminating in the expulsion of both Bishop Bernardo Thiel and the Jesuit order in 1884. See Backer (1975).

10. See Aguilar Bulgarelli (1980); Oconitrillo (1982); Rovira Mas (1988).

11. The church and the U.S. Embassy worked actively to promote a settlement. Archbishop Sanabria's basic position was that a way must be found to stop the bloodshed. The U.S. position was more complex and profoundly ambivalent (see Schifter, 1986; Longley, 1997; Yashar, 1997). The United States was increasingly concerned about the communist presence in the Picado and Calderón governments, but Calderón had been a highly reliable ally in World War II and was furthermore a close friend of Nicaraguan president Anastasio Somoza, another faithful United States ally. However, Somoza was temporarily at odds with the United States over the Nicaraguan presidential succession. The United States also distrusted Figueres's close alliance with President Juan José Arévalo of Guatemala, a reformer viewed with suspicion in U.S. government circles. Figueres's strong anticommunism recommended him, but his advocacy of extensive reforms elicited uneasiness. He was not well known to U.S. policymakers. Thus the United States was dealing with conflicting cues (indeed, the State Department and the ambassador were not always of the same persuasion) in a situation that was not perceived as central to U.S. interests. It is thus not surprising that as the crisis heated up in the late 1940s, the United States did not play an active role. But with the advent of civil war, and the reduction of the alternatives to Calderón (and the Communists) or Figueres, U.S. policy crystallized in favor of a negotiated departure of Calderón. The U.S. ambassador, along with the papal nuncio, was critical in arranging such an agreement in the final days of the war, thus averting an assault on San José itself.

12. In contrast, the communists and other left parties, constitutionally outlawed in 1949, were not permitted unrestricted electoral participation until 1970. The constitutional proscription of communist parties was finally officially lifted in 1975. However, unlike Calderón, the Left received no policy satisfaction: all they got was the privilege of participating. See Oconitrillo, 1982; Salom, 1987.

13. Costa Rica, smaller than the other countries studied in this chapter, is correspondingly more vulnerable to external pressure. Since 1949, the dominant Costa Rican elites have generally shown an understanding of how to maximize their scope for autonomous action relative to the United States. Costa Rican foreign policy is consistently pro-American, regardless of the party in power, and every Costa Rican government since 1948 has been anticommunist. The Costa Rican commitment to democracy is a prominent feature of the country's self-image and is stated in liberal terms that are congenial to U.S. ears. The relatively strong Costa Rican state has generally been administered with reasonable efficiency, and the economy has been managed to avoid the worst pitfalls, such as hyperinflation. This history of prudent competence has afforded the Costa Rican elites with enough maneuvering room to maintain the welfare state and state control of banking and insurance, even though these features are in tension with U.S. conventional wisdom.

14. On Colombian history, see Bushnell (1993); Guillén Martínez (1979); Dix (1987); Hartlyn (1988); Archer (1995). On Venezuela: Salcedo-Bastardo (1979); Lombardi (1982); Kornblith and Levine (1995).

15. This positivist slogan was widespread in the region at the time; it was enshrined in the flag of the Brazilian Republic established in 1889.

16. On the elite settlement in Venezuela, see Arroyo Talavera (1988); López Maya and Gómez Calcaño (1989); Levine (1989); Karl (1987); Blank (1984).

17. On the consolidation of democracy in Venezuela and current problems, see Arroyo Talavera (1989); Brewer-Carías (1988); Carrera Damas (1988); Cruz

(1988); Martz and Myers (1986); Levine (1989); Kornblith and Levine (1995); Peeler (1995a); Goodman et al. (1995).

18. In contrast, a U.S.-style plurality electoral system would give the Left little incentive to seek legalization, since the prospects of winning seats in Congress would be minimal.

19. See U.S. Senate (1975).

20. See Guillén (1973).

21. In contrast, Allende's 36 percent in 1970 was within the normal range for the Chilean Left.

22. This crisis was caused fundamentally by the sudden rise in world petroleum prices in the late 1970s, covered by extensive Third World borrowing from commercial banks. See Stallings and Kaufman (1989).

23. The principal strategy of Arias aimed for an autonomous Central American peace settlement, which was finally concluded in 1987 after the United States had been diplomatically outmaneuvered (Rojas and Solís, 1988). The diplomacy of the Arias Peace Plan is an excellent study in how small powers can exercise substantial autonomy relative to great powers.

24. See numerous issues of *La Nación,* 1995–1996.

25. See Peeler (1995a).

26. For a fuller discussion of the crisis of the 1990s, see Chapter 5.

27. On the recent evolution of Colombia, see Camacho (1986); Comisión de Estudios (1988); Santamaría and Silva Lujan (1986); Hartlyn (1988); Peeler (1995a); Archer (1995).

28. See Peeler (1995a).

29. There is no visible reason why Colombia should not have as bad a debt problem as most other Latin American countries, but in fact it does not, and the explanation probably lies at least partially in hidden drug profits that filter into the legal economy. Consult Thoumi (1995).

30. Democratic stability in Chile after 1932 depended on the continuing exclusion of illiterates from the franchise. Their enfranchisement in 1970, when coupled with the political effects of agrarian reform in the 1960s, was seen by many on the Right as a mortal threat to its political viability. The crisis of 1970–1973 was due in no small part to this inability or unwillingness of the Right to adapt to a fully democratic franchise.

31. Argentina poses an interesting contrast to Chile and Uruguay. The relatively stable elitist civilian regime in Argentina around 1900 was similar to regimes in power during the same period in Chile and Uruguary. But the Argentine elite could not adapt to the extension of universal male suffrage in 1912 and modest democratizing efforts of Ypólito Yrigoyen after his election in 1916. The Radical-dominated constitutional regime was overthrown by the army in 1930. Perón's attempt to mobilize and incorporate the working class was resisted by military coups in 1955, 1962, 1966, and 1976. Adaptation to mass political participation has come only since the latest democratic restoration, in 1983. See Chapter 3.

32. Higley and Gunther (1992) define an elite settlement as an explicit agreement to control competition and keep peace between rival political elites. Convergence is a less explicit process of coming to accommodation. Democracies, they argue, must be founded on one or the other form of agreement among elites. Note the contrast between the absence of elite settlements at the foundation of the early democracies in Uruguay and Chile and the centrality of such settlements in the reestablishment of democracy in these two countries in the 1980s (see Chapter 3). In the latter cases, establishment of democratic regimes was clearly intended.

33. See Mainwaring and Scully (1995), the chapters by Kornblith and Levine on Venezuela, Yashar on Costa Rica, Scully on Chile, González on Uruguay, and Archer on Colombia. See also Rovira Mas (1994); Fernández (1994) on Costa Rica.

34. See, e.g., Lehoucq (1996); López (1996).

3

Later Democracies:
Patterns of Regime Change

Between 1978 and the present writing, most of the countries of Latin America that were not already liberal democracies became so. The only exceptions, and thus the only Latin American countries not treated in this chapter, are Colombia, Costa Rica, and Venezuela (see Chapter 2) and Mexico, Paraguay, and Cuba (see Chapter 4). The rest made this transition in an epoch of wrenching economic crisis and reorganization, as the old consensus of state-led development was everywhere replaced by a new orthodoxy, the "Washington consensus," in favor of global free trade and a reduced state role in economic and social matters.

Much of the literature on Latin American and comparative politics in the last fifteen years has been concerned with this great transition.[1] Given that and the need to discuss fourteen countries in this chapter, there is no choice but to deal with this topic in a comparative and analytical manner rather than case by case. As we proceed, major sources on each country are cited. Even as we proceed comparatively, it is essential to keep in mind that notwithstanding the global and regional conditions that affected all of the countries and in spite of the similarities to be noted, each country has its own history, its own political and economic structures, and its own unique set of actors. To understand any case fully will require going beyond this comparative analysis and becoming familiar with the country on its own terms.

This chapter begins with a review of the authoritarian regimes from which the transitions began and considers the domestic and international conditions that led to the end of those regimes. The actual transitions to democracy are analyzed in considerable depth. The principal challenges confronting the new democracies are reviewed in Chapters 5 and 6, and assessments will be made of their prospects.

AUTHORITARIAN REGIMES OF THE 1970S

Most of Latin America was under authoritarian rule during the 1970s, but the character of those regimes varied widely, and that, in turn, profoundly affected the course of the transitions and the prospects for the emerging democratic regimes. *Personalist dictatorships* held sway in Nicaragua (until 1979), Paraguay (until 1989), and Haiti (until 1987).[2] This is the most traditional form of dictatorship, in which one person monopolizes supreme political power, subordinates the armed forces and other institutions, and rules by force and fraud until overthrown. Typically, the relatives and allies of the dictator monopolize the economic benefits that flow from control of the state. The societies subjected to this kind of regime are among the poorest and least developed of the region; one consequence is that the populations are relatively unorganized and inactive politically. Lack of mass political mobilization is both a condition for a personalist dictatorship and a consequence of it. However, two of the three dictators in this set, Anastasio Somoza Debayle in Nicaragua and Jean-Claude Duvalier in Haiti, lost power precisely when an effective mass mobilization occurred. The third, Alfredo Stroessner in Paraguay, was simply removed in an elite coup when he became aged and infirm.

The authoritarian regimes of Hugo Banzer in Bolivia (1971–1979) and Joaquín Balaguer in the Dominican Republic were basically similar to the personalist type, but with variations.[3] Banzer did come to power as leader of the armed forces, but he exercised power as a personalist dictator and went on after his overthrow to become one of the principal power brokers of Bolivian politics in the 1980s and early 1990s. Balaguer was not a military man but rather an old collaborator of the dictator General Rafael Leonidas Trujillo. After the U.S. invasion in 1965, Balaguer maintained himself in power by fixing elections from 1966 to 1978. However, his regime was not hard-line authoritarian: competitive elections were held, and most civil liberties were respected. It was clear, nevertheless, that the only acceptable outcome was Balaguer's continuation in power.

The remaining authoritarian regimes of the 1970s were products of the armed forces as institutions, though their characteristics varied greatly. In the most developed countries (i.e., the Southern Cone) and in Brazil, the regimes (labeled "bureaucratic authoritarian" by Guillermo O'Donnell, 1979) were committed to a sweeping purification and reorientation of society. This project entailed, as a matter of policy, extensive repression and violations of human rights, directed ostensibly against the political Left, and justified as a necessary part of an unconventional war against subversion.[4] To varying degrees (most of all in Chile), these regimes adopted neoliberal economic policies that tended to reduce the state's dominance of the economy, but their primary emphasis was on national security, not economic reform. Because these regimes were totalitarian in aspiration (not, however, in practice), the task of building democracies to succeed them was more demanding than elsewhere, even though these countries remain among the most developed in the region.

In the three Central American cases of Guatemala, El Salvador, and Honduras, the armed forces as institutions ruled and displayed a rhetorical affinity to the authoritarian regimes of the Southern Cone.[5] But in Central America, at a lower level of development, the totalitarian aspiration was remote from reality. Instead, the rightist institutional Central American regimes tended toward a simple iron-fisted defense of the established social order, along with naked corruption much more extensive than what was found in the Southern Cone.

In the late 1960s and early 1970s, in the central Andes, the armed forces experimented with populist regimes, dedicated to challenging the economic elites and forcing through some economic redistribution.[6] The most sweeping attempt was made by General Juan Velasco Alvarado in Peru (1968–1975); similar but shorter-lived and less systematic efforts were made by Generals René Barrientos, Alfredo Ovando, and Juan José Torres in Bolivia (1964–1971) and by General Guillermo Rodríguez Lara in Ecuador (1972–1976). In Ecuador and Peru, these populist regimes were ousted by more conservative military rulers, who then initiated the transition to democracy. In Bolivia, the rightist government of Hugo Banzer, after overthrowing Torres, did not begin in 1971 with the intent of negotiating a transition but nevertheless did initiate a transition in 1979.

The youngest of the Latin American republics, Panama, became independent from Colombia in 1903, under U.S. protection. It immediately signed the Panama Canal treaties with the United States and has had U.S. troops on its territory ever since. New treaties ratified in 1979 provided for Panamanian sovereignty over the canal and an end to U.S. troop presence in 1999. Although the U.S. presence is pervasive in the politics of all the Central American and Caribbean countries, it has nowhere been so dominant for so long as in Panama. Even considering the periods of competitive elite politics that bore some resemblance to democracy (e.g., in the period between World War II and the military coup of 1968), it is difficult to make a case that Panama ever had a true liberal democracy. The central feature of the political system was a chronic tension between a conservative commercial elite closely tied to the United States and a succession of populist leaders who appealed to the urban and rural masses. The first of these was Arnulfo Arias, who came to prominence in the 1930s, built a substantial popular following, and was elected president four times. Three times, however, he was removed from office by military coups, the last being in 1968.

The leader of the 1968 coup was General Omar Torrijos, who was much impressed by the contemporaneous nationalist and reformist military regime of General Velasco Alvarado in Peru. Torrijos moved, rather more effectively than Alvarado, to mobilize a mass following on the basis of a populist appeal. He promoted various programs that had the effect of channeling more resources to the poor at the expense of the rich, but like other populists, he did little to change the basic economic and social structure. He did succeed—as Velasco Alvarado had not—in building a mass political constituency. Indeed, he largely took over the social sectors that had provided the political base for Arnulfo Arias. His popularity was further enhanced by the successful negotiation of the new canal treaties with the Carter administration.[7]

REGIONAL AND GLOBAL CONDITIONS

Beginning in the late 1970s, strong international pressures bore on all of Latin America to achieve (or to retain) formal liberal democracy,[8] with special emphasis on respect for human and political rights,[9] and to move away from state-centered models of development toward freer markets, freer international trade, and a major reduction in the size and power of the state. The new economic approach was called "neoliberalism," because it amounted to a reaffirmation of the classic economic liberalism of Adam Smith and the major British political economists of the early nineteenth century.

The United States, as the hegemonic power of the hemisphere, played a crucial role in placing both political and economic reform on the international agenda.[10] On the political front, U.S. policy under President Jimmy Carter (1977–1981) emphatically demanded respect for human rights on the part of our allies as well as our enemies, thereby putting pressure on the Latin American military regimes. Although conservative Republican Party members such as Jeane Kirkpatrick and Ronald Reagan were critical of Carter's human rights policy because it undermined friendly anticommunist authoritarian regimes, by late 1982 Reagan himself began to make the promotion of formal democracy a key component of U.S. policy, especially in Latin America. By the mid-1980s, progress toward formal democracy came to be essential for a strong relationship with Washington.

The Reagan administration also promoted, from its inception, the sorts of free-market, laissez-faire economic reforms described above. This policy, entirely consistent with the ideology of the administration, was rendered all the more effective because it coincided with the most profound and widespread economic crisis of the century in Latin America.[11] The large petroleum price increases imposed by the Organization of Petroleum Exporting Countries (OPEC) in 1978–1979 seriously strained the economies of oil-importing countries, causing most to borrow heavily. Meanwhile, exporters such as Mexico and Venezuela borrowed heavily on optimistic projections of petroleum revenues. Thus both exporting and importing countries found themselves burdened with heavy debts. Starting in 1982 with Mexico, most Latin American countries, including both oil producers and oil consumers, found themselves either defaulting on their international debts or in grave danger of doing so. Unable to secure new credit, states across the region found that they could finance their bureaucracies and social services only by printing money, thereby provoking unprecedented levels of hyperinflation and thus deepening the economic crisis.

Although several governments tried a variety of economically heterodox approaches to solving the crisis, none were successful. The only way of getting additional credit was by conforming to the neoliberal strictures established by the major international lenders (International Monetary Fund, World Bank, Interamerican Development Bank), which in turn are controlled by the United States and its advanced capitalist allies, who provide most of the capital of the lending institutions. Thus virtually everywhere by the late 1980s, economic policy was moving in a neoliberal direction. Government expenditures were cut, government workers laid off, state-owned companies privatized. Protective tariffs were lowered or eliminated and the national economies reoriented from domestic consumption to exports.

These sweeping economic changes were, to say the least, unpopular. Because in most cases the onset of the economic crisis—and the early attempts to deal with it—took place under military rule, the wave of democratization clearly owes some of its impetus to the historical accident that compelled the military rulers to take the blame for the crisis. But by the same token, the longer the crisis continues without visible improvement in most people's lives, the more discredit will accrue to the new liberal democratic regimes.[12] The course of development in each of these countries during the 1980s and 1990s has much to do with how successfully the various governments—whether authoritarian or democratic—dealt with the challenge of economic crisis.

Thus, the authoritarian regime of Augusto Pinochet in Chile was able to last until 1989 in part because its neoliberal economic policy was successful in controlling inflation and promoting growth. Even though unemployment was high and income inequality growing, it was difficult for the opposition to mobilize while the economy was relatively prosperous. At the other extreme, economic difficulties helped to bring an end to the military regimes in Peru and Bolivia by 1979. Relative economic success by President Alberto Fujimori in Peru (1990–) and by President Carlos Menem in Argentina (1989–), following gross failures by their predecessors, permitted each to gain constitutional amendments allowing a second consecutive term and then actually to win reelection by comfortable margins.

HOW AUTHORITARIAN REGIMES ENDED

Adam Przeworski (1991, 1996) developed a useful model, called "extrication," of the negotiation processes by which authoritarian rulers may decide to end their regime and initiate a transition to democracy. He posited that in an authoritarian situation there are four relevant categories of actors. Within the regime are (1) hard-liners and (2) reformers. The former prefer maintenance of the regime to any change; the latter prefer change to the status quo but do not wish to go all the way to democracy. Outside the regime, in the opposition, are (3) moderates and (4) radicals. The moderates prefer full democracy but are willing to negotiate with regime reformers to secure extrication, even if some guarantees must be given that restrict democracy. The radicals prefer full democracy and oppose any negotiation with the regime (see Przeworski, 1991, chap. 2; cf. Casper and Taylor, 1996).

Many of the transitions of the late 1970s and early 1980s exhibited elements of this model, though each had its own unique character. In Peru (1975), Ecuador (1976), El Salvador (1979), Honduras (1981), and Guatemala (1984), military coups ousted hard-liners and installed reformers who were willing to negotiate a transition.[13] In the Dominican Republic (1978), Uruguay (1980), Brazil (1984), and Chile (1988), electoral defeat convinced incumbent rulers to move toward a more reformist position, accepting the electoral outcome and beginning negotiations with the opposition on the terms of transition.[14] In Bolivia, incumbent dictator Hugo Banzer decided on his own to terminate his regime and called elections (1979).[15] But the resultant electoral victory of a leftist coalition (1979, 1980) was resisted for two years by other factions of the armed forces and the business sector, who presided over a series of short-term military and civilian governments until acceptable terms for permitting Hernán Siles Zuazo to take office were agreed upon.

In four other cases, the model of a negotiated extrication was not applicable. This model depends on regime reformers and opposition moderates getting the upper hand and negotiating extrication. In these cases, hard-line regimes were simply overtaken, either by events beyond their control or by their own mistakes: they did not extricate themselves; they were overthrown. In Nicaragua, the transition was initiated after the revolutionary overthrow of Somoza in 1979. There was no effective negotiation between the authoritarian regime and the opposition.[16]

In Argentina, the weakening military regime, in an effort to avoid having to negotiate extrication, staged the disastrous invasion of the Malvinas/Falkland Islands (1982). Defeat insured that they had no choice but to initiate a transition to democracy. There was very little to negotiate, and they could not prevent the election and inauguration of Raúl Alfonsín, the candidate most outspoken in opposition to the regime.[17]

In Haiti, the dictator Duvalier was ousted by his own army in 1986, in what may best be interpreted as a coup by hard-liners determined to renovate the regime in order to keep themselves in power, in the face of a growing popular movement for social justice and democracy. Under increasing

U.S. and international pressure, the hard-liners in power made repeated tactical retreats while retaining ultimate power. They permitted the election of the populist priest Jean-Bertrand Aristide in 1990 but overthrew him less than a year later. Only with an international military intervention led by the United States in 1994 was Aristide returned to serve out his truncated term under close international supervision. The supervision had the dual purposes of preventing a coup against Aristide and containing Aristide's radicalism.[18]

Finally, in Panama, the populist Omar Torrijos was killed in a plane crash in 1981 and was succeeded by the gangster populism of Manuel Noriega. A Torrijos ally, he had come up through the military intelligence system and was commander of the Panama Defense Force in 1981. General Noriega, although less popular than Torrijos, took care to maintain his populist base as well as his military base. In that sense he was the political heir of Torrijos (and, indirectly, Arias). Noriega never held the presidency of Panama; he ruled through a succession of puppet presidents and parliaments that were fraudulently elected.

Noriega had long been a paid asset of the Central Intelligence Agency (CIA), useful for his contacts in Cuba in particular. He was known to be corrupt and reputed to be involved in the drug trade, but as long as he kept a low profile, he was apparently considered too useful to be dispensed with, especially as the Central American crisis became more intense in the 1980s. At first, the Reagan administration chose not to make an issue of either political corruption or criminal connections. However, by the end of Reagan's term in 1989, Noriega was getting more publicity. More and more press reports appeared that documented his drug connections, his CIA connections, and his political corruption. In 1989, he was very heavy-handed in assuring victory for his designated presidential candidate, even though opposition candidate Guillermo Endara was widely reputed to have won. Also in 1989, a federal prosecutor persuaded a grand jury in Miami to indict Noriega on drug-trafficking charges. It is unlikely that the Bush administration orchestrated or even authorized the prosecution of Noriega, since that could only be politically embarrassing in view of Noriega's past associations. Nevertheless, once he had been indicted, the administration had little choice but to abandon Noriega and demand his removal from power. By early 1990, after sanctions and intense political pressure had not moved him, Bush apparently believed that direct military action to remove and arrest Noriega was necessary for his own credibility and that of the United States. The ensuing invasion was a military success, and after eluding capture for a few days, Noriega was carted off to jail in Miami.[19]

The ending of every authoritarian regime here reviewed, whether brought about by negotiation (the majority) or by overthrow (four), left a legacy of significant structural limits or conditions on the successor regime. These might include amnesties for human rights abuses enacted by the outgoing regimes, or constitutional limits on the successors' freedom of action or control over the armed forces (as in Chile). Restrictions might also be more informal, as in the continuing political power of the armed forces to resist policies not to their liking or the economic and political power of the United States, as regional hegemon, to have its wishes respected by governments dependent on it, such as those in Haiti, Panama, or Central America.

Only in the case of Argentina might it be argued that the end of authoritarianism left the successor regime completely free of restrictions. Yet even in this case it is clear that, at most, this was true for a few weeks at the beginning of the Alfonsín government. Alfonsín might have been able, at the beginning, to impose radical reform on the armed forces, but he showed no interest in doing so. Within months, the military had recovered sufficient power to actively resist his efforts to control them and to exact important concessions from him.

TRANSITIONS TO DEMOCRACY

The establishment of democratic regimes necessarily overlapped the processes by which authoritarian regimes were terminated. Nevertheless, it is useful analytically to distinguish the two processes. Authoritarian regimes can be ended without necessarily resulting in the constitution of a democratic regime. The Mexican and Cuban Revolutions are clear examples of that, as are coups d'état that replace one set of authoritarian rulers with another. Negotiated extrication need not lead to democracy either, though in the late twentieth century most extrication processes are at least clothed in democratic symbols and rhetoric.

What, then, have been the routes and methods by which so many Latin American countries have made the transition to democracy in the last twenty years? How can we explain the rarity, thus far, of authoritarian relapses, even in the less developed countries whose democracies appear quite fragile?[20]

We should emphasize that the achievement of liberal democracy came to be accepted, by the mid-1980s, as inherently desirable by virtually the entire political spectrum of political elites and activists, except die-hard right-wing supporters of the military regimes.[21] This was an especially significant change for the far Left, which had long held to the marxist-leninist view that liberal democracy was a sham that served only to mask bourgeois domination. But it was the far Left that suffered by far the most under military repression. The survivors increasingly adopted the view that the protection of individual rights that is entailed in liberal democracy, far from being a sham, was vitally important. Moreover, it became ever more clear to people on the Left that the goal of a socialist revolution was receding ever further into the future and that liberal democracy would at least give them an arena in which they could articulate their critiques of capitalism. Some considered that, at least in the short term, they had little choice but to pursue neoliberal economic policies if they gained control of the government. Many on the Left were no more immune than those on other parts of the spectrum to the lure of patronage and other perquisites of office.

The new valuation of democracy was not only a phenomenon of the Left. Politicians and scholars of the Center and Center-Right also often had their commitment to democracy strengthened by the experience of authoritarianism. Particularly in Central America, the Central Andes, and the Caribbean, in countries with no history of stable democracy, the last period of authoritarianism seems to have enhanced appreciation for democracy among centrists who might, in the past, have seen political conflict as a struggle for durable hegemony, not for transitory advantage within a constitutional order.

A key implication of this new valuation of democracy was that political conflicts—whether over ideology, policy, or patronage—needed to be dealt with in a civil manner designed to avoid the outbreak of political violence. Competition for power is the essence of liberal democracy, but civil competition cannot be sustained if the stakes are so high that losing is unacceptable or if the rules are so biased that victory is unattainable. The older democracies had in their time faced the same issue; then as now, a key tool in most transitions to democracy was the pact among rival elites that guaranteed both fair regulation of competition and policy moderation (Peeler, 1985; Higley and Gunther, 1992). In half of the fourteen cases considered in this chapter, the transition was facilitated by some sort of pact or pacts that served to regulate competition and conflict. Transitional pacts varied according to who participated in them and the range of issues governed by them. The broadest type, called an "elite settlement" by Michael Burton, Richard Gunther, and John Higley (1992), would include all or almost all significant elites and would address all major issues among the elites, either by resolving them or by agreeing to suspend conflict over them. If the outgoing authoritarian elite remained politically significant, it would be included in an elite settlement.

Elite Settlements and Other Pacts

Uruguay and El Salvador may be construed as having approached this ideal type, the elite settlement. In Uruguay, two of the three principal parties negotiated the Naval Club Agreement with the military regime after the latter was defeated in a constitutional referendum in 1980.[22] The agreement carefully specified and controlled the transition process, so that, for example, the parties were able to reestablish the former electoral law, and the armed forces received guarantees against prosecution for human rights violations. When the Blancos, who had boycotted the negotiations, finally accepted the terms of the agreement, it became the foundation for the Uruguayan transition to democracy.

In El Salvador, more than a decade of civil war followed the initial overthrow of the authoritarian Carlos Humberto Romero government in 1979.[23] With strong aid from the United States, an attempt was made during that period to complement the war against the marxist insurgency by establishing a minimally democratic regime based on the center-right Christian Democrats and the far-right National Renewal Alliance (ARENA). Leftist parties were either in rebellion or were repressed. However, after 1989, with the Cold War waning and the Reagan administration out of office, the United States (and the Cuban and Nicaraguan patrons of the insurgent Farabundo Martí Front for National Liberation [FMLN]) began to press strongly for a negotiated settlement. This was achieved in 1992 and is currently being implemented. The FMLN has gained access to the political process, but few of the substantive social reforms it advocated have begun. The armed forces and ARENA have had to give up their goal of annihilating the Left and to accept a broadening and deepening of political participation. Essentially all significant elites were parties to this settlement brokered by the hegemonic power, the United States.

The transitions in Brazil[24] and Peru[25] show some affinity with elite settlements but cannot properly be so regarded. In each case, the new regime was shaped not by the sorts of closed-door, small-group negotiations that produced the Uruguayan and Salvadoran pacts but instead by highly public, massive constituent assemblies (in 1979 in Peru and 1987 in Brazil). The assemblies were certainly broadly representative of all significant sectors of the respective societies, and they did lay down the definitive constitutional parameters of the emerging democratic regime. In these ways they were similar to elite settlements, but they really were a different phenomenon entirely. Whereas the elite settlements were quite detailed documents intended to be implemented, the constitutions were to a considerable extent symbolic statements of aspirations, part of a long Latin American tradition of laws as statements of values rather than as governing rules (see Chapter 1).

Three other countries, Chile,[26] Bolivia,[27] and Nicaragua,[28] have made significant use of elite pacts but not of true elite settlements or of definitive constituent assemblies. In Chile, General Pinochet had worked hard to destroy or undercut the leftist and centrist political parties after the coup of 1973. In 1980, against a weak and divided opposition and using fraud and strong-arm tactics, he gained victory in a referendum on his new authoritarian constitution. Subsequently, a still-divided opposition led an unsuccessful campaign in the early to mid-1980s to force Pinochet to resign. The constitution of 1980 mandated that Pinochet, as president, submit himself to a plebiscite in 1988, without opponents, on the question of his continuing in office for another eight years. The opposition leaders of the Center and Center-Left (principally Christian Democrats and socialists) formed the "Concertación por el No" to fight for rejection of Pinochet. Although right-wing parties remained committed to Pinochet, and left-wing parties (mainly the communists, still outlawed) were excluded from the Concertación, Pinochet was in fact defeated, 55 percent to 43 percent. This obliged Pinochet to activate the provision of his own constitution that provided for competitive elections a year later, in 1989. The Concertación reconstituted itself as the Concertación por la Democracia to fight the competitive election, bringing victory to their candidate, Patricio Aylwin, with 55 percent of the vote. Two rightist candidates obtained a total of 34 percent. The Concertación remained together through Aylwin's government and in 1993 obtained 58 percent of the vote for its nominee, Eduardo Frei (son of the former president). Arturo Alessandri (grandson of former president Arturo Alessandri and nephew of another former president, Jorge Alessandri) received 24 percent, and a second rightist candidate got 6 percent. Two leftist candidates received a total of 10 percent (Godoy Arcaya, 1994). The Concertación then continued during the Frei government.

The Concertación is not an elite settlement.[29] The Right remains devoted to Pinochet and largely unreconstructed in its preference for a right-wing authoritarian regime. The Right participates as the principal opposition in the post-Pinochet constitutional regime primarily to defend the authoritarian features of that regime that limit the maneuvering room of the elected governments.[30] Although the Left tacitly cooperated with the Concertación in the 1988 campaign, important leftist sectors continue to reject the legitimacy of the post-Pinochet regime. The Concertación is simply a center-left coalition for both electoral and governmental purposes. It drew together important political forces that had opposed each other prior to 1973, thereby achieving a decisive electoral edge and a working majority in the Chamber of Deputies. The Concertación has been essential to the political defeat of the Right in elections and to whatever grudging and partial retreats the Right has made in policy since 1989. The fact that Christian Democrats and socialists have been able to work constructively together since then has laid to rest the ghost of sectarian polarization that contributed so much to the demise of democracy in 1973. But precisely because the Concertación is not an elite settlement, a future victory by either Left or Right could endanger the stability of the already diluted Chilean democracy.[31]

In Bolivia, too, pacts among elites have been vital to the transition to and practice of democracy, especially since 1985, but they have not been elite settlements. At the end of the Banzer regime in 1979, the elites were so deeply fragmented by competing ambitions, interests, and ideologies that no elected government could be produced until 1982. Moreover, the government of Siles Zuazo (1982–1985), with its fragile unity and narrow base in parliament, could not complete its term and had to agree to early elections. As of 1985, then, there was little reason to expect that, after six years, the transition in Bolivia would lead to a stable democracy.

The election of 1985 was not a good sign. The former dictator, Banzer, led Víctor Paz Estenssoro, the old caudillo of the revolution, 28.6 percent to 26.4 percent. Siles Zuazo's outgoing vice president, Jaime Paz Zamora, was third with 8.9 percent. The constitution provides that if no presidential candidate receives more than 50 percent of the vote, the newly elected Congress shall elect the president from the top three contenders. With no candidate even close to a majority in Congress, an impasse threatened until Paz Estenssoro and Banzer agreed to a pact whereby Banzer would support Paz Estenssoro and receive substantial patronage in return. This would not be a true coalition government, however. Banzer thought he had an agreement from Paz Estenssoro to support Banzer for president in 1989; in the event Paz Estenssoro could not or would not prevent his economy minister, Gonzalo Sánchez de Lozada, from running as the nominee of Paz Estenssoro's Nationalist Revolutionary Movement (MNR). The result was another electoral impasse: Sánchez de Lozada led with 23 percent, followed closely by Banzer with 22.7 percent and Paz Zamora with 19.6 percent. This time, a pact was struck between Banzer and Paz Zamora to elect the latter, denying the victory to Sánchez de Lozada and establishing a coalition both in parliament and in the government. Finally, Sánchez de Lozada gained the presidency in 1993, winning 33.8 percent of the vote against 20.3 percent for Banzer, who was running as the candidate of a coalition of Banzer's National Democratic Alliance (ADN) and Paz Zamora's Revolutionary Left Movement (MIR). Although a congressional vote was still called for under the constitution, in view of the margin of victory Banzer did not insist. Nevertheless, Sánchez de Lozada still faced the problem of building a coalition to govern. He had broadened his electoral constituency by nominating indigenous leader Víctor Hugo Cárdenas of the Tupac Katari Revolutionary Liberation Movement (MRTKL) as vice president. Now he moved to bring in other relatively new political forces, such as the Solidarity Civic Union, led by beer magnate Max Fernández, and the Free Bolivia Movement (MBL, a center-left offshoot of MIR). Both of these parties took seats in the government (Gamarra and Malloy, 1995; Mayorga, 1994b, 1995a).

The marginalization of the Bolivian Left after the debacle of Siles Zuazo in 1985 was key to the subsequent success of having three elected governments in a row complete their terms, for the range of political perspectives that had to be accommodated was temporarily narrowed. The remaining leaders and parties, from center-left to right, found it easier to arrive at pacts among themselves, not only because of a narrower ideological range but also because they focused increasingly on pragmatic matters of patronage rather than the ideological import of policy. Without the radical critique and alternative vision posed by the Left, it was possible for Bolivian politics to gain a certain stability through a pattern of shifting presidential coalitions in Congress, in which, over the long run, any party or movement might find itself in partnership with any other for largely pragmatic reasons. René Mayorga (1995) labeled this new pattern "parliamentarized presidentialism," and he argued that it is the recurrent necessity of negotiation among rival elites that is the most important key to the newfound stability of Bolivian democracy.

Nicaragua's transition has also been substantially affected by a key pact that was conceived as an elite settlement but failed to become one. As the earlier discussion of the end of the Somoza regime makes clear, I regard the transition to democracy in Nicaragua as beginning in 1979, when the Sandinistas came to power.[32] A tumultuous decade of revolution and counterrevolution, of foreign intervention and economic destabilization and decay, led finally in 1990 to an agreement between the Sandinista government and the National Opposition Union (UNO),[33] which permitted the elections of 1990 to take place in relatively peaceful conditions. The electoral victory of Violeta Barrios de Chamorro as the UNO candidate came as a surprise to virtually everyone. The Sandinistas had assumed they still retained overwhelming popular support as the embodiment of the Revolution. Their opponents, including the U.S. government, assumed that the Sandinistas would cheat. Both sides were wrong.

Most of the leaders of both UNO and the contras clearly expected that Chamorro's victory would lead to the definitive expulsion of the Sandinistas from power and the reversal of all major revolutionary policies and programs. The dominant expectation was literally counterrevolutionary. But the newly elected Chamorro confronted the reality that the Sandinistas remained the largest, best-organized political force in the country, quite capable of rendering Nicaragua ungovernable. Moreover, the state, and especially the armed forces and police, had been rebuilt from the ground up by the revolutionary regime and were thus completely populated by people committed in varying degrees to revolutionary aspirations. They could not all be replaced at a stroke without risking a disastrous worsening of the very economic and social chaos that had led to her victory.

Her solution, engineered by her closest adviser (and son-in-law) Antonio Lacayo, was a pact with the Sandinistas. Although as a party the Sandinistas would move into the opposition, the pact provided that command of the armed forces and police would remain with the Sandinista incumbents (the armed forces commander was Humberto Ortega, brother of the retiring president, Daniel Ortega). The commanders in turn committed themselves to loyally serving the new president. The military and police commitment also implicitly promised that the Sandinistas' mass followers would be reined in, discouraged from pushing agitation to the point of destabilizing the new government. Chamorro's pact with the Sandinistas could have been the base for a potential elite settlement, but its achievement would have required that she hold her own coalition together. That proved impossible, though, and the majority of UNO deputies in the Assembly defected and became, in effect, her principal opposition, whereas the Sandinistas in the Assembly teamed with the pro-Chamorro minority to give her a small majority at the beginning of her term. Defections would erase even that fragile majority by 1995.[34]

The abortive elite settlement remains very important in the Nicaraguan transition. Had UNO remained united and carried out a thorough counterrevolution, it might easily have led to a renewal of civil war and would certainly have pushed even more Nicaraguans to the edge of desperation. With the end of the Cold War, the end of the Sandinista government, and the manifest weakness of the isolated Cuban regime, extensive U.S. aid (widely expected by UNO leaders) was unlikely to make it through the hazards of the policy process in Washington. The real choice was between a truly counterrevolutionary government that could not govern and a compromise government that could govern at least minimally. Chamorro did not accomplish a great deal in her term, but she did finish it and hand power to an elected successor. That would have been much less likely without the Sandinista pact.

Interestingly, the Sandinistas were not particularly helped by the pact. They have suffered a severe split, and they are but a shadow of the ruling party of the mid-1980s. Nor has Chamorro been helped. Her heir apparent, Lacayo, was blocked from running by a constitutional amendment prohibiting presidential candidacies of close relatives of the sitting president. Thus, even though the pact was important to a peaceful transition in Nicaragua, it was deeply illegitimate in the eyes of most UNO leaders. It was ironic, therefore, that after right-wing liberal Arnoldo Alemán defeated Daniel Ortega in the presidential runoff in 1996, a split in Alemán's coalition gave control of the Assembly to a tacit alliance between the Sandinista Front for National Liberation (FSLN) and dissident liberals.[35]

Transitions Without Pacts: Hegemonic Influence

The other seven countries in our set made transitions to democracy without major reliance on pacts. However, five of the seven made the transition under the decisive sponsorship and guidance of the United States as regional hegemon. These five small countries of Central America and the Caribbean are Guatemala, Honduras, Panama, the Dominican Republic, and Haiti.[36]

The shape of the transition in these five countries can only be understood in the context of U.S. policy, although within that context each country has its own internal conditions that also must be understood. Within our structure/action framework, this is a situation in which action by the United States constitutes structure for the small states involved, in that U.S. policy is a condition they must adapt to, without having much control over it. The moderating role played in some other countries by pacts among elites has in these cases been played by the hegemon.

The course of Guatemalan history for half a century was in substantial part determined by the CIA-sponsored overthrow in 1954 of the reformist government of Jacobo Arbenz, second reformist president after the overthrow of the dictator Jorge Ubico in 1944.[37] Until 1985, the country was under the direct control of a series of reactionary military governments closely allied with the agroindustrial elite and tacitly supported by the United States.[38] The Mayans, who are a majority of the population, were permitted no autonomous political participation or organization. There had been a revolutionary insurgency in Guatemala since the early 1960s; by the early 1980s, for the first time, it was making some headway with the indigenous population of the western highlands. At the same time, the United States, under Carter and (after 1982) Reagan, made it known that its counterinsurgency policy in Central America required that its allies have elected civilian governments. The initial military response to these twin challenges was the maverick dictatorship of General Efraín Ríos Montt (1982–1983), who pursued repression of unparalleled brutality in indigenous villages while also promoting those in the villages who were willing to adhere to the government and serve in local defense patrols that cooperated with the army. However, Ríos Montt's aggressive, fundamentalist Protestantism worried the Catholic hierarchy as well as more traditional conservatives in the armed forces. Additionally, the bloody toll of repression in the villages was reaching the international press, seriously embarrassing the armed forces. Consequently, in 1983, Ríos Montt was ousted, and the military high command embarked on a transition to elections, which took place in late 1984. Christian Democrat Vinicio Cerezo was inaugurated in 1985.

The legal political parties (all from the Right and Center, none from the Left) had very little leverage on the military and certainly could not have compelled the latter to surrender power. However, with the well-known preference of the United States for a civilian government, the high command found it prudent to permit a constitutional transition while never yielding control over counterinsurgency or internal military affairs. Frequent massacres, disappearances, and other human rights violations continued. Over their long hegemony, the armed forces had acquired substantial business interests, of which they retained control. Individual generals also used their positions to acquire lands and other property. The civilian presidents after 1985 could exert no control over any of this, but no coup was likely as long as the international array of forces continued to favor a constitutional, civilian regime.

After 1989, the same international forces that led to peace negotiations in El Salvador bore down on Guatemala, but with less success. Negotiations began between the government and the alliance of insurgents, the Guatemalan National Revolutionary Union (URNG), but had achieved no settlement by the mid-1990s. Nevertheless, a movement broadly sympathetic to the guerrillas, the Guatemalan National Democratic Front (FDNG), was allowed to register as a legal party for the first time.

In 1995, general elections were held that indicate several contradictory changes in Guatemalan politics. First, the FDNG won six of eighty seats in Congress, providing the Left with a legal public forum for the first time since 1954. On the other hand, the political comeback of General Ríos Montt continued. Prohibited by the constitution from election as president because of having led a coup d'état, Ríos Montt nonetheless founded a political movement, the Guatemalan Republican Front (FRG), which gained enough seats in the 1993 congressional elections to allow him to be elected president of Congress. His party's candidate for president, Alfonso Portillo, finished second in the first round of the presidential election of 1995 (with 22 percent) and barely lost the runoff in January 1996, with 49 percent of the vote to 51 percent for Alvaro Arzú of the conservative National Advancement Party (PAN). Arzú, however, has a majority in Congress, if he can hold it together. Abstention among eligible voters was remarkably high, even for Guatemala: 63 percent. It is particularly notable that Arzú won in urban areas, whereas Portillo won in rural areas, including the western highlands that suffered so much repression under Ríos Montt.[39]

These results signify, first of all, that authoritarianism is still extremely strong in Guatemala and the Left is still quite weak. Ríos Montt, however, is not the candidate of the armed forces, most of whose officers are thought to distrust him. The resurrection of Ríos Montt suggests that the armed forces may be losing some control over the political process. Although the armed forces did intervene in 1993 to force out a president who attempted a Fujimori-style coup, the military currently shows little interest in governing (as long as their prerogatives remain untouched). To stop Ríos Montt, they might have to intervene again, this time in defiance of a popular mandate. Democracy in Guatemala in the 1990s remains an illusion kept in place by an international structure centered on U.S. foreign policy.

The international structural pressure for a political settlement of Guatemala's long-standing insurgency was actually utilized by President Arzú to compensate for his internal political weakness, as he boldly moved forward with negotiations with the URNG in spite of misgivings within the armed forces and on the political Right. With great difficulty, these negotiations were brought to a successful conclusion at the end of 1996. Should the agreements be carried out, they will constitute an elite settlement similar to that negotiated earlier in El Salvador. It is premature, however, to move Guatemala out of the category of countries that made transitions without pacts.[40]

Honduras also found itself caught up in the international politics of counterinsurgency during the 1980s, and it is to that involvement, in large part, that it owes its transition to a precarious democracy. Until the 1980s, Honduras was without question Central America's poorest country, distinguished by a relatively weak landed class, minimal industrialization, and the economic and political dominance of the great banana companies, particularly United Fruit. A long series of alternating hegemonies between the traditional Liberal and National Parties marked the country's political history; the ruling party normally operated in alliance with the army. The mass of the population, poor, dependent, and mostly illiterate, had little to do with politics, except for a few thousand banana workers organized in unions. The United States traditionally showed little interest in Honduras as long as it treated United Fruit well.

This pattern came under strain in the early 1980s as the Sandinista revolution focused the minds of U.S. policymakers on Central America. Honduras, as Nicaragua's northern neighbor, had obvious geopolitical significance. In 1981, the United States successfully discouraged General Policarpo Paz García from perpetuating himself in office and induced the military to begin a transition to an elected civilian regime. The United States channeled quantities of aid into Honduras second only to the aid sent to neighboring El Salvador—and the latter country was fighting a major guerrilla war, whereas Honduras was not. The price of the aid for Honduras was that the United States was lent several bases, and Honduras turned a blind eye to operations of the Nicaraguan contras from Honduran territory. A succession of reasonably honest elections produced four successive civilian, constitutional presidents drawn from both traditional parties, after 1981. These presidents, though, never succeeded in controlling the military or stopping human rights abuses.[41] Although the economic elite was much weaker than in Guatemala or El Salvador and the political elite less predatory, it remained clear in the mid-1990s that democracy in Honduras was likely to persist only as long as its international support.

The transition to democracy in Panama was of course profoundly conditioned by the U.S. invasion that ousted Manuel Noriega (see previous discussion). Opposition presidential candidate Guillermo Endara arrived on a U.S. transport and was duly sworn in as constitutional president. Thus was Panama's transition to democracy begun. However, Endara's government was weighed down by economic crisis and received relatively little aid from the United States. Not surprisingly, then, free elections in 1994 brought to the presidency Ernesto Pérez Balladares, head of the old Torrijos-Noriega party. Pérez Balladares dissociated himself from Noriega and showed himself disposed to comply with the basic lines of neoliberal economic policy; his populism, in short, was much diluted. Indeed, reflecting Panamanian nervousness as the final canal transition approached, Pérez Balladares began negotiations to keep at least some U.S. troops in Panama after 2000. In 1996, Pérez Balladares was shaken by reports in the international press that his campaign had received drug money, a charge that also appeared plausible with respect to several other candidates or parties.

Given its levels of education and economic development, one would expect democracy to have been more successful in Panama than it has in fact been. It seems likely that the constant presence of the United States as a political actor in Panama has retarded democratic development in at least two ways. First, it has provided economic elites with a crutch that allows them to neglect the political learning that is necessary to operate a democracy successfully. Second, it has provided a ready-made foil for populists and nationalists that allowed many Panamanians to persist in an oversimplified analysis of national problems. Thus, after nearly a century of national independence, democracy in Panama remains, at best, in its infancy.

During the same epoch (the first third of the twentieth century) when the United States acted to secure Panamanian independence (and the canal), the United States also intervened militarily in several other Caribbean and Central American countries, including the Dominican Republic.[42] The stated purpose in each case was the preservation and enhancement of political stability, governmental efficiency, and sound pro-business economic policy. The political effect was baleful without exception, leading in every case but Puerto Rico to prolonged dictatorships and the complete failure to establish stable democracies.[43]

In the Dominican case, the U.S. occupation was followed, in 1930, by the seizure of power by General Rafael Leonidas Trujillo, U.S.-trained commander of the U.S.-trained army. Trujillo would rule with tacit U.S. support until his assassination in 1961. What began as a transition to democracy was truncated by a military coup that overthrew recently elected President Juan Bosch in 1963. A popular uprising in 1965 led by military supporters of Bosch was put down by a massive U.S. occupation. The following year, with U.S. blessings, elections were held that were won by Joaquín Balaguer, a longtime collaborator of Trujillo. Balaguer had a real constituency among business elites, the military, and public functionaries inherited from Trujillo, and he did not hesitate to use the usual range of manipulation and intimidation in order to magnify that constituency and twice gain reelection (1970, 1974). He enjoyed strong support from the Johnson and Nixon administrations, but when it became apparent that he had failed to control the 1978 election, initial efforts to annul it or to falsify results were actively discouraged by the Carter administration. As a result, the opposition Dominican Revolutionary Party (PRD) gained control of the government and held it for two presidential terms, until 1986, when the aged Balaguer was returned to office. Reelected in 1990, his victory in the disputed elections of 1994 was accepted by the PRD only on the condition that his term end with new elections in 1996, in which he would not be a candidate. Electoral fraud is less widespread than it used to be, and there have been several reasonably honest elections, but it is by no means certain that the post-Trujillo establishment will give up power. With electoral politics being refereed by the United States, there was no necessity for the competing political forces to agree among themselves. The pact of 1994, recognizing Balaguer's victory but curtailing his term, is the first instance of elite pact making in the Dominican Republic, and the United States was, at a minimum, a very interested observer. In 1996, PRD candidate Francisco Peña Gómez led in the first round but confronted a surprising alliance of the two patriarchs, Balaguer and Juan Bosch, in support of the runoff opponent, Leonel Fernández, the candidate of Bosch's party, the PRD. The result in the 30 June runoff was a 51 percent victory for Fernández and the likelihood of continued behind-the-scenes influence for Balaguer.[44]

Nearly twenty years after the decisive turning point of 1978, the country's economic and political establishment continues to be addicted to Balaguer. Dominican democracy, approaching two decades of continuity, must still be accounted fragile and externally sponsored. It is, in all its fragility and contradiction, the best example of the United States having successfully promoted democracy.

Haiti endured an even longer U.S. occupation than the Dominican Republic or Nicaragua: the Marines did not depart until 1934. The resultant dictatorship did not last as long; it was overthrown in 1946. The dominant dictator of recent Haitian history, François Duvalier, emerged in the 1950s, relatively independent of U.S. influence. However, once he had consolidated his hold on power, successive U.S. administrations worked with him as the best guarantor of stability in Haiti. He was succeeded after his death by his son, Jean-Claude, who was ousted in 1986. The subsequent years of turmoil have been reviewed earlier in this chapter. After President Jean-Bertrand Aristide was restored to office by the U.S.-led intervention of 1994, Aristide was able to effectively dismantle the old army and police and to begin training a new police force. However, neither Aristide's forces nor the international troops succeeded in disarming the large number of supporters of the old regime who participated in unofficial terrorist squads. The public peace and the security of the new democratic regime thus remained in check. Aristide's ability to provide concrete benefits to the poor majority of the population was limited by the small amount of external aid and by the continued power of his opponents in the Congress. General elections were held under international observation in late 1995, which led to victory for Aristide's Lavalas Party and for its presidential candidate, René Preval.

The real test of the new Haitian regime has begun: the charismatic

Aristide has left office, and the foreign troop presence is winding down. Can this genuinely popular movement, supported by an overwhelming majority drawn largely from the poorest classes, reach a new accommodation with the propertied classes of Haiti and with the policymakers of Washington? Or will the former power holders persist in seeing the new regime as a mortal threat? The old rulers, having had their military arm amputated, lack the means to retake power on their own, but as long as they hope for a U.S. intervention on their side, they are unlikely to accept a new and less favorable balance of internal power.[45] If such a new pact is not worked out, then, the United States will remain the moderator of Haitian politics.

The cases reviewed in this section show clearly that the evolution of political regimes can be decisively affected, particularly in small and weak countries, by external structural influences, both intentional and unintentional. In several cases, U.S. intervention helped to end dictatorships, and recent U.S. policy has certainly promoted free and fair elections and respect for human rights, but such influence has limits. By definition, democracy as rule by the people cannot be externally imposed because then it would not be the people ruling but the outside power. However, liberal democratic formal institutions, with their emphasis on limited government, individual rights, and political competition, clearly can be insisted upon by an outside hegemonic power. Political elites acting within such an externally structured context may in time learn to operate the system with less and less supervision and may indeed learn to appreciate its virtues.

Transitions Without Pacts: Relative Autonomy

The other two cases of countries that made transitions without pacts were much less subject to outside intervention and thus more fully explicable in terms of internal conditions. Beyond their relative autonomy and the relative unimportance of pacts in their transitions, however, Argentina and Ecuador share very little.

In Argentina, the military government, having confronted severe economic crisis and military defeat in the Malvinas/Falklands War, was unable to negotiate terms of the transition.[46] They made some attempts to do so, but the Radical Party and other elements of the opposition refused to agree to the military conditions. In the end, the transition occurred on the terms demanded by Alfonsín and the Radicals. There was also no pact with the principal opposition party, the Peronists. Indeed, the scope of the unprecedented Radical Party electoral victory of 1983 led some radical leaders to entertain thoughts of a new epoch of radical political hegemony, like that before 1930. From this perspective, the Peronists were not a legitimate opposition force but rather a historical aberration that could finally be eliminated. Similar sentiments of what one may call a hegemonic vocation were of course widespread among Peronists, but their very defeat caused them to begin reevaluating their long-standing assumption that they were the natural tribunes of the people. The attitudinal basis for a civil relationship between a governing party and a loyal opposition began to evolve only after the radicals suffered electoral reverses in provincial and congressional elections. By the late 1980s, it became clear to both radicals and Peronists that an Argentine democracy would necessarily be a multiparty democracy.

The Peronist victory in the 1989 elections led to the first transition in Argentine history from a democratically elected president to a democratically elected successor from the opposition. As such, it marked the success of the Argentine transition to democracy. Yet the particular conduct of Carlos Menem as president raises important issues for the future of democracy in Argentina, issues that will be discussed in Chapter 5.

The Ecuadoran military extricated itself from the government by 1978, arriving at only minimal procedural agreements with the various civilian political leaders. The latter, for their part, embarked on the electoral competition for political power without an explicit or implicit pact regulating that competition.[47] Ecuador never had institutionalized political parties; rather, individual leaders formed personalist movements around themselves, relying on some combination of patronage, economic interest, regional loyalty, class conflict, and charisma to maintain the loyalty of their followers. The most durable cleavage continued to be between the coast and Sierra (or between Guayaquil and Quito), but in each region many leaders competed with each other for elite and popular support. The new democratic era simply meant that this kaleidoscopic political competition would take place, for a time indeterminate, within liberal democratic procedures. Whereas in Peru the first ten years of democracy were dominated by well-institutionalized parties, in Ecuador there were only personalist movements. Whereas in Bolivia the most powerful elites could hold their parties together while they negotiated pacts that enhanced stability, in Ecuador a succession of minority presidents found themselves isolated, immobilized, and impotent. An important reason for this difference was that Ecuador uses a runoff election in the event that no presidential candidate wins an absolute majority, whereas Bolivia relies on congressional election in such an eventuality. As René Mayorga (1995b) argued, the Bolivian system requires pact making to win elections, but that of Ecuador does not. Thus most Ecuadoran presidents reach office with a Congress controlled by the opposition, whereas Bolivian presidents could not have been elected without piecing together a congressional majority.

The democratic regime has survived in Ecuador, in spite of the failure of every elected president since 1978. Although the evolution of democracy there seems to owe little to external influence, its persistence is probably due to military reluctance to seize power in light of predictable unhappiness in Washington at such an eventuality. Political elites show little sign of commitment to the principles and practice of liberal democracy. Their continued acceptance of it is a matter of political convenience: in the present domestic and international environment, none of them can establish hegemony.

The Argentine and Ecuadoran cases show much less influence of external structures on the transition, but that influence is by no means negligible, at least in raising the probable cost of any reversion to open authoritarianism. Internal structures, such as Argentina's highly institutionalized parties and Ecuador's inchoate party system (see Chapter 6), were important in shaping the contours of the transition in each country, contours within which political action occurred.

Elites and Transitions to Democracy: An Overview

Adam Przeworski (1991, p. 80) argued that

> all transitions to democracy are negotiated, some with representatives of the old regime and some only among the pro-democratic forces seeking to form a new system. Negotiations are not always needed to extricate the society from the authoritarian regime, but they are necessary to constitute democratic institutions. Democracy cannot be dictated; it emerges from bargaining.

The preceding discussion tends to confirm the truth of this assertion, though it should be added that in the cases of the smaller countries of the Caribbean Basin, a key negotiator has been the U.S. government, whose policy has favored, at the least, competitive and honest elections (except for the early Reagan years). Even such a powerful actor cannot always impose liberal democracy, but it can raise the costs of resisting democratization, and thereby obtain, most of the time, formal compliance from the internal elites. Still, it is common to find that human rights continue to be violated, usually by the armed forces or semiofficial death squads. Electoral fraud may be less widespread but is still commonly alleged, and often with reason. The political culture of tolerance has as yet only shallow roots.

The remaining cases, mostly South American, confirm that democracies have emerged from elite bargaining of various sorts, ranging from something close to a comprehensive elite settlement to agreements taking in only part of the relevant universe of elites or addressing only some of the outstanding issues. Because liberal democracy requires elites to forswear force and fraud and to accept control of the government by their opponents, they need to have confidence that their opponents will stand by the same commitments. In the absence of such mutual assurance, democratic institutions will inevitably be fragile, as in the cases of Ecuador, Nicaragua, and Haiti, for example.

At a more general level, these cases tend to support the centrality of elites to any political processes. This is not to say that the rest of the population (i.e., nonelites) does not matter (see the next section), but only that political action by nonelites has an impact on the society as a whole to the extent that it is either mobilized or channeled by elites. I am using "elite" here as a synonym for leadership, which obviously may emerge from nonelite sectors. Even spontaneous popular riots acquire an "elite" in this sense, persons who are at least momentarily able to guide or focus the attention of the rioters on one object rather than another. Not a few riots or public manifestations have in fact been systematically promoted by leaders opposed to the dominant elites of society, who may be seen, effectively, as counterelites.

Political success or failure for all these elites and counterelites depends heavily on whether they can really demonstrate mass support. To be able to do that, they must somehow relate themselves effectively to the felt needs and preoccupations of some sector of the society and then induce that sector to support them as they bargain with other elites.

Nonelites: The People and Transitions to Democracy

Roles played by the middle-class minorities (professionals, successful merchants, and bureaucrats, whether public or private) and by the poor majorities (workers, peasants, small merchants, and the marginal poor) constitute a variable and highly significant element in the several transitions treated in this chapter.

Nonelite actions with national impact on the transitions to democracy may be divided into several categories: (1) popular riots and rebellions, (2) social movements, (3) political mobilization, and (4) abstention. By popular riots and rebellions, I mean relatively spontaneous violent protest or resistance against public authorities or policies. Established opposition elites do not promote or control such riots or rebellions, though counterelites may emerge from them. Several countries have experienced such episodes, commonly in response to the economic strains imposed by neoliberal adjustment policies. In general, if directed against authoritarian regimes, (e.g., in Nicaragua in 1978) these actions might strengthen hardline elements but could also provide popular support to insurgencies like the FSLN. If directed against democratic regimes (as in Venezuela in 1989), the actions tended to put in doubt the legitimacy of those regimes.

Social movements are collective actions of people beyond the level of the family but not part of any existing party or other political institution.[48] Social movements emerge to meet felt needs of the people involved and may become institutionalized over time. One type of social movement that was highly relevant to democratic transitions was organizations of relatives of the disappeared or of other victims of authoritarian violations of human rights. The classic example was the movement called the Madre de Plaza de Mayo in Argentina, who began in the late 1970s to appear in the principal plaza of Buenos Aires in front of the presidential palace (la Casa Rosada), marching silently every week with signs demanding that the government provide information as to the whereabouts of missing sons, daughters, spouses, or grandchildren.[49] By forcing the issue of the disappearances onto the public agenda, these women publicly cast doubt on the legitimacy of the military regime and provided a vivid example of courage in the face of repression. Their very status as mothers made it extremely difficult and politically costly for the regime to repress their protests or to retaliate against them, though several were in fact killed. Similar social movements developed in other countries, most notably Chile and Guatemala.

In the transition processes, competing elites repeatedly attempted the political mobilization of nonelites. A key choice for nonelites, then, was how to respond to these appeals. If authoritarian regimes could count on enough popular support (as in Chile in the 1980 constitutional referendum), they could perpetuate themselves in power. Even when they lost elections (as in Uruguay's 1980 constitutional referendum or the 1988 presidential plebiscite in Chile), a substantial popular vote would strengthen their hand in negotiating the transition. Conversely, opposition elites needed highly visible popular support to be effective in making demands on the military authorities. Popular demonstrations against the military regime in Argentina after its defeat in the Malvinas War helped to push it toward the exit, and the strength of Alfonsín's electoral victory in 1983 helped him avoid making concessions before his inauguration. A key question, in short, is, for which causes were people willing to mobilize themselves (Casper and Taylor, 1996)?

The other side of that coin was abstention, the decision on the part of citizens to abstain from voting or other political action, to take what Albert Hirschman (1970) called the "exit" option. Clearly, one reason so many transitions to democracy were successful during this period was that large numbers of citizens did mobilize to support the cause of democracy: they did not abstain, withdraw, or exit. However, as we shall see in Chapter 6, a key problem of the resulting liberal democracies has been to maintain levels of participation adequate for purposes of legitimacy but not so intense as to threaten stability.

Finally, it is important to remember that nonelites may respond to and engage in politics in ways that may profoundly affect their own lives and their immediate communities, without breaking the surface of national politics. Every time people within a community or neighborhood organize to address a common problem, such as the water supply or crime, they are engaged in politics in the very direct sense that they are making collective decisions and taking collective action to address common issues. The national arena is not the only place for politics. Indeed, politics at the base, grassroots politics, may be, can be, the most authentically democratic of all.[50]

CONCLUSION

The complex and diverse transitions from authoritarian to liberal democratic regimes over the last two decades in Latin America cannot be convincingly understood within any one theoretical framework. For every meaningful generalization, there are exceptions and caveats. If we emphasize elite choices and negotiations (as do Linz and Stepan, 1978; O'Donnell and Schmitter, 1986; or Higley and Gunther, 1992), we must nevertheless acknowledge the weight of economic and social structure, the global conjuncture of political and economic forces, and, of course, tradition and culture. If we try to make economic and social structure primary (like Rueschemeyer, Huber Stephens, and Stephens, 1992), we will still run afoul of contingencies of human choice and policy. Explanations based on global pressures for democratization cannot deal with the immense variation in timing and result. If, like Claudio Véliz (1980) or Howard Wiarda (1992), we make culture and tradition determinative, we will find it hard to account for real cases of democratization. If we emphasize mass political action and social movements, we confront the inevitable emergence of elites.

The orientation of this book, as defined in the Preface, is that the search for a single universal cause is misconceived. Human societies are inherently complex, and causation in society is necessarily multiple and recursive. That is, any social phenomenon is both cause and effect. Human beings take actions that affect their environment; the environment at the same time affects them and limits the range of actions they can take. Action is neither an illusion nor an inconvenient anomaly: it is fundamental to being human. Thus an adequate understanding of complex human phenomena such as transitions to democracy cannot begin by trying to "control for" human action in order to see more clearly the effects of the predictive variables. It must be part of our understanding that people take actions that are not predetermined and that have real effects. At the same time, we should be foolish to think that such actions are unaffected by the actors' environment. It remains a key task of analysis to sort out the interplay of various environmental influences in distinct cases.

For the problem at hand, it is clear that we must acknowledge central roles for distinct sectors of the political elites, in making choices about how they interact with each other, how they confront economic and political challenges and crises, and how they respond to popular demands. We will not be able to understand the transitions without taking account of these choices. But the structural context of the choices is just as important:

international political and economic pressure, the severity and timing of economic crises in each country, the character and intensity of popular political mobilization. All these and other structural factors will shape and limit elite choices. A society's history, as processed through its culture, structures how both elites and nonelites define their situation and respond to it. Thus, the pervasiveness of clientelistic behavior among elites and nonelites (in Brazil or Ecuador, for example) has deep historical and cultural roots that make it hard for people to behave in any other way in the political arena. By acting clientelistically, they in turn shape the character of the emerging regime in their country. Choices are shaped and limited by structural context; they are not determined. Choices may change the structural context, but they cannot transcend it.

NOTES

1. Major comparative studies include O'Donnell, Schmitter, and Whitehead (1986); Diamond, Linz, and Lipset (1989, 1995); Baloyra (1987); Higley and Gunther (1992); Przeworski (1991); Huntington (1991). Major comparative studies focused on Latin America include Malloy and Seligson (1987); Drake and Silva (1986); Wiarda (1990); Mainwaring and Scully (1995); Camp (1996a); Conaghan and Malloy (1994); Jonas and Stein (1990); Needler (1987); Tulchin (1995).

2. On Nicaragua, see Booth (1985); Walker (1986, 1991). On Haiti, see Mintz (1995); NACLA (1987). On Paraguay, see Abente (1995); Lewis (1993a).

3. On the Banzer period, see Malloy and Gamarra (1987, 1988); Dunkerley (1984); Kelley and Klein (1981); Klein (1992). On the Balaguer period, see NACLA (1982); Black (1986); Espinal (1987); Conaghan and Espinal (1990); Kryzanek (1996).

4. See especially O'Donnell (1979); Collier (1979). On Argentina, see also Rouquié (1994); Cavarozzi (1983, 1986). On Brazil, see also Stepan (1988, 1989); Martins (1986). On Chile, see also Valenzuela (1978, 1989); Valenzuela and Valenzuela (1986); Arriagada (1988); Garretón (1989). On Uruguay, see Gillespie (1986); Rial (1986); Dutrénit Bielous (1994); González (1995).

5. On Central America, see Torres Rivas (1993); Pérez Brignoli (1987); Weaver (1994). On Guatemala, see Calvert (1985); Handy (1984); Jonas (1991). On El Salvador, see Baloyra-Herp (1985); Montgomery (1995). On Honduras, see Morris (1984); Peckenham and Street (1985).

6. On Peru, see Stepan (1978); Palmer (1980); Rudolph (1992). On Bolivia, see Malloy and Gamarra (1987, 1988); Ladman (1982). On Ecuador, see Isaacs (1993); Martz (1987).

7. During the same period, the military regime of Osvaldo López Arellano in Honduras showed substantial affinities with this type.

8. A useful survey on international dimensions of democratization is Whitehead (1996).

9. Human rights, as codified in international law and treaties, would include, for example, the right not to be tortured, arbitrarily imprisoned, or caused to disappear. Political rights would include freedom of speech and the press and honest, competitive elections.

10. See Schoultz (1981, 1987); Stallings and Kaufman (1989); Hartlyn, Schoultz, and Varas (1992); Smith, Acuña, and Gamarra (1994a, 1994b); Remmer

(1991b); Haggard and Kaufman (1995); Bresser Pereira, Maravall, and Przeworski (1993).

11. The causes of the crisis are beyond the scope of this book. See Stallings and Kaufman (1989); Stamos and Pool (1989).

12. See, for example, the lead article by Chauvin (1995) in *Latinamerica Press*.

13. On Peru, see Rudolph (1992); McClintock and Lowenthal (1983). On Ecuador, see Isaacs (1993). On El Salvador, see Montgomery (1995). On Honduras, see Morris (1984). On Guatemala, see Calvert (1985); Jonas (1991). For a comparison of Ecuador and the Dominican Republic, see Conaghan and Espinal (1990). Note that especially in El Salvador, Honduras, and Guatemala, pressure was intense from the United States for a transition to democracy. This pressure developed because the United States was preoccupied with the revolution in Nicaragua from 1979 on and wished to avoid the embarrassment of propping up authoritarian allies in the isthmian region. Cf. Allison and Beschel (1992).

14. On the Dominican Republic, see NACLA (1982); Black (1986). On Uruguay, see Rial (1986). On Brazil, see Martins (1986); Fleischer (1986); Soares (1986). On Chile, see Caviedes (1991); Garretón (1995). The Dominican case was marked by direct and public pressure from the Carter administration for President Balaguer to recognize his defeat.

15. On Bolivia, see Malloy and Gamarra (1987, 1988); Mayorga (1991).

16. On Nicaragua, see Booth (1985); Walker (1986, 1991); Torres and Coraggio (1987). Anti-Sandinista elements of the opposition, with the help and encouragement of the United States, did attempt to negotiate an extrication that would leave in place some checks on Sandinista power, but these efforts came too late to affect the outcome of the insurrection.

17. On Argentina, see Cavarozzi (1986); Vacs (1987); Wynia (1986).

18. On Haiti, see Mintz (1995); NACLA (1994a); Rohter (1996a).

19. On Panama, see Ropp (1982, 1996); Priestley (1986); Pérez (1995).

20. Major analyses of the transition in Latin America include O'Donnell, Schmitter, and Whitehead (1986); Higley and Gunther (1992); Przeworski (1991); Haggard and Kaufman (1995); Malloy and Seligson (1987); Baloyra (1987).

21. Public opinion was also typically favorable toward democracy in the abstract, but important sectors in most countries also showed sympathy for authoritarian rule. Often, the same individual might simultaneously articulate both attitudes. See, for example, Leslie Anderson (1995); Basáñez (1994); Booth and Richard (1996).

22. On the transition in Uruguay, see Gillespie (1986, 1992); Rial (1986); Dutrénit Bielous (1994); González (1995); Caetano and Rilla (1995); Caetano, Rilla, and Pérez (1987).

23. On the peace settlement in El Salvador, see Montgomery (1995).

24. On the Brazilian constituent assembly, see Bruneau (1992); Crespo Martínez (1991); Lamounier (1994a); Rizzo de Oliveira (1988); Stepan (1989).

25. On the Peruvian constituent assembly of 1979, see McClintock and Lowenthal (1983).

26. On the development and political role of the Concertación in Chile, see Cavarozzi (1992); Garretón (1993a, 1995); Drake and Jaksic (1991); Angell (1993); Oppenheim (1993); Petras and Leiva (1994); Puryear (1994); Scully (1995).

27. On the role of pacts in the Bolivian transition, see Gamarra and Malloy (1995); Gamarra (1994); Mayorga (1992, 1994a, 1994b, 1995b).

28. On the Chamorro/FSLN pact in Nicaragua, see Vargas (1995); LaRamée (1995). For a comparison with Guatemala, see Jonas (1989).

29. But cf. Cavarozzi's argument in Higley and Gunther (1992). Patricio Silva, in a private communication, argues that "although the Concertación as such is not an elite settlement, it represents a political project (democracy with free market economy) which is, in itself, the basis of a general agreement between the Concertación sector and right-wing elite sectors."

30. For example, there are nine unelected senators, appointed by the Pinochet government before leaving office, whose terms expire only in 1998. Pinochet is specified in the constitution as commander of the army, unremovable by the president, until 1998, and he will hold a life seat in the Senate thereafter.

31. The Concertación is thus in a position similar to the democratic center in the German Weimar Republic of the 1920s: continuation of the democratic regime depends on the continuing electoral strength and cooperation of the center parties. As is well known, when the Center failed in Germany, the result was Nazism.

32. This is a controversial judgment. Huntington (1991) represents the more customary position of U.S. policymakers and allied scholars, that the FSLN revolutionary government was itself authoritarian or even totalitarian. Thus it would follow that the transition began in 1990 with the electoral defeat of the Sandinistas. Nevertheless, along with most Nicaragua specialists, I hold that a careful review of the record of the Sandinista decade shows that there was indeed a serious project of democratization that sought to incorporate the essential elements of liberal democracy and to go beyond them. Consult Coraggio (1985); CIERA (1984); Ruchwarger (1987); Coraggio and Deere (1987); Tirado López (1986). The Sandinista model was neither purely liberal nor totally marxist-leninist; rather, reflecting the amalgam that was the FSLN, it displayed features of both in an uneasy and contradictory mix. The "popular organizations" were arms of the FSLN and were patterned directly on Cuban paradigms. However, there was never an attempt to create a marxist-leninist single party like the communist parties of Cuba or the Soviet Union. Rather, the party system and electoral system were intended to be competitive and were so. Many Sandinistas expected that the Front would achieve a durable electoral dominance as the natural leaders of "the people." Some may have secretly aspired to a Mexican-style party hegemony. But in any case they held two general elections (1984, 1990) under intense scrutiny from international observers. Both were widely judged free and fair. They lost the second, and they surrendered power. See Walker (1991).

33. UNO was a loose and fractious alliance of most of the elites opposed to the Sandinistas. It had been pieced together with strong leadership and financial support by the United States as a means of presenting a united civil opposition, even while both the U.S. government and UNO maintained a tacit alliance with the various armed counterrevolutionary groups (contras), which were also largely created and financed by the U.S. government.

34. The U.S. government was of course quite unsympathetic to Chamorro's gambit and used its influence to bolster the opposition. For an interpretation very critical of both the Sandinistas and the Chamorro government, see Lara and Herrera (1996).

35. For election results, see *La Nación* (Costa Rica), 5 December 1996 (Internet edition). For the coalition split, see *Miami Herald,* 28 November 1996, p. 25A, cited in *Central American Newspak* (9–22 December 1996, pp. 10–11).

36. On the transition in Guatemala, see Rosada Granados (1992); Jonas (1989, 1991). On the transition in Honduras, see Rosenberg (1989); Paz Aguilar (1992). On the crisis and transition in Panama, see Smith (1992); Ropp (1996). On the transition in the Dominican Republic, see Black (1986); Conaghan and Espinal (1990). On the post-Duvalier transition in Haiti, see Mintz (1995); NACLA (1994a); Rohter (1996a).

37. Schlesinger and Kinzer (1982); Immerman (1982).

38. There was one presidential term (1966–1970) when a civilian president held office under effective military control.

39. There has been much speculation about the explanations for this voting pattern. In the absence of reliable survey data, the most plausible explanation may be a combination of factors. In some villages, repression may have been worse before or after Ríos Montt. Those killed or exiled obviously cannot vote, and those who remain may be beneficiaries of the violence in that they may have received land previously occupied by the victims. Even more speculatively, it is conceivable that some indigenous voters, accustomed to patrimonial, clientelistic authority relations, voted for the man who had shown himself strongest, Ríos Montt, hoping thereby to put themselves on his side rather than against him. Finally, the abstention rate must be factored in. In addition to plain apathy and political ignorance, it is likely that a significant number of nonvoters in indigenous areas may have feared to come to the polls at all or may have been unwilling to vote for the available alternatives or fearful of voting for FDNG. It is impossible, with available information, to disentangle all these factors. It is not, in any case, unreasonable to think that Ríos Montt might have won, had he been permitted to run. See Jeffrey (1996).

40. On the Guatemalan accords, see Rohter (1996c).

41. Such abuses were much less frequent than in neighboring El Salvador and Guatemala. President Carlos Roberto Reina (1992–1996) did begin to have some success in this area.

42. Other countries included Haiti, Cuba, Puerto Rico, and Nicaragua. See Bradford (1993); Cerdas Cruz (1992); McClintock (1992); Pastor (1992).

43. Puerto Rico is not treated in this book. After the Spanish-American War (1898), the island was made a U.S. dependency and denied the opportunity for independence. Since World War II, it has been self-governing, theoretically entitled to independence, but economically quite closely tied to the United States.

44. *Latinamerica Press,* 30 May, 13 June, 11 July 1996.

45. The Reagan and Bush administrations rhetorically supported democratization in Haiti while doing a great deal behind the scenes to undermine Aristide and to prevent him from returning once he had been overthrown. The Clinton administration was more positive toward Aristide and finally did bring about his return. Important sectors of the Clinton administration were nevertheless very suspicious of Aristide and sought to bolster potential opponents once Aristide had returned. See Rohter (1996a); NACLA (1994a).

46. On the Argentine transition, see Cavarozzi (1986); Vacs (1987); Wynia (1986); Halperín Donghi (1994).

47. On the Ecuadoran transition, see Isaacs (1993); Conaghan and Espinal (1990); Conaghan and Malloy (1994); Conaghan (1995).

48. On social movements and politics in Latin America, see Eckstein (1989); Escobar and Alvarez (1992); Jaquette (1994); McManus and Schlabach (1991); Corradi, Fagen, and Garretón (1992). For an important general analysis, see Tarrow (1994).

49. On the Madres de Plaza de Mayo and other human rights movements in Argentina, see Guzmán Bouvard (1994); Jelin (1994); Quiroga (1993).

50. Grassroots politics also can be deeply undemocratic, when a small elite dominates everyone else. For example, shantytowns in Rio de Janeiro and elsewhere are commonly controlled by criminal gangs. Cf. Hellman (1994).

4

Authoritarian
Regimes in Transition

Most Latin American countries made the transition to liberal democracy in the 1980s and 1990s. Three countries (Paraguay, Mexico, and Cuba) have not made such a transition, but each authoritarian regime[1] is nevertheless undergoing significant political change that could lead to democratization. These three countries have been swimming against the current of the international structural conjuncture that has favored transitions to democracy over the past two decades. Advocates of democratization in these countries carry the heavy weight of traditions and institutions hostile to their goal. Still, the combination of external and internal pressures has brought change in each case. It is possible that democracy may flow from this change but by no means inevitable.

These three cases, as disparate as they are, have in common the fact that they do not meet the criteria for liberal democracy. Rather than shared political hegemony among competing elites, they have been characterized by self-perpetuating monopolies on political authority. Such political monopolies, of course, have been the rule throughout Latin America until recently, and in that sense, Paraguay, Mexico, and Cuba are closer to the regional tradition than their neighbors that have made the democratic transition. Caudillismo and its adaptations are very much alive in these cases. The Paraguayan dictatorship of Alfredo Stroessner (1954–1989) was the closest of the three to pure, personalistic caudillismo; although Stroessner ruled through the institutions of the armed forces and the Colorado Party, he exercised thorough personal control over both and used that control to perpetuate himself in power. The Mexican system, in contrast, decisively ended self-perpetuation in power after 1940, thereby achieving an ingenious and effective institutionalization of caudillismo without personalism. The Cuban revolutionary regime has also evolved a single ruling party, in this case with a legal monopoly (unlike Mexico or Paraguay, where other parties may exist). However, the Cuban leadership has not chosen to break with personalism as the Mexicans did; on the contrary, the personal leadership of Fidel Castro remains, after nearly forty years, the central feature of the revolutionary regime.

The three regimes are different not only because of very distinct social structures and political traditions; they also differ in their levels of popular social and political mobilization and in their levels of state capability and performance.[2] Paraguay is characterized by the least-mobilized populace; correspondingly, the Stroessner regime remained stable over decades without ever developing high levels of state capability. Mexico's regime has much higher capabilities and thus was able to promote, channel, and control political participation much more intense than that which has characterized Paraguay. Cuba's revolution has explicitly depended on organizing and mobilizing the populace in support of the revolutionary project, and the regime has successfully developed the capability to guide and control the people thus mobilized. All three regimes have thus enjoyed prolonged political stability because of a balance between political mobilization and state capabilities.

Each has nevertheless been destabilized in the past decade, and each is undergoing extensive political change whose outcome remains uncertain. Destabilization occurs when the structural balance between political mobilization and state capabilities is upset due to a relative loss of state capabilities, either because the state itself becomes weaker or because political mobilization increases. Destabilization has both endogenous and exogenous causes. Endogenous, or internal, causes may include the inevitable effects of aging on the effectiveness of a personalist leader like Stroessner or Castro. Mexico's much more institutionalized, depersonalized regime illustrates another structural cause of destabilization: rigidity due to institutional aging. Finally, even if the state does not lose capability, the populace may become more politically mobilized as a result of development of economic and social structures (e.g., rising incomes, improved education, better communications). Political mobilization may be particularly stimulated when expectations have been raised and then dashed.

Exogenous, or external, structural causes of destabilization include global economic conditions such as the great debt crisis of the early 1980s, which undermined the capability of all regimes, authoritarian and democratic, to meet the expectations of their populations (cf. Chapter 3). An exogenous political cause of destabilization was the foreign policy emphasis of the United States on human rights and democratization. In the specific case of Cuba, U.S. policy since the early 1960s has been explicitly intended to destabilize the revolutionary regime and, in conjunction with endogenous factors, seems finally to be having some such effect. As has been pointed out before, although U.S. policy and practice is action from the point of view of the United States, it is structure from a Latin American point of view because it represents a constraint not easily affected by Latin American action.

As we saw in Chapter 3, most authoritarian regimes found it necessary to respond to these structural pressures (internal and external) by carrying through full transitions to democracy. The three regimes considered in this chapter, however, were more resistant and have thus far avoided going the whole way to liberal democracy. They have, however, each undergone substantial liberalization short of full democratization. Here again the insights of Adam Przeworski (1991, chap. 2) prove quite useful, because he focused our attention on the probable interest calculations of distinct sectors of both the authoritarian regime and its opposition. Recall that he distinguished between hard-liners and reformers within the regime and between moderates and radicals in the opposition. Once endogenous and exogenous causes have increased instability in the authoritarian regime and the corresponding opportunities for change, actors in the distinct sectors of state and opposition have choices to make. It is useful to proceed on the assumption that each sector will prefer some outcomes over others and will act rationally to promote their preferences. Thus, in Przeworski's scheme, regime hard-liners are assumed to prefer the authoritarian status quo over any other outcome and to reject a democracy without guarantees for themselves and their supporters. Conversely, the opposition radicals are assumed to prefer democracy without guarantees and to reject the authoritarian status quo. In view of these diametrically opposed extremes, much depends on the relative strength of regime reformers and opposition moderates and upon their orders of preferences. Figure 4.1 shows Przeworski's assumed preferences of regime reformers and opposition moderates and the results of distinct alliance strategies. Note that reformers are assumed to prefer liberalization of the authoritarian regime both over the status quo and over democracy, whether with or without guarantees. Moderates, in contrast, prefer democracy without guarantees. If both reformers and moderates choose to negotiate with each other, democracy with guarantees is a reachable outcome, as we saw in Chapter 3 in studying numerous cases of negotiated transitions to democracy.

Figure 4.1   Authoritarian Transitions: Interaction of Regime Reformers and Opposition Moderates

		Moderates ally with	
		Radicals	Reformers
Reformers ally with	Hard-liners	Authoritarian status quo 2,1	Authoritarian liberalization 4,2
	Moderates	Democracy without guarantees 1,4	Democracy with guarantees 3,3

Source: Przeworski (1991), p. 69. Reprinted by permission of Cambridge University Press.
Note: The first numeral in each cell is the relative value of the outcome to reformers, and the second, the relative value to moderates, where 4 is the most desired outcome.

The present cases of authoritarian regimes in transition, however, cannot be assumed to be headed toward democracy (although they may be). Instead, the outcome thus far in all three cases approximates the upper right cell of Figure 4.1 (authoritarian liberalization): the regime remains authoritarian but more liberal than before. In terms of Przeworski's scheme, regime reformers remain in alliance with hard-liners while taking advantage of the relative moderation of the opposition to press liberalizing reforms on the hard-liners. Przeworski rightly pointed out, however, that as liberalizing reforms proceed, regime reformers have declining incentives to remain allied with the hard-liners and more incentives to negotiate with the opposition moderates, especially if the reformers believe they have sufficient popular support to survive in a democracy with guarantees.[3] Thus the eventual outcome in these cases could well be a democracy with guarantees, even though the immediate outcome is a liberalized authoritarianism.

We now turn to a more detailed review of the three cases.

PARAGUAY: REFORMED CAUDILLISMO

As in Colombia, Uruguay, and Honduras, politics in Paraguay continue to center on two traditional parties with roots in the nineteenth century, the Colorados and the liberals. As in those countries, the traditional pattern has been for a caudillo associated with one of the two parties to establish a durable hegemony in which control of the army and of elections permitted perpetuation of the caudillo and his or her party in power. The party out of power was persecuted but not destroyed, and leaders of cooperative opposition factions might be incorporated into the government. Elections served only to legitimize the tenure of the incumbents and their chosen successors. The opposition could come to power only by force of arms and only when the ruling coalition was in disarray.[4] The Colorados and liberals emerged during the generation after Paraguay lost the War of the Triple Alliance (1865–1869) and by the late 1880s were clearly defined elite factions. Whereas before the war Paraguay was dominated by a series of purely personal dictatorships (José Gaspar Rodríguez de Francia, Carlos Antonio López, and Francisco Solano López), its subsequent history has been a series of personal dictatorships with clearly defined partisan affiliations. The Colorados were the initial heirs to power after the war, and a succession of Colorado factions held power until they were ousted in a coup in 1902. By 1904 the liberals were clearly established in power, and successive liberal factions ruled until the conclusion of the Chaco War (1932–1935). Disillusionment with the liberal government's corruption and poor preparation for that war facilitated a coup in 1936 (by reformers called Febreristas), a countercoup against the Febreristas in 1937, and finally the return of the Colorados to power after 1940. After a prolonged struggle for power among Colorados, General Alfredo Stroessner seized power in a coup in 1954. He subsequently established a strongly personalist and emphatically Colorado regime that lasted until his overthrow in 1989.

Stroessner's rise to power reflects how personalism and caudillismo survive in the context of a twentieth-century professional military institution.[5] A cadet at the time of the Chaco War, Stroessner served with enough distinction to call attention to himself. Over the succeeding, tumultuous decade, he largely stayed out of politics and concentrated on professional advancement. By 1947, he was a lieutenant colonel in command of a key artillery regiment. Over the next seven years, he steadily gained political weight as he picked the winners in a series of political and military conflicts, making increasingly crucial contributions to his allies' victories. Finally, in 1954, as commander of the army, he was in position to seize power for himself, and he did.

It was still necessary for him to manage the multiple factions of the Colorado Party and the armed forces, but by 1954, all opposition political parties had been suppressed, with their leaders in jail or exile. Stroessner, as a military leader with Colorado affiliation, thus inherited a de facto Colorado monopoly on power. A succession of maneuvers brought the key Colorado factions under his control in the late 1950s, and guerrilla resistance from liberal and Febrerista exiles was put down in the early 1960s. By the late 1960s, both the Febreristas and the liberals sued for peace and were permitted to return to the country and to operate legally, as long as they did not challenge the legitimacy of Stroessner's new authoritarian institutional order.

The constitution of 1940 already provided extensive powers to the president, and these were enhanced by amendments adopted in 1967. The president could be indefinitely reelected and disposed of an essentially unlimited authority to declare a state of siege and rule by decree. In fact, during almost all of the Stroessner period Paraguay was under a state of siege. The strategy of control was built on the twin pillars of the army and the Colorado Party, both purged of elements less than completely loyal to Stroessner. Other institutions, such as the Catholic Church, labor and peasant unions, and other interest groups, were subjected to repression whenever they became unacceptably critical. Individual dissent was brutally repressed. At the same time, opponents willing to come to terms with the regime were willingly co-opted. The overall goal, according to Carlos Miranda (1990), was to limit political mobilization against the regime. The regime engaged in very little positive mobilization of its own supporters; overall, the regime was founded upon the maintenance of low levels of popular political mobilization. Its economic strategy emphasized free enterprise and free trade; business interests willing to collaborate with the regime (as most were) benefited in a climate of minimal regulation and repression of organized labor. Paraguay became the South American center for contraband trade, and Stroessner and his senior associates made substantial profits from that trade.

The Stroessner regime was subject to the same global and regional stresses during the 1980s as the rest of the region.[6] In the late 1970s, the Carter administration brought considerable pressure on Stroessner for liberalization, and as a result the opposition gained some space. Still, while all its neighbors were making transitions to democracy, Paraguay seemed fundamentally unchanged. Economic growth slowed substantially in the 1980s but for the most part did not reverse (in contrast to several Latin American countries, where the decade as a whole showed negative gross domestic product [GDP] growth).[7] Nevertheless, Paraguay did undergo a pronounced relative slowdown compared to the boom times of the 1970s, and this may well have softened support for the regime. Table 4.1 shows GDP growth rates during the 1970s and 1980s.

Table 4.1   Paraguay: GDP Growth

Year	GDP Growth (percentage)
1971	5.4
1972	6.4
1973	7.2
1974	8.2
1975	6.3
1976	7.0
1977	12.8
1978	10.9
1979	10.7
1980	11.4
1981	8.5
1982	–2.5
1983	NA
1984	3.1
1985	4.0
1986	0.0
1987	4.3
1988	6.2

Source: Roett and Sacks (1991), pp. 72, 80.
Note: Data through 1982 are from Paraguayan government sources, whereas those from 1984 on are from the Interamerican Development Bank.

Perhaps the most important factor in the weakening of the regime, however, was the physical aging of its principal. Stroessner's declining vigor and worsening health became ever more evident in the late 1980s. Although all major figures in the regime had been picked for their loyalty to him, the inevitability of his passage from the scene surely caused many to consider how the essential features of the regime might be continued without him. From the mid-1980s, serious factional conflict focused on the issue of Stroessner's succession emerged within both the Colorado Party and the armed forces. The principal party factions were the *militantes* (partisans of a continuation of Stroessner's personalist style under his son, Gustavo) and the *tradicionalistas* (advocating depersonalization and liberalization of the regime after Stroessner). There were other smaller factions as well. Most senior army officers appear to have opposed the *militantes* (Miranda, 1990, p. 131) and favored a civilian successor. It is important to remember, however, that all Colorado and military factions favored continuation of the Colorado-military hegemony in some form; at most, they were liberalizers, not democratizers.

Opposition political forces (parties, labor unions, and civil society) also became more active and assertive in the late 1980s, increasingly participating in the debate over the post-Stroessner future. Organizations ranging from the business community to the peasantry mobilized politically to criticize the government and make demands, and the government's efforts to exercise repression were ineffective and counterproductive. The Catholic Church hierarchy became increasingly vocal in its criticism of the regime. The National Accord of major opposition parties, founded in 1979, was increasingly active and successful in mobilizing supporters to demand liberalization and democracy. In short, political mobilization was increasing at the same time as the unity and capacity for action of the regime was being undermined. Stroessner was still able to win the presidential elections of February 1988 due to his control of the machinery,[8] but his position had become quite weak. A year later, on 2 February 1989, the commander of the army, General Andrés Rodríguez (a close associate of Stroessner and even a relative by marriage) staged a coup that, after some fighting, sent Stroessner into exile in Brazil.

The Rodríguez coup marked a clearly defined accession to power by liberalizers, or reformers, within the regime.[9] Rodríguez immediately called new general elections for 1 May 1989 and invited the participation of all parties. He pledged the restoration of democracy and of respect for human rights, but there was never a serious possibility that anyone but Rodríguez would win the 1989 election. Rodríguez refrained from consolidating his personal power in the succeeding years, did indeed show increased respect for human rights and civil liberties, and presided over relatively clean elections in 1993. Table 4.2 shows electoral data for 1989 and 1993.

Between the two elections, Paraguay moved from a dominant, or hegemonic, party system to a competitive one in which non-Colorados could win a majority of congressional seats and a united opposition could win the presidency. However, the Colorados were weakened by internal divisions, and the most powerful army general (Lino César Oviedo) stated just before the 1993 election that the armed forces were determined to

Table 4.2 **Paraguay: Presidential Election Results, 1989 and 1993 (percentage)**

Party	1989	1993
Colorado	74	40
Authentic Radical Liberal	20	32
Other	4	25

Sources: 1989: Abente (1995), p. 315; 1993: *Latin American Weekly Report* (27 May 1993), p. 240.

continue cogoverning with the Colorados, regardless of the electoral outcome. Thus, it is premature to judge Paraguay as having completed a transition to democracy, though it is clearly a very different polity than in 1989.

Much will depend on the conduct of government and opposition during the administration of Juan Carlos Wasmosy, the winner in 1993.[10] Possessed of a remarkably weak mandate from elections whose legitimacy was widely doubted, Wasmosy also faces continued disunity within the Colorado Party. The camp of his principal rival, Luis María Argaña, has become, as Esteban Caballero (1995, p. 12) said, an opposition within the governing party itself. The government was based on a fragile alliance of other Colorado factions and was overshadowed by a potential military strongman, Army Commander General Lino César Oviedo, who acted increasingly in concert with Argaña to undermine Wasmosy. In April 1996, Wasmosy dismissed Oviedo in the course of a military uprising. Wasmosy later argued that Oviedo had refused to accept his dismissal and had tried to seize power. Oviedo countered that Wasmosy had unsuccessfully solicited his cooperation in an *autogolpe,* or seizure of power by the president himself. Wasmosy then ordered the jailing of Oviedo, who surrendered, but only after being nominated as the Colorado candidate for president in 1998 and only after calling on the president to resign. In short, the old military-Colorado alliance that sustained Stroessner is far from dead.

There were also more positive developments for political stability and an eventual movement toward a full-fledged liberal democracy. There was substantial international support, both economic and political, for what was widely seen as significant progress toward democracy; this support enhanced the stature and leverage of the Wasmosy government. After the 1993 elections, the leader of the principal opposition party, Domingo Laíno of the Authentic Radical Liberals, initiated discussion of a pact of governability between the government and the opposition. This negotiation both enhanced Wasmosy's electoral legitimacy and provided him with a legislative majority in spite of the Argaña schism. However, by mid-1996, that majority seemed to be in jeopardy.

The economic and social problems of the population remained serious, and levels of political mobilization continued to rise, posing a significant challenge to the government. For example, in March 1995, thousands of peasants demonstrated peacefully in the principal cities, voicing criticism of the government's agrarian policy and demanding a comprehensive agrarian reform; just prices for produce; and the construction of roads, schools, and clinics. According to the report, the actions were carried out by more than forty peasant organizations. Other sectors of civil society, such as labor and the church, have also become more organized and active, continuing a trend from the latter Stroessner years. In May 1996, major labor unions staged a successful forty-eight-hour general strike to protest government economic policies. Governing Paraguay is no longer, as it was twenty years ago, a matter purely for elites.

That Paraguay is in transition is beyond question. Establishment of a credible liberal democracy is a very real possibility, especially if some working accommodation can be reached between the armed forces and the Colorados on the one hand and key elements of the opposition on the other. It is not clear that the collaboration between Wasmosy and some opposition elements will acquire the scope and weight necessary to ensure such a transition. Important elements among the leadership of both the armed forces and the Colorados continue to reject the basic premises of liberal democracy; these hard-liners may be expected to try to reassert control, but they are at a disadvantage in the international climate of the mid-1990s. The persistence of social injustice and economic insecurity does not in itself constitute a barrier to establishment of liberal democracy, but as the Venezuelans have found, such economic and social weaknesses may make it very difficult to maintain and consolidate a more authentic democracy.

MEXICO: INSTITUTIONALIZED CAUDILLISMO

The political order under which Mexico's Institutional Revolutionary Party (PRI) and its direct predecessors have ruled uninterruptedly for nearly seventy years deserves recognition from political scientists as one of the most ingenious and successful in modern history.[11] As with most other Latin American countries, Mexico's nineteenth-century history was the story of a series of caudillos (Santa Anna, Juárez, and Díaz), whose prolonged hegemonies were punctuated by periods of instability, internal conflict, and external intervention. General Antonio López de Santa Anna pursued a classic caudillo's career in the context of the unique conditions of Mexico's independence struggle and its early independence.[12] As a young, Mexican-born Spanish officer, he fought with distinction to defeat the radical insurgencies of the priests Hidalgo and Morelos and their followers between 1810 and 1821. He then provided crucial support for the conservative independence movement of Emperor Agustín de Iturbide, only to side, in 1822, with republican rebellions that ended the short-lived empire. Perhaps the most powerful general in Mexico in the 1820s, he was the principal arbiter of power and politics in Mexico for a generation until he was ousted for the last time in 1855. He spent a considerable part of this time out of power or in exile, but when he was out of power, he was always available to the opponents of those in power. Beginning as a liberal and ending as a conservative, Santa Anna was before anything devoted to his own power. Quite unlike the figure of Diego Portales in Chile, Santa Anna neither imposed order nor limited corruption. Instead, his entire epoch was marked by kaleidoscopic struggles among elite factions, each seeking to control the government for the material benefits they might derive. The environment of corruption and incompetence certainly made Mexico vulnerable to the secessionist aspirations of American colonists in Texas (1836) and facilitated Mexico's defeat both in the Texas war for independence and in the later war with the United States (1846–1948). In sum, Mexico as a nation gained little from the era of Santa Anna, save the political experience of living with—and under—a classic caudillo.

Liberal forces overthrew Santa Anna in 1855 and initiated the era of La Reforma. Even more strongly than elsewhere in Latin America, liberalism in Mexico was committed to breaking down the surviving elements of the old colonial social order and establishing a new order based on individual liberty (economic even more than political) and limited government. Mexican liberalism had a strongly anticlerical thrust, reflecting the historic power of a conservative hierarchy in this former viceroyalty. The liberals implemented legal reforms that abolished the *fueros,* or legal exemptions, of the church and the armed forces and sharply restricted collective or corporate ownership of property. Both measures had serious negative implications for the church and provoked impassioned opposition from the church and its conservative allies.

The most prominent liberal leader was Benito Juárez, Zapotec by birth, lawyer by education, governor of Oaxaca at the time of the liberal takeover. Like Santa Anna before him, Juárez came to dominate the politics of a generation but never could rest easy in power. After serving as justice minister and chief justice of the supreme court, he succeeded to the presidency in 1858, only to face a conservative revolt that forced him out of Mexico City until 1861. Then, the conservatives gained the support of Napoleon III to enthrone Prince Maximilian of Austria as emperor of Mexico in 1862, with the aid of French troops (and the engagement of U.S. forces in the Civil War). Only in 1867 was Maximilian ousted and Juárez restored. He then remained president until his death in 1872.

It is not customary to regard Juárez as a caudillo, and he clearly was a very different kind of leader than Santa Anna. For example, Juárez had principles that he cared about and acted upon, whereas these were not evident in Santa Anna. There is no particular evidence that Juárez sought to enrich himself in office, but that seemed to be very nearly the essence of Santa Anna's motivation. Yet, Juárez had to be in some measure a caudillo, for in mid-nineteenth-century Mexico there was no other way to lead. A leader who had power and failed to use it to keep power merely invited his own overthrow. Juárez was repeatedly called upon to fight to get and keep power, and he did so ably. Moreover, after 1867, he was quite willing to use his control of the electoral machinery to ensure his reelection and to exclude his adversaries.

La Reforma and Benito Juárez had a more substantial and largely positive legacy, as compared with Santa Anna. It is true that the reforms undermined indigenous communal property and laid the groundwork for a massive concentration of land. The church as a potential check on state power was decisively weakened. Yet, the church had rarely served, in practice, as a defender of the poor and weak; more often, it defended the rich and privileged. La Reforma also established definitively the legal equality of every citizen, an indispensable basis for liberal democracy. La Reforma was the first political project in Mexico that aspired to something like liberal democracy. That it fell woefully short of its aspirations cannot surprise us, given the context, but Juárez is still venerated as few other Mexican presidents have been; he is comparable in this respect only to Lázaro Cárdenas (see later discussion).

Porfirio Díaz was a successful and popular liberal general who challenged Juárez for the presidency in 1867 and again in 1871. When the latter election was settled by a deal in Congress that shut Díaz out, he revolted and was driven into the hills. After Juárez died in 1872, his successor, Sebastián Lerdo de Tejada, granted amnesty to Díaz and was elected to a full five-year term. When, in 1876, he sought reelection, Díaz revolted again, this time with the slogan, "Effective Suffrage, No Reelection." Díaz seized power, got himself elected constitutional president, and secured adoption of a constitutional amendment prohibiting presidential reelection. He indeed did leave office in 1880 and returned as an elected president in 1884, thereafter establishing a dictatorship that would last until 1910. Díaz, then, was the third and last of the great nineteenth-century Mexican caudillos.

The Porfiriato, as it came to be called, would transform Mexico. Under the strong influence of positivist doctrines of progress through a postreligious secular order, political life was kept under tight control while economic opportunity was opened to those Mexicans with capital and especially to foreign investors. Infrastructure, such as railroads, telegraph lines, and ports, were developed by foreign capital at the invitation of the government. Large commercial plantations took over lands from indigenous communities and smallholders, creating a growing class of landless peasants. And it was all done in the name of progress.

Díaz was the first Mexican caudillo actually to consolidate himself in power. After 1876 he was clearly the strongman of the regime, and after 1884 he was the undisputed master for twenty-five years. He used and perfected all the techniques of caudillismo, including fraudulent elections, rule through puppets and clients, political repression, intimidation, and brute force. Once it became clear who was in charge, anyone who was ambitious would likely try to adhere to the regime so as to gain patronage or other advantages. The regime was particularly receptive to foreign investors, many of whom developed quite cozy relationships with Díaz and his close associates. He got particularly strong support from some U.S. business interests (e.g., railroads) and from the Republican Party administrations that represented them. The longer Díaz continued in power, the more pervasive and obvious was corruption within the regime.

Opposition to Díaz tended to come from liberals who objected to the dictatorship; from Indians, peasants, and small farmers adversely affected by the developmentalist policies of the regime; from urban and industrial workers whose wages were kept down and whose working conditions were neglected; and from propertied interests excluded from the Díaz trough. Eventually, by the first decade of the twentieth century, the regime was showing the age of its principal. In 1910, Díaz engaged in one more attempt to perpetuate himself in power through electoral manipulation. His principal opponent, Francisco Madero, rose in rebellion after the blatantly fraudulent election, once again raising the banner, "Effective Suffrage, No Reelection."

Madero's rebellion quickly attracted popular support, both in Mexico City and elsewhere, and Díaz was soon forced to resign and leave the country. The Mexican Revolution, one of the seminal upheavals of the twentieth century, had begun.[13] The next decade would see civil war, political instability, and social turmoil as competing caudillos with contrasting regional and social bases struggled for national primacy. Though the period seemed like previous epochs of civil war, there were deeper issues at stake. Some of the caudillos, most notably Emiliano Zapata in the southwest and Pancho Villa in the north, raised basic demands of social justice such as agrarian reform. Urban and industrial workers demanded rights and benefits long denied by the Díaz regime and its business allies. Nationalists rallied around demands for national control of petroleum and mining. The call for an authentic popular democracy was widely heard. Most of these demands were embodied in the historic 1917 constitution, though few were consistently implemented. The gap between rhetoric and reality in the Mexican Revolution has always been wide.

Madero was overthrown in a counterrevolutionary coup by General Victoriano Huerta in February 1913, backed by many Porfiristas and by the ambassador of the lame-duck Taft administration in Washington, Henry Lane Wilson. However, a month later when Woodrow Wilson was inaugurated, Ambassador Wilson was relieved and U.S. policy reversed. Over the next year, the United States worked in tacit alliance with Huerta's opponents to bring him down (most notably by occupying Veracruz and denying customs revenues to Huerta). The outcome was decided, however, on the field of battle, when a loose coalition of revolutionary generals (most notably including the constitutionalist army of Venustiano Carranza and Alvaro Obregón, the northern radical Pancho Villa, and the southern radical Emiliano Zapata) combined to drive him from the country in July 1914.

Carranza successfully maneuvered to become provisional president and turned his attention to the destruction of Villa and Zapata, whose agrarian radicalism he distrusted. By 1915, each had been confined to his regional base, and each would later be assassinated. The radical thrust of the revolution had been blunted. The constitution of 1917, framed and adopted under Carranza's hegemony, could then safely articulate radical goals (such as agrarian reform and nationalization of petroleum) in the knowledge that serious implementation would be continually postponed. Of course, it included the prohibition of presidential reelection.

Struggles for power then emerged within Carranza's constitutionalist coalition. Carranza could not succeed himself in 1920 but hoped to secure the election of a chosen successor through his control of the electoral machinery. He failed to do that, however, when his circle of supporters divided into two camps, one supporting General Pablo González and the other behind General Alvaro Obregón. Civil war erupted again. Carranza was forced to flee and was assassinated, and Obregón gained control and won the election.

Between 1920 and 1928, Obregón and his chief lieutenant, General Plutarco Elías Calles, reestablished stability by controlling other caudillos and alternating in the presidency (thereby sharing power and avoiding immediate reelection). Calles was elected with Obregón's support in 1924. After a term marked by the pro-clerical *Cristero* rebellion, Calles was induced by Obregón to push through a constitutional amendment that lengthened the presidential term to six years and permitted former presidents to hold the office a second time. Under this latter provision and benefiting from Calles's control of the machinery, Obregón easily won the election of 1928 but was killed the next day by a *Cristero* assassin.[14]

In the face of this sudden turn of events, Calles chose not to directly extend his term of office or to have himself reelected. Either course would have violated the basic revolutionary principle of no reelection. Yet, caudillos rarely retire; they hold onto power until they are overthrown. That certainly had been the pattern in nearly twenty years of revolutionary struggles. Calles sought, then, to rule from behind the scenes after he left office, naming a series of puppet presidents between 1928 and 1934 and summarily removing them whenever they showed signs of independence. The substance of this strategem was pure traditional caudillismo, but Calles developed an innovative instrument for carrying it out: the official revolutionary party.

The National Revolutionary Party (PNR) was intended to draw together the diverse strands of the revolutionary family to defend the revolution against counterrevolutionary forces such as the *Cristeros*. That was the official goal. Unofficially, its mission was to monopolize control of the government and to assure that its candidates continued to win elections. The party's *jefe máximo* (supreme chief) was Calles. In its inception, then, the revolutionary party was little more than a personalist machine. It is true that there were still many people who held to the ideals of the revolution, many of whom adhered to the PNR as the best instrument to defend the revolution and hold open the possibility of a future revolutionary transformation. But Calles and his closest collaborators had become "an incestuous clique of millionaires enriched by graft and plunder" (Williamson, 1992, p. 397).

The last of Calles's puppet presidents was Lázaro Cárdenas (1934–1940), a puppet who would not be manipulated.[15] Cárdenas worked to remove Calles allies from positions of influence and then, in 1936, forced Calles into exile. So far, it was all according to the script of caudillismo. Cárdenas then sought to rebuild popular support for the party (and for himself) with a series of popular but controversial measures, including the most extensive agrarian reform since 1910, nationalization of the petroleum industry, and social welfare and security programs benefiting the workers. He also rebuilt the revolutionary party along corporatist lines, with organized sectors representing the major interests of peasants, workers, military, and "popular" (the last being predominantly state employees). The party was to be the mechanism by which these diverse interests could be reconciled. The military sector was eventually eliminated, once the last major regional caudillos were domesticated or suppressed. The business interests were notable by their absence. Officially, the Mexican Revolution continued to be nationalistic and even a bit socialistic: it would not do for business to appear within the revolutionary tent. Indeed, Cárdenas's relations with business were tense, and understandably so, given his major policy initiatives. Also absent from the party was the church, for the regime remained officially anticlerical. Nevertheless, Cárdenas achieved a certain modus vivendi with the Catholic hierarchy, choosing not to go out of his way to persecute the church when he had trouble enough on other fronts.[16]

If Cárdenas's economic and social policies were radical, constituting the high-water mark of revolutionary change in Mexico, his crafting of the revolutionary party was profoundly conservative and virtually assured that there would never again be a president as radical as Cárdenas himself. The party's structure not only represented all major constituencies of the revolutionary coalition but organized them for patronage, thereby domesticating them and assuring that they could be controlled by the top leadership. Further, Cárdenas definitively established the principle that presidents would serve for one six-year term and no more. The constitution and the official party enabled them to be virtual dictators while in office and to designate their successors, but they would not continue to rule from behind the scenes after leaving office. Cárdenas himself stuck firmly to this principle, and so have his successors, down to the present day.

The significance of this practice was that by depersonalizing caudillismo, the fundamental cause of instability was removed. The ambitious need no longer conspire against the incumbent government if they are denied a seat at the table; they need only wait six years, tend their political connections, and hope for better placement in the next government. The essence of the Mexican regime under Cárdenas and thereafter has remained caudillismo, but it is liberated from the life cycle of any single incumbent (cf. Stroessner and Castro) and freed from endemic turmoil. It is among the most stable regimes in modern history and, by the same token, among the most resistant to change.

After Cárdenas, the Mexican political system entered a prolonged era of political stability, lasting from 1940 to 1968.[17] Presidents followed presidents (five in all), each designating his successor, each retiring to the background. The PRI retained overwhelming electoral dominance and captured virtually all elective offices. The party's sectoral organizations, in tacit alliance with big business and foreign investors, moderated popular demands while ensuring that everyone who played the game got at least small rewards. That included several small leftist parties that were rewarded for participating in elections so as to enhance the legitimacy of the process. The only serious opposition was from the rightist National Action Party (PAN), which, notwithstanding its strength in the North, was rarely an electoral victor. One reason was that the PRI machine was quite capable of controlling electoral outcomes whenever necessary. Nevertheless, Mexico during this period was by no means a harsh dictatorship: the press had broad—but not unlimited—freedom, and civil liberties were usually— but not always—respected. Elections were held on schedule and were formally competitive. Most people, particularly workers and peasants, pursued the logic of caudillismo and attached themselves to the official party in hopes of some material benefit. To the superficial observer, Mexico might have appeared a democracy before 1968, but it was really what Guillermo O'Donnell and Philippe Schmitter (1986) called a *dictablanda,* or soft dictatorship (as distinguished from a *dictadura,* or hard dictatorship).

The prolonged crisis of the Mexican regime began with a clearly defined event, the massacre of students in the Plaza of Tlatelolco, Mexico City, in 1968.[18] Students animated by the example of the Cuban Revolution and encouraged by a widespread climate of revolutionary agitation in Latin America at the time sought to take advantage of international attention focused on the Olympic Games in Mexico to highlight the gross injustices in Mexican society. Rising tensions culminated in the bloody repression of a massive demonstration in Tlatelolco. The repression was ordered by President Gustavo Díaz Ordaz and carried out under the command of Interior Minister Luis Echeverría. Echeverría was rewarded with the presidency for the 1970–1976 term.

It is reasonable to date the Mexican political crisis from 1968 because Tlatelolco showed the regime reduced to the use of massive force to control the public arena and further displayed the regime using such force against demands that were central to the legitimacy of the revolutionary heritage. The emperor had no clothes. President Echeverría sought to cover himself with the tried and true tactics of "populist philanthropy" (Williamson, 1992, p. 403), spending heavily on agrarian reform, food, education, housing, and health while also promoting economic expansion. These positive policies, combined with repression, indeed seemed to have brought the situation under control by the mid-1970s, without the need for substantive political concessions. Samuel Schmidt (1986) made the case that Echeverría chose to enhance the political legitimacy of the regime at a time of political crisis, even though that meant incurring heavy economic costs and strained the regime's relationship with the Mexican and foreign bourgeoisie.

As a result of these heavy commitments to agrarian reform and social programs, the Mexican state found itself severely overextended when Echeverría's successor, José López Portillo, took office. However, López Portillo was saved from having to impose an unpopular austerity program by the very timely confirmation of massive petroleum deposits along the coast of the Gulf of Mexico. López Portillo then had a ticket for even more extravagant social spending; in fact, his government borrowed heavily on projections of growing oil production and rising prices. Prosperity continued into the early 1980s. Then, as petroleum prices unexpectedly entered a severe slump, Mexico found itself unable to service its international debt. The strategy of overextending economically to confront the crisis of political legitimacy had reached its limit, and the Mexican crisis ripped the cover off what came to be known as the Third World debt crisis.[19]

López Portillo's first response was pure demagoguery: blaming international bankers for the crisis, he pushed through the immediate nationalization of the banking system. But he also designated as his successor Miguel de la Madrid Hurtado (1982–1986), the first of a line of sober economic technocrats who would hold the presidency through the end of the century. De la Madrid began the process of reorienting Mexican economic policy from the politically driven populism of the 1970s toward an increasing commitment to neoliberal orthodoxy. The goal was to reestablish business confidence in the regime so as to attract investment and promote the resumption of economic growth. Neoliberal adjustment was as painful in Mexico as elsewhere in Latin America, and the costs were borne disproportionately by the poor, the peasants, and the workers. As elsewhere, the rich got richer and inequality increased. The incumbent regime suffered politically in Mexico as in other Latin American countries; though it retained the resources and capabilities to keep itself in power, it would do so with difficulty and at high cost. The economic crisis and the neoliberal response were the progenitors of a renewed political crisis that emerged in 1988.

Dissidence within the PRI grew much stronger under de la Madrid's neoliberal policies and led finally to one of the party's most serious splits.[20] A sector associated with Porfirio Muñoz Ledo and Cuauhtémoc Cárdenas (son of Lázaro Cárdenas), frustrated in their attempt to prevent the nomination of another economic technocrat in 1988, split off and ultimately formed the National Democratic Front (FDN; it was transformed after the election into the Democratic Revolutionary Party, or PRD) as a vehicle for Cárdenas's presidential candidacy. Disillusionment with poor economic conditions, social injustice, and political corruption reinforced Cárdenas's appeal and that of Manuel Clouthier, nominee of the PAN. The PRI nominated Carlos Salinas de Gortari, another economist trained in the United States and the principal architect of de la Madrid's economic policy. The PRI's electoral machine, unenthusiastic about the nominee but needful of winning the election to guarantee continued patronage, was caught by surprise by an apparent Cárdenas victory and had to resort to naked manipulation under cover of a highly suspicious computer failure in order to achieve a bare majority for Salinas (50.7 percent), as against official totals of 31 percent for Cárdenas and 17 percent for Clouthier (see Table 4.3). Salinas thus entered office with less political legitimacy than the PRI had had at any time since 1970 but without the economic means to spend his way out of the hole, as Echeverría had done.

Table 4.3   Mexico: Presidential Election Results, 1940–1994 (percentage)

Year	PRI	PAN	FDN/PRD	Other	Turnout
1940–1976 (mean)	86.0	10.6[a]	–	7.0	55.0
1982	71.0	15.7	–	9.4	66.1
1988	50.7	16.8	31.1	1.4	49.4
1994	50.2	26.9	17.1	5.8	74.0

Sources: Craig and Cornelius (1995), p. 258; Klesner (1995), pp. 138, 145.
a. Mean for 1952–1970. PAN did not contest the other elections.

Salinas had little choice but to stay the neoliberal course and hope that there would be enough economic growth to undercut the opposition. He staked Mexico's economic future—and the PRI's political future—on negotiation of the North America Free Trade Agreement (NAFTA) with the United States (and Canada, which had already signed such a pact with the

United States). He found in the Bush administration (1989–1993) and its successor, the Clinton administration, willing partners committed to the basic principles of neoliberal economics. Although there were many skeptics in all three countries and many interests that would be threatened, ultimately in 1993, Clinton was able to push through the ratification of the treaty as negotiated by the Bush administration. Salinas, still with a PRI congressional majority, was then able to do the same in Mexico. But the promised benefits of free trade were slow to appear, and Mexican economic conditions continued to be poor, while the social fabric was shredding.

Under these conditions of chronic crisis and endemic corruption, the regime sustained a series of new blows to its economic and political health, though it continued to have the means to survive. On 1 January 1994, just as NAFTA was going into effect, the Zapatista Army of National Liberation (EZLN) initiated an armed uprising in the southernmost state of Chiapas.[21] Although this revolt was superficially similar to many marxist-leninist insurgencies across Latin America since the 1960s, it soon became clear that the Zapatistas were something new. Having surprised the police and army and captured several towns and extensive territory, the masked spokesman of the Zapatistas, "Subcomandante Marcos," announced a cease-fire and offered to negotiate with the government. It soon became clear that the predominantly Mayan insurgents and their predominantly mestizo and white leaders were not seeking the revolutionary seizure of power. Rather, they sought to call attention to unjust conditions in Chiapas and elsewhere in Mexico and to the lack of true democracy. They intended, through armed negotiation, to oblige the government to address these issues. Negotiations did begin but were inconclusive over the next two years as the Zapatistas resisted government attempts to either co-opt or intimidate them, and the government refused to make meaningful concessions.[22] In October 1995, the EZLN called for abstention in the state elections, and indeed the abstention rate was notably high. One result was that the PAN (not notable for its strength in Chiapas) won the mayoralty in the capital city, Tuxtla Gutiérrez, and the PRI saw its statewide percentage drop from over 90 percent to about 55 percent. The center-left PRD was a major loser in a state where they expected to do well, and they criticized the Zapatistas for their unilateral boycott of the election.

Meanwhile, politics on the national scale grew more byzantine and more deadly. In the space of a few months, assassination claimed the lives of an archbishop; the PRI's presidential candidate, Luis Donaldo Colosio; and a former PRI party chairman. The alleged triggermen were apprehended in each case, but efforts to trace down the real authors went nowhere. There was possible drug cartel involvement in each case, but even more troubling was the possibility that some or all of the killings amounted to political account settling (Paternostro, 1995).

Salinas chose to replace the slain Colosio with yet another economic technocrat, Ernesto Zedillo, who faced strong opposition from the PAN (Diego Fernández) and the PRD (Cárdenas). With a weak candidate and widespread disillusionment and disaffection, the PRI faced the same dilemma in 1994 as in 1988: to avoid losing even more legitimacy, the regime needed a credibly honest election but would thereby run a serious risk of losing. The results were similar to those of 1988 in that Zedillo officially received just over 50 percent of the votes, but this time the PAN came in second and the PRD third (see Table 4.3). There were allegations of fraud, but few maintained that Zedillo was not the true winner.

There were, moreover, important signs of the continuing decline of the PRI's hegemony at the local and regional levels.[23] The PRI saw a long-term decline in the proportion of congressional districts that were safe.[24] (In the 1997 congressional elections, the PRI finally lost its majority in the Chamber of Deputies, receiving 38 percent of the vote and 239 of 500 seats. The PRD and PAN each received about one-quarter of the votes; together with the Greens and the Workers Party, the combined opposition was able to organize the new Chamber [*Latin American Weekly Report*, 15 July 1997, 326].) The party system has become more differentiated regionally (PAN especially strong in the north, PRD in the Federal District and the south). Finally, PRI's hold on rural districts, while still stronger than its national average, has weakened notably. Since it is in the rural areas that the logic of clientelism is most powerful, this last finding is a harbinger of trouble for the PRI.

After the elections on 23 August 1994, Zedillo was no sooner inaugurated than a massive selloff hit the Mexican peso in December 1994. Weighed down by economic distortions and policy errors of more than a decade, the peso lost more than half its value against the dollar in the course of a month. The Clinton administration realized that a continuing uncontrolled crisis could have serious effects on the U.S. economy, along with potential devastation of the Mexican economy. Therefore, after committing funds already at his disposal, he worked hard to get an aid package through Congress but confronted deep skepticism from both parties. With final approval of the plan, featuring loan guarantees of $40 billion, the battered Mexican economy began to stabilize, but with lasting damage to the population's standard of living and to the government's credibility. Former President Salinas was virtually forced into exile, and his brother, Raúl, was arrested on charges of financial corruption (and on suspicion of involvement in the murder of former PRI chair José Francisco Ruiz Massieu). Corruption, deception, and incompetence seemed to be the trademarks of the PRI regime. Zedillo's initiation to office, in short, was nothing short of disastrous.

In addition to coping with the peso crisis and its political fallout and continuing inconclusive negotiations with the Zapatistas, the Zedillo government also sought and secured, in January 1995, a pact with the principal opposition parties to guarantee the credibility of future elections. Although the pact was nothing more than a mechanism for consultation and negotiation among the parties concerning alleged electoral irregularities, it represented a major step toward political accommodation for Mexico and brought to mind similar pacts that were turning points in the establishment of democratic regimes in Venezuela in 1958 and in Uruguay in 1984. The actual record in the rest of 1995 was mixed. Elections in Tabasco in January and Jalisco in February raised serious questions about the fairness of the processes, and in May the PAN captured the governorship of Guanajuato and came so close to victory in Yucatán as to make accusations of fraud quite credible. By June, the pact appeared to be on its deathbed, a victim of a continued perception, by the opposition parties, of electoral fraud in various state elections. Although reformers within the regime have gained increasing leverage since 1968, they are not yet ready to cast their lot with opposition moderates. The PRI machinery appears still all too committed to using any means at its disposal—and it still has many means—to gain victory. The opposition parties remain unwilling to accept that any PRI victory could be other than fraudulent. The conditions for a viable pact are not yet present.

Nevertheless, the Mexican party system—and the political system as a whole—are clearly changing. The PRI is without doubt losing ground, and the PAN and PRD are gaining (but see Knight, 1994, for a more skeptical view). The Zapatistas also seem to have considerable strength, at least in Chiapas. Mexico can no longer be regarded as a hegemonic party regime, even though the PRI remains the ruling party, nationally and in most states. The power of the party and its ability to compete electorally are completely dependent on control of patronage (i.e., jobs and other benefits). If the PRI should ever lose control of the national government, it no longer has the base of popular commitment with which to make a comeback.

This reality suggests that the final citadel, the presidency, will not lightly be surrendered to the opposition by electoral means. This regime of depersonalized caudillismo will likely hang on to the bitter end. A transition to democracy may have to wait until a much weakened regime succumbs to some sort of institutional rupture. However, it is also possible that the opposition, with a much stronger electoral base after 1997 and with substantial international support, will be able to demand an honest election even at the presidential level in 2000. President Zedillo's words and actions are inconclusive for predicting the role he may play in the campaign for the elections of 2000. On the one hand, he insisted that the PRI accept its loss of the Congress in 1997, but on the other hand, he kept control of the party leadership rather than pushing it into a democratic leadership election after the defeat of 1997.

CUBA: REVOLUTIONARY CAUDILLISMO

Cuba was one of the first territories in the Americas to come under colonial rule and one of the last to escape. Even after Spanish rule was ended in 1898 as a direct result of the Spanish-American War, Cuba faced more than three decades of an explicit subordination to the United States embodied in the Platt Amendment to the Cuban constitution imposed on the Cubans by the United States, which gave the United States the right to intervene in Cuban internal affairs without the consent of the Cuban government. After the abrogation of the Platt Amendment in 1934, Cuba's political evolution continued to be overshadowed by the United States, which tacitly backed the Batista dictatorships of the 1930s, 1940s, and 1950s. In short, as in several other Caribbean and Central American states previously discussed, one cannot understand Cuba's development without seeing it in the light of external intervention.[25]

As in other countries, the strong U.S. influence helped to produce an economy profoundly dependent on the U.S. economy (dominated by sugar exports to the United States), and a political elite willing to accept subordination to U.S. policy. In the first generation after independence from Spain, Cuba was ruled by a succession of unstable civilian governments subject to U.S. pressure and occasional direct intervention. Gerardo Machado y Morales, elected president in 1924, established a dictatorship that lasted until his overthrow (with U.S. mediation) in 1933. The leader of the successful coup was Sergeant Fulgencio Batista, who became the new strongman. Batista facilitated the installation of a reformist provisional government, led by Ramón Grau San Martín, in September 1933, then overthrew Grau in January 1934. The United States then abrogated the Platt Amendment. Batista was thereby—whether intentionally or not—confirmed in power. Batista would continue as Cuba's dominant caudillo for over twenty-five years until his overthrow in 1959; however, he formally occupied the presidency only from 1940 to 1944 (constitutional) and 1954 to 1959 (extraconstitutional). Particularly after seizing power in 1952, Batista's government was characterized by escalating corruption and repression.

In short, prior to 1959, Cuba in its brief independent history experienced a generation of corrupt, quasi-independent elite politics and two dictatorships. Of democracy it knew nothing. Or, more precisely, the Cuban experience was that formal democracy meant nothing more than fraud and corruption. A natural response of politically aware Cubans was an intense nationalism that drew its inspiration from the repeated insurrections of the colonial era, and most particularly from that led by José Martí, starting in 1895. Not unexpectedly, the principal object of nationalist resentment in Cuba was the United States. Nationalist themes were central to Grau San Martín's rhetoric in the 1930s, though his practice in his only elected presidency (1944–1948) was corrupt and far from nationalistic. Revulsion against Grau and his Auténtico (Authentic) Party led to formation of the Ortodoxo (Orthodox) Party by Eduardo Chibás in 1947.[26] Chibás seemed to be a promising reformist candidate for the 1952 presidential elections, but he committed suicide in 1951. When Batista then preempted the elections by seizing power in 1952, it was Ortodoxo elements led by a young law graduate, Fidel Castro, who attempted to spark a popular uprising by attacking the Moncada Barracks in the eastern provincial capital of Santiago, in 1953. The attackers were repulsed, captured, and tried. Castro's statement at his trial would later become a famous articulation of Cuban revolutionary nationalism, *History Will Absolve Me* (1976). Sentenced to prison, Castro and his collaborators were granted amnesty by Batista in 1955, after the latter was elected president, unopposed, in 1954. Exiled in Mexico, Castro, his brother Raúl, and their small group of followers worked to prepare a new insurrection. Among their new recruits was a young Argentine physician, Ernesto "Ché" Guevara. Acquiring an old yacht, the *Granma,* Castro and his followers sailed to eastern Cuba in 1956, where many were killed or captured on landing. The survivors, including Castro, made their way to the Sierra Maestra mountains above Santiago and established an increasingly successful insurgency. Offensive operations began in 1957, and other guerrilla fronts opened in 1958. Popular disaffection was reflected in an abortive general strike in April 1958, and there were also several instances of unsuccessful military uprisings against Batista. The United States imposed an arms embargo against Batista in March 1958. After a government offensive against the Sierra Maestra failed in mid-1958, Batista's position steadily deteriorated. Finally, with Castro's forces closing in on Havana, Batista was removed by a military coup. A general strike then forced the military government to yield power to Fidel Castro on 1 January 1959. The Cuban Revolution was in power.

Castro's movement, the 26th of July Movement (named for the date of the Moncada assault), was very much in the tradition of the nationalist insurrections of the nineteenth century and quite consciously patterned on the insurrection of José Martí, a key inspirational figure for Castro (Liss, 1994, pp. 33–35). Like the older movements, this one was led by a single charismatic leader, sought to articulate the aspirations of the whole people, and saw itself as resorting to arms after all peaceful avenues were closed to it. At one level, it represented a caudillismo of opposition, focusing energy through a single extraordinary leader dedicated to the destruction of the incumbent regime. At a second level, whereas a highly elitist caudillismo dominated Cuban politics from 1925 to 1959, Castro's movement was distinctly oriented toward mobilizing and speaking for the great, oppressed mass of the population. The movement was not, prior to coming to power in 1959, either implicitly or explicitly socialist (much less communist or marxist-leninist). *History Will Absolve Me* and other documents call for an authentic liberal democracy and very moderate economic and social reforms (Liss, 1994, pp. 15–21). The prerevolutionary communists (organized as the Popular Socialist Party) in fact opposed Castro until late 1958.[27]

Decisions made in Cuba and the United States in the first two years of the revolution set a pattern that would persist to the end of the century. Castro and his close collaborators (especially Raúl and Ché) certainly had every reason to expect that the United States would be the principal enemy of the revolution if they attempted to make Cuba truly independent for the first time. They apparently saw, therefore, little point in trying to conciliate the United States after the initial weeks of positive press that followed the ouster of Batista. A succession of increasingly radical economic reforms certainly raised anxieties in Washington and on Wall Street, but key U.S. policymakers and intelligence officials were suspicious of Castro from the beginning. Planning began almost immediately for a covert intervention using Cuban exiles to overthrow the revolutionary government, an operation that would be patterned on the successful intervention in Guatemala in 1954 (Immerman, 1982; Schlesinger and Kinzer, 1982). This operation, planned and initiated by the Eisenhower administration, took shape as the abortive Bay of Pigs invasion of April 1961, in the early weeks of the Kennedy administration.

Cuba reestablished diplomatic relations with the Soviet Union in 1960, but a true alliance with the Soviets would not emerge until after the definitive break with the United States. The break came in the course of 1960, as extensive nationalizations of U.S. properties provoked the initiation of the trade embargo that the U.S. government has maintained, at varying levels of intensity and with varying levels of success, up to the late 1990s. Diplomatic relations were broken in early 1961. After the Bay of Pigs made clear the extent of the security risk posed by the United States, Cuba moved much closer to the Soviet Union. Castro declared himself a Marxist-Leninist on 1 December 1961. The Cuban Missile Crisis of October 1962 was occasioned by the emplacement of Soviet ballistic missiles in Cuba and the U.S. demand that they be removed. That the crisis was resolved between President John F. Kennedy and Premier Nikita Khrushchev over the head of Castro was an early sign that, for Cuba, the price of independence from U.S. control would be dependence on the Soviets for security. In spite of its many frustrations, though, the Soviet alliance continued to be a better bargain than accommodation to the United States, since the Soviets were basically supportive of the Cuban revolutionary project, in stark contrast to the United States. In sum, it was better to be dependent on an increasingly arthritic post-Stalinist Soviet Union than on a reactionary, anticommunist United States. The revolution would have no chance to succeed as a radical, socialist transformation of Cuban society except by defying the United States. The only source of the means to that end was the Soviet Union.

In retrospect, we can see that the Cuban Revolution has gone through six major phases, listed here with approximate dates (cf. Pérez-Stable, 1993): (1) radical nationalism (1959–1961); (2) institutionalizing the revolution (1962–1965); (3) the radical experiment (1965–1970); (4) reinstitutionalization based on the Soviet model (1971–1986); (5) rectification: reasserting autonomy in the face of Soviet decline (1986–1991); (6) the Special Period Time of Peace: partial adaptation to the capitalist world economy in order to secure the survival of the socialist revolution (1991–1996). It is possible that a renewed political retrenchment began in 1996. A very noticeable common feature throughout has been that each major shift of direction has been announced, defined, and—apparently—controlled by Castro and a relatively unchanging inner circle. Very little of prerevolutionary Cuban society has survived nearly four decades of revolutionary transformation, but caudillismo still lives. Each of the major shifts represents an action on the part of the leadership to control the course of the revolution, usually by acting on structure. Either they have been coping with and resisting the effects of existing structures, or they have been constituting new structures, or both.[28]

Radical Nationalism (1959–1961)

Before the revolution became explicitly and officially socialist, revolutionary policy and practice concentrated on extending the organization and mobilization of the populace (never attempted systematically before 1959) and on reform measures widely advocated by radical nationalists in Latin America, such as land redistribution and nationalization of exploitative foreign companies (especially U.S.). There was an initial attempt to escape from Cuba's exaggerated dependence on sugar exports by promoting industrialization, but it soon became apparent that the capital for industrial investment could only come from continued and expanded sugar export. Like other Third World countries, Cuba would find it difficult to escape from its niche as an agricultural exporter. There was a largely successful attempt to mobilize the vast majority of the population in support of the revolution by providing them with both tangible benefits (e.g., land, schools, health services) and symbolic reinforcement (e.g., the efforts of the Federation of Cuban Women [FMC] to promote true equality for women for the first time). During this period, most of the upper classes and professionals, along with substantial numbers of middle-class Cubans, fled to Miami, creating the nucleus of what would become a numerous and politically potent Cuban exile community in Florida. It was from this sector that the CIA recruited the Bay of Pigs invasion force. For the vast majority of Cubans, however, peasants, rural and urban workers, and those from the middle sectors, this first stage of the revolution brought a clear improvement in their situations and, perhaps more important, the promise of even more improvement to come. The revolution was hope.

Institutionalizing the Revolution (1962–1965)

Once the leader had declared himself to be Marxist-Leninist, the way was clear for the development of revolutionary institutions. This process began in 1960 with the creation of the major mass organizations (i.e., Committees for the Defense of the Revolution [CDR], the FMC, the Association of Rebel Youth [AJR], the National Association of Small Farmers [ANAP]), which came under increasingly explicit political control from the Center after 1962. By 1965, the Communist Party of Cuba (PCC) had been established as the institutional capstone of the revolutionary order. The strong emphasis on the egalitarian distribution of goods and services continued and would become the single most distinctive achievement of the Cuban Revolution.

The Great Experiment (1965–1970)

Castro and his revolutionary colleagues appear to have chafed under the tutelage of the Soviets, fearing that excessive bureaucratization and institutionalization were sapping the enthusiasm and spontaneity of the early popular mobilization, thereby producing an incipient version of the gray Soviet bureaucracy. Theirs was still the radical vision of revolution as a moral transformation of society. They wanted to build new human beings who could transcend the limits of capitalist individualism, with its utility-maximizing rationality. They were dependent on the Soviet Union, but it must nevertheless have been clear that the Soviet road to socialism would not lead to such a moral transformation. Premature institutionalization threatened to strangle the revolution. From about middecade, without eliminating the institutions they had just created, they placed much greater emphasis on spontaneity and voluntarism in moving the revolution forward. Rather than rely on plodding organizations, they sought to mobilize the power of the revolutionary will to create the new society through the very act of refusing to be contained by the conventional wisdom. Rejecting the Soviets' pragmatic use of considerable elements of markets and material incentives for the promotion of social goals, Castro and the Cuban leadership sought to create the new socialist person by directly appealing to moral incentives and rejecting the use of material incentives for the promotion of work and production. The market was rejected as a regulatory mechanism for distribution because it gave preference to those with more money and because it encouraged the survival of material incentives. Finally, substantial resources continued to be devoted to housing, education, and medical care, which remained free and available to all. Food and other scarce but essential goods were rationed in order to assure equitable access.

The centerpiece of the great experiment was the declaration of an unprecedented ten-million-ton sugar harvest as a goal for 1970. The point was precisely that a seemingly impossible feat could be accomplished with moral exhortation and sheer revolutionary will. Through the late 1960s steadily increasing effort went into preparations for the 1970 harvest, with personnel being encouraged to take leaves from their regular jobs in order to work as volunteers in the harvest. The result was serious decline in all sectors of the economy except sugar. The 1970 harvest, though a record, fell far short of ten million tons, and Castro was forced to admit the folly of the effort.

Another feature of the great experiment was Cuban activism in the promotion of revolutionary insurgencies in the rest of Latin America. Ché Guevara slipped out of Cuba in the mid-1960s and worked actively in several countries to promote revolutionary insurrections. Cuban assistance and encouragement was evident across the continent in a considerable increase in insurgent activity. Correspondingly, however, the United States started to pay much more attention to this revolutionary threat in the region, training Latin American armed forces in counterinsurgency doctrine drawn from the Vietnam experience. The result in general was stalemate: the insurgencies consistently failed to overthrow incumbent governments, but the armed forces were generally unable to finish off the insurgencies. One case in which the insurgency was wiped out was in Bolivia in 1967, where Ché himself was leading a guerrilla band that was surrounded and annihilated. Ché's body was triumphantly displayed to the world press. Thereafter, the direct fomentation of Third World revolutionary uprisings was deemphasized.

Reinstitutionalization: The Soviet Model (1971–1986)

After the failure of the ten-million-ton sugar harvest, Castro and the revolutionary leadership admitted serious errors and reversed course again. Picking up the thread of institutionalization from the early 1960s, the emphasis shifted to an orderly, centrally planned economy that would be specifically oriented toward meeting the needs of the other planned economies of the Soviet bloc. Although the ten-million-ton campaign was rejected as having been an irrational allocation of resources, Cuba still needed to export sugar as its principal source of credits within the Soviet bloc and foreign exchange within the world capitalist economy. Other major exports included nickel and tobacco. Cuba would now be systematically integrated into the system of exchange within the socialist bloc, and it would continue to play the role of agricultural and raw material exporter. With the credits thus earned, Cuba could purchase petroleum, machinery, and other goods it did not produce. The favorable terms of exchange with the Soviet Union and its allies enabled the Cuban regime to continue to fund its commitment to the egalitarian provision of social services and essential goods. The population thus continued to have a good standard of living, with educational attainments and health standards comparable to those in advanced capitalist countries—but more equitably distributed.

Institutionalization also proceeded in the political realm. For the first time, experimentation began on an institutionalized system of popular representation (Popular Power) distinct from the mass organizations. Popular Power was initiated on the provincial level in Matanzas province in 1974, and extended to the whole country with the promulgation of the revolution's first constitution in 1976. Local assemblies of Popular Power were directly elected, and there was competition for available seats. However, the PCC supervised nominations to screen out unacceptable candidates. Local assemblies then elected provincial assemblies, which in turn elected the national assembly. No parties except the PCC were permitted.

The party itself also underwent institutionalization, developing a hierarchical structure patterned on that of the Soviet Union and holding its first party congress in 1975, sixteen years after the seizure of power.[29] During the 1970s, Cuba thus moved quite markedly toward patterns of political and economic organization that recapitulated those of the Soviet Union and Eastern Europe. The institutions of central planning and the single-party monopoly seemed increasingly secure, and the process of constructing the revolutionary society seemed increasingly a matter of orderly development through known stages. The voluntarism of the great experiment was increasingly remote.

Rectification (1986–1991)

By the early 1980s, Cuba's relationship with the Soviet Union was increasingly troubled, as the senior Soviet leadership aged and became less flexible. The advent of the Reagan administration in Washington posed the most direct security threat to Cuba since the 1960s, but the Soviets were increasingly hard put to respond to the expensive arms race initiated by the U.S. administration. The Soviet leadership, in short, was old and rickety, and the economy showed increasing signs of breakdown. The Solidarity uprising in Poland in 1979 had been put down by the Polish communists under Soviet pressure, but only by means of a military coup and martial law. A prolonged period of uncertainty ensued when Soviet president Leonid Brezhnev died in 1982: Presidents Yuri Andropov and Konstantin Chernenko each ruled for barely a year before also dying. Finally, reformers within the Soviet leadership gained the upper hand, and Mikhail Gorbachev was elected president in 1985.

Gorbachev quickly gained popularity in the West with his candor about the parlous state of the Soviet economy; his receptiveness to the negotiation of arms control agreements; and his promotion of twin reform agendas, glasnost (openness) and perestroika (restructuring). Like other reformers within authoritarian regimes, Gorbachev never intended to surrender the communist monopoly on power. Rather, he intended to consolidate that monopoly by forcing through changes that would render the regime more genuinely popular and more able to respond to challenges. That he miscalculated the effects of his reforms is now well known. Perhaps Eastern Europe would have broken with communism anyway in 1989, and perhaps the communist regime in the Soviet Union would have fallen anyway in 1991, but it certainly appears that Gorbachev's reforms at least eased and probably hastened these transformations.

Castro and the Cuban leadership appear to have understood quite quickly the implications of Gorbachev's reforms. By 1986, Cuba was charting a course increasingly independent of the Soviet Union. Reforms there would be, but neither perestroika nor glasnost. Instead, Castro began leading the way back, he said, to a more authentically Cuban socialism. The promotion of revolutionary consciousness and mass mobilization were reemphasized, and central planning was reduced in importance. The limited scope for free markets (e.g., for peasants to sell their produce) and material incentives was once again restricted. The thrust of economic policy, in turn, was a partial return to the heady days of the great experiment. The goal was to improve economic performance by eliminating the rigidities of Soviet-style central planning and again mobilizing popular commitment to the revolution (Pérez-Stable, 1993, pp. 157–158).

Political rectification supported the shifts on the economic front. The thrust was to shift power from administrative bureaucrats to the workers and to the PCC. Of course, the identity between workers and the party was implicitly assumed. Workers' revolutionary consciousness was to be promoted, and they were to be encouraged to criticize instances of corruption or inefficiency in the state bureaucracy and firms. The party, Marifeli Pérez-Stable (1993, p. 163) pointed out, was not a legitimate object of criticism. There was no question of political liberalization being extended to criticism of the regime itself. There was no Cuban Gorbachev.

It is ironic, though, that even as Castro became increasingly vocal in his criticism of Soviet errors and failings and especially of Gorbachev's reformism, Soviet support for Cuba continued with few changes until 1990. The rectification process was in effect fueled by continuing Soviet economic support for Cuba. Finally, in 1990, the Soviets announced that they could not continue to subsidize the Cuban economy. Future exchanges would be on the open market in hard currency. By the end of that year, it was apparent that Cuba was facing its worst economic crisis since 1959. Drastic changes were called for.

The Special Period in Time of Peace (1991–1996)

Shorn of Soviet support and the shelter of the Soviet bloc trading system, Cuba confronted the global reality of low sugar prices and high petroleum prices. Cuba simply could not sell enough in the global marketplace to buy the petroleum and manifold other goods it needed to keep its economy and its society stable.[30]

An untenable situation demanded a bold response, and once again it was Castro alone who could define that response. In late 1990, he announced the Special Period in Time of Peace, effectively an economic emergency in which a variety of special measures were to be authorized for the purpose of confronting the disastrous economic crisis and thereby assuring the survival of the revolution itself. In general, the special period meant abandonment of those aspects of rectification that worked against the market. Thus, farmers' markets were again authorized as a means to promote agricultural production. Possession of dollars by private citizens was decriminalized. Individuals were permitted to engage in small businesses on their own account (but not to employ nonfamily members) in a widening range of fields. Such expedients, directly contrary to the revolutionary ethos that the regime had sought to promote, were simply a recognition that the state no longer had the means to employ—and pay—everyone in the labor force. An even more radical departure was to open the economy to foreign investment in the form of joint ventures between the Cuban state and foreign corporations, in which the latter would control management. This occurred particularly in the tourist sector, which emerged as a major source of foreign exchange but needed extensive upgrading in order to achieve its potential. The regime also opened other sectors to foreign investment, including mining and even sugar. A considerable investment boom ensued, led by Canadian, European, and Latin American firms anxious to get in on the ground floor while the United States was still prohibiting its own citizens and firms from doing business there.[31]

These changes, however necessary, had serious negative effects. Most notable was the growing gap between those with access to dollars (e.g., people employed in the tourist sector) and those without such access (e.g., workers and professionals in the state sector). More broadly, liberation of market forces had the predictable result of increasing income inequality even among Cubans without access to dollars. Less tangible but supremely important to the Cuban leadership, liberation of the market carried with it a reemphasis on precisely the individualistic and materialistic values that the regime had been seeking to discourage.

Economic change was to some extent matched by political change, though there was more continuity from the rectification period on the political side. In late 1992, the National Assembly adopted a major reform of Popular Power—direct election of provincial and national deputies. Nominations for these higher assemblies were vested in candidacy commissions reporting to municipal assemblies. The latter (which formerly elected the provincial delegates) now will nominate exactly as many candidates as there are seats available. Voters may vote for as many as they wish, and candidates must receive at least 50 percent of the vote to be elected. The party was to cease participating directly in nominations, but it was still clear that the political elite retained substantial control over the nomination process (Bengelsdorf, 1994, pp. 171–173).

There was a significant opening, or liberalization, in the political arena, reflected in increased acceptance of independent nongovernmental organizations (especially religious and secular study institutes, or "think tanks") that were fundamentally "with the Revolution," but independent of party or state control. Leaders from some of these organizations were accepted as delegates to the National and Provincial Assemblies of Popular Power. These organizations (a good example is the Centro Félix Varela, directed by the philosopher Juan Antonio Blanco) were permitted to do their own publishing, to establish extensive contacts outside Cuba, and to sponsor conferences in Cuba where the exchange of ideas could be quite free. There was no question of changing the leading role of the PCC, and dissidents who did not accept the basic parameters of the revolution as defined by the party were still repressed and often imprisoned or exiled. Still, a limited liberalization was undeniable, at least up to early 1996.

A New Rectification? (1996–)

Within the regime, and indeed within the personality of Fidel Castro, persist strong tendencies opposed to liberalization or reform and insistent on maintaining the integrity of the original revolutionary project. As in its ascendancy in the late 1960s and late 1980s, this revolutionary fundamentalism may now be regaining the upper hand. The fundamentalist response has been aided by a marked deterioration in Cuba's already tense relations with the U.S. government and with right-wing Cuban exiles. Conservatives in the U.S. Congress had been working for some time on the Helms-Burton Act, designed to further tighten economic pressure on Cuba. Their allies among the Cuban exiles, meanwhile, pursued a campaign of deliberately provocative (but unarmed) overflights of Cuban territory and in one case dropped propaganda on Havana. On 24 February 1996, Cuban Air Force interceptors shot down two such planes after they refused to land. Although the provocation was deliberate and repeated, Cuba had, under international law, no right to shoot down an unarmed plane.

There are some indications that the downing of the aircraft may have been more than a simple overreaction to a deliberate provocation. On the same day the government canceled permission to the Cuban Council, a grouping of dissidents and human rights activists, to hold a meeting in Havana. A few months earlier, such a meeting might have been permitted. Then, after the Helms-Burton Bill had been passed and signed by President Clinton (a reversal by the president attributable entirely to the downing of the planes), the Central Committee of the PCC met in closed session to consider the situation. Leaks (probably intentional) conveyed a picture of a party digging in and reasserting its prerogative to define and enforce revolutionary purity. Castro is reported to have issued a call for a new period of ideological struggle, asserting that "revolutionary ideology has never been more necessary than today." Raúl Castro is said to have argued that Cuba must at all costs avoid Gorbachev-style reforms, and to have criticized intellectuals and journalists even in the party's own institutes. Concern was not limited to shutting off the political opening: the issue of the growing numbers of self-employed workers was also apparently cited as a problem. Foreign investment, though admittedly important to Cuba's recovery, was deemphasized in favor of mobilizing capital from within Cuba.[32] In sum, the aircraft incident has at least provided a stimulus and an opportunity for hard-line elements within the revolutionary regime to reassert their primacy (even as it has also reinforced the right-wing hard-liners in the United States).

The future of the Cuban regime remains highly uncertain. The aircraft downing of 1996 could mark a new stage of rectification, or it could be merely a short-term deviation. Taking a longer view, the periodic shifts of emphasis, from revolutionary consciousness to pragmatism and back, are basic to understanding the history of the revolution. The shifts are basic, as Carollee Bengelsdorf (1994) made clear, because the revolutionary project contains inherent contradictions that produce their own countercurrents. The subtitles of her chapters summarize these contradictions: "The First Decade: Paternalist Centralization and Anarchist Decentralization," "The Seventies: Centralized Decentralization," and "The Eighties: Unchanging Change." The fundamental dilemma is that while the goal is the development of a revolutionary consciousness in the people that will permit the building of authentic socialism, the means is a continuing centralization of effective power in the hands of a tiny revolutionary elite and, ultimately, in the hands of Fidel Castro. The people cannot be trusted until they have achieved true revolutionary consciousness, and they cannot do that as long as they are without the power to shape their own society and their own lives. The revolutionary purists thus appear trapped in a cycle in which they must repeatedly act to cut off excessive pragmatism in order to preserve the hope of a revolutionary future, although they can never actually achieve that future because of the contradictions of their own situation.

The pragmatists, or reformers, are those who would adapt Cuba to global structural "realities." In the 1970s, pragmatism meant accommodating to the Soviet Union. Now, it means insertion into the global marketplace. Either way, if they succeed, the radical promise of the Cuban Revolution will be betrayed. Presently, there are enormous pressures and incentives for Cuba to forsake its revolutionary project and make its peace with global capitalism and liberal democracy. The reformers may not intend to go all the way, but they risk reaching a point of no return where the opposition can no longer be suppressed. At that point Adam Przeworski's (1991) analysis will become relevant to Cuba. That is, reformers, having gained the upper hand, might find that they need to collaborate with opposition moderates to avoid being purged by the hard-liners.

Castro himself seems quite genuinely to have sympathies with both hard-liners and reformers. His periodic shifts of emphasis probably reflect his own analysis of the immediate requirements of the revolutionary project. Finally, however, his commitment is to an uncompromising vision of the revolution. He is willing to make tactical shifts to ensure the survival of the revolution, but he will not accept reforms that he thinks will undermine the essence of the revolution. And he is the one who defines that essence.

Cuba will change fundamentally; we know that because Castro is mortal, and this revolutionary caudillo continues to be the very core of the revolution. His authority is far more extensive and transcendent than that of Stroessner, and there has been no effective institutionalization of his authority or routinization of his charisma. There is a constitutional successor (Raúl) who will have effective control of party, army, and state; that control may suffice to entrench a new "revolutionary" autocracy. If so, it will be nothing like Fidel Castro's revolution.

Finally, there is the grim possibility that the United States, in collaboration with Cuban exiles, might attempt, covertly or overtly, to impose a post-Castro regime. That would almost certainly mean a devastating war in Cuba.

CONCLUSION

Not one of these three surviving authoritarian regimes is on a sure course for a democratic transition. All three are in transition, but toward what we cannot know. Ironically, the least developed of the three, Paraguay, may be the most likely to make a successful democratic transition. It is certainly the furthest along at this point. Its advantages include a relatively unmobilized population. Its weaknesses include a tradition of unvarnished caudillismo and a ruling elite whose commitment to democracy is not very deep. But as long as the international structure of incentives favors democracy, the Paraguayan elite may be expected to play the game, including a progressive easing up on the opposition parties. Given some time, the habits of liberal democracy might take deeper root.

Mexico's depersonalized caudillismo has proven highly durable, and it may yet survive the current epoch of political change. As suggested previously, it seems unlikely that the PRI political establishment will ever permit itself to lose the presidency by electoral means. However, as the opposition gains strength, there is a possibility of a split in the ruling party leading to a palace coup in alliance with opposition elements. Such an event could open the way to democratization, but it might not. Similarly, a popular mobilization could become massive enough in Mexico (unlike Paraguay) to force the PRI out of power. This does not seem very likely at present, but then, who predicted the emergence of Cuauhtémoc Cárdenas as a viable challenger in 1988?

The autumn of Cuba's revolutionary patriarch poses perhaps the most intriguing possibilities, because the Cuban regime combines high levels of organizational development and popular mobilization with a completely personalistic, charismatic supreme leader.[33] The Cuban population certainly has the cultural sophistication to operate within a liberal democracy, should they want to do so, but many citizens and the majority of the ruling elite reject liberal democracy as a poor substitute for the aspirations of the revolution. A transition to liberal democracy is possible after Castro, given the right set of circumstances. More likely is a continuation of a progressively depersonalized revolutionary regime, along the lines of China after Mao.

NOTES

1. I use "authoritarian regime" to mean a persistent system of rule in which rulers gain and retain political power by coercion rather than consent and are not effectively checked by laws. The distinction between authoritarian and totalitarian regimes, commonly used from the 1940s until the 1980s, is no longer relevant, because it depended on the supposedly total control exercised by the latter. If control were total, then totalitarian regimes could not be overthrown from within, whereas authoritarian regimes could be ousted from within because they exercised less extensive control. Since the breakdown of communist rule in Eastern Europe and the Soviet Union, we know that supposedly totalitarian regimes were susceptible to overthrow from within. They thus cannot be differentiated on principle from authoritarian regimes. Cf. Linz (1975); Kirkpatrick (1982, 1990).

2. Huntington (1968) emphasized that political stability depends on a relative balance between levels of mobilization and institutionalization. Almond (1973) similarly argued that stability depends on the political system's capability to produce outcomes that respond to demands coming from the society.

3. Of course, they may miscalculate, as Gorbachev did in the Soviet Union in 1991.

4. On Paraguayan politics and parties in general, see Abente (1995); Roett and Sacks (1991); Mora Mérida (1981); Lewis (1982, 1993a, 1993b); Miranda (1990).

5. See Lewis (1982, 1993a); Miranda (1990).

6. On the decline and fall of Stroessner, see Miranda (1990), chap. 7; Roett and Sacks (1991), chap. 6.

7. Roett and Sacks (1991), chap. 4. Indeed, it is notable that the two South American countries that longest resisted the trend toward democratization were Chile and Paraguay, each with relatively healthy economies.

8. He did not, like Pinochet later in the same year, make the mistake of holding an honest election.

9. On the Rodríguez period, see Abente (1993, 1995); Sondrol (1992); Black (1993).

10. On the Wasmosy period, see Caballero (1995).

11. Major sources on Mexican politics include Craig and Cornelius (1995); Cornelius (1996); Camp (1996b); Hellman (1983, 1994); NACLA (1997); González Casanova (1970); Schmidt (1986); Morris (1995); LaBotz (1995); Roett, ed. (1995); Woldenburg (1995); Cordera and Sánchez Rebolledo (1995); Cansino (1995);

Knight (1994); Acosta Silva et al. (1995); Carrigan (1995); Muñoz Patraca (1994); Fox (1994); Davis (1994); Coppedge (1993).

12. For a brief summary of this period, see Bushnell and Macaulay (1994), chap. 4.

13. On the Mexican Revolution, see Knight (1986, 1992); Williamson (1992), chap. 10; Hellman (1983); Meyer (1981); Alba (1967); Brandenburg (1964); Cumberland (1968); Dulles (1972); Cornelius (1973).

14. Williamson (1992, p. 396) noted that Calles was suspected of having a hand in the assassination of his ally and rival.

15. On Cárdenas, see Knight (1986, 1992); Cornelius (1973); Williamson (1992), chap. 10.

16. The principal opposition party of modern Mexico, the National Action Party (PAN), was founded in 1939 and sought to draw in these various strands of conservative opposition to the revolutionary regime: religious people and the clergy, businesspeople, and in general anyone disillusioned with the regime. See Craig and Cornelius (1995), pp. 269ff.

17. For this period, see Brandenburg (1964); Hellman (1983); Alba (1967).

18. On the post-1968 crisis, see Craig and Cornelius (1995); Schmidt (1986); Hellman (1983); Morris (1995); Camp (1996b); Woldenburg (1995); Cordera and Sánchez Rebolledo (1995); Coppedge (1993); Fox (1994).

19. See Pool, Franko-Jones, and Stamos (1991); Stallings and Kaufman (1989); Haggard and Kaufman (1995).

20. Additional sources on Mexican politics since the mid-1980s include Paternostro (1995); Camp (1995); Pacheco Méndez (1995); Basañez (1994); Klesner (1995); Knight (1994); NACLA (1994b, 1997); Rosen (1996a); Muñoz Patraca (1994); Acosta Silva et al. (1995); Cansino (1995); Aziz Nassif (1995); Schulz and Williams (1995); Cornelius (1996).

21. Writing on the Zapatista rebellion has been voluminous. Useful sources include Carrigan (1995); Hernández (1994); García de León (1995); Rosen (1996b); Zermeño (1995); Stephen (1995); Nash (1995); Dietz (1995).

22. In February 1995, the government announced the probable identity of Subcomandante Marcos: Rafael Sebastián Guillén, born in 1957 to a middle-class family in Tampico, a former honors student of philosophy and sociology at the National Autonomous University in Mexico City and at the Sorbonne. He allegedly had participated in the Nicaraguan and Guatemalan insurgencies and had been in the Soviet Union. For an enlightening interview with Marcos, see McCaughan (1994).

23. See Gómez and Bailey (1990); Craig and Cornelius (1995); Klesner (1995); Pacheco Méndez (1995).

24. In 1994, sixty-four senators were chosen in single-member district, plurality elections; PRI won them all. Thirty-two were chosen by proportional representation (twenty-four to PAN, eight to PRD). Three hundred deputies were chosen by single-member district, plurality elections, and PRI won 275. In 1997, PRI won only 164 single-member seats. Two hundred deputies were chosen by proportional representation, again allocated mostly to PAN and PRD (Klesner, 1995, p. 138; *Latin American Weekly Report,* 15 July 1997, p. 326). The use of proportional representation is an electoral reform adopted in 1977 to increase the presence of opposition parties in Congress, while continuation of the majority of seats under the single-member district, plurality rule assures the PRI a majority as long as it holds a plurality in most places (Craig and Cornelius, 1995, p. 284).

25. Major sources on Cuban history include Pérez-Stable (1993, 1994); del Aguila (1994); Simons (1996); Pérez (1995); Williamson (1992), chap. 12.

26. The Auténticos' formal name was the Partido Revolucionario Cubano. The Ortodoxos' formal name was the Partido del Pueblo Cubano.

27. Castro himself may have been a Marxist in 1953, but if so, he took care not to give himself away before his followers were prepared to understand. See Liss (1994, p. 17) for this interpretation.

28. Additional major sources on revolutionary Cuba include Bengelsdorf (1994); Halebsky and Kirk (1992); Eckstein (1994). For a provocative comparison of the Cuban Revolution with those of Nicaragua, Bolivia, and Grenada, see Selbin (1993). For a thorough analysis of women and the revolution, see Smith and Padula (1996).

29. Subsequent congresses were held in 1980, 1986, and 1991.

30. Major sources on the special period include NACLA (1995b); Edelstein et al. (1995); Roman (1995); Cross (1995); Walsh (1996); Blanco (1995); Blanco and Benjamin (1993); Reed (1995); Fitzgerald (1994).

31. In fact, the U.S. Congress passed laws in 1992 and 1996 that sought to further tighten the economic noose on Cuba and in particular to impose penalties on foreign firms that persisted in doing business in Cuba. This latter provision, of course, drew unanimous condemnation from governments and corporations outside the United States and from important sectors and interests within that country as well. Although the politics of U.S. policy toward Cuba is beyond the scope of this work, the effects of that policy continue to be central to an understanding of the Cuban situation.

32. This Central Committee meeting is reported in Rohter (1996b).

33. I refer to Gabriel García Márquez, *The Autumn of the Patriarch*.

5

Economy, Society, and Democracy

In this chapter we consider the economic and social environment of democracy in the 1980s and 1990s. We deal with how the massive economic crises of the past fifteen years have constrained economic policy and strained the abilities of democratic governments to serve the interests of their people and thereby fortify their own legitimacy. We examine how various governments sought to resist external pressures for neoliberal economic reforms, how they sought instead to act along more or less heterodox lines, and how their attempts to assert autonomy largely failed.

The effects of economic crisis and economic reform were generally quite negative for the majority of Latin American populations. Income distributions became less equal, real incomes declined, and unemployment rose. Yet democratic regimes dealt with adversity just as well as authoritarian ones, and the stability of democratic regimes was not significantly undermined by coping with economic crises.

In the second part of the chapter we consider social structure and its relevance for democracy. Extensive attention is paid to civil society, as the main way citizens have to act politically, to participate in the political life of their society. Civil society includes organizations and movements that are concerned with politics but not so integrally involved as political parties. For most nonelites, it is through civil society that meaningful action is possible in the political arena.

ECONOMIC REFORM AND DEMOCRACY

Reference was made earlier to the great debt crisis of the 1980s and to the roughly simultaneous emergence of the "Washington consensus" among international lenders and aid donors, favoring not only fiscal austerity and reduction of trade barriers but also extensive privatization of state enterprises and a general reduction of the state's role in economy and society. The stress of the debt crisis and the concomitant reforms undoubtedly helped to push many of the authoritarian regimes out of power and thus facilitated the transitions analyzed in Chapter 3. However, the new liberal democratic regimes have themselves confronted many of the same stresses, for recovery has been slow, income and property have become measurably more concentrated, middle-class jobs in the state sector have been eliminated, and the quality and coverage of social programs have declined. These stresses are justified in neoliberal theory as necessary to a fundamental economic readjustment, which will in the long run lead to higher growth rates that will benefit the whole society.[1]

In the context of this analysis of democracy, it is not necessary to involve ourselves in the argument among economists as to the merits of the neoliberal model and its predictions. However, we must take account of neoliberalism and the Washington consensus as political facts of the 1990s, as demands placed upon all governments in Latin America (indeed, all developing countries). How have responses varied between countries or between governments? What political characteristics or structural features help to explain this diversity? What have been the results of neoliberal policy reform? And finally, what for our purposes is the central question: how have neoliberal economic reforms affected democratic regimes?

How Have Responses Varied?

Responses to neoliberal pressures for reform have varied, both between countries and between governments in the same country.[2] Policies of both authoritarian and democratic governments have ranged from defiant populism (e.g., Velasco Alvarado and Alan García in Peru) to highly orthodox neoliberalism (e.g., Pinochet and Aylwin in Chile). The populist approach was characterized by the maintenance and expansion of subsidies ensuring the popular standard of living (e.g., price controls, social services, public employment). Populist policies tended to produce fiscal deficits because tax collections could not keep up with program costs, and severe inflation usually emerged. Exports tended to be discouraged by support for high wages and artificially high currency values. Imports were typically blocked by high tariffs in order to promote import substitution industrialization, on the theory that protection of internal markets was the only way for local industry to establish itself. Severe deficits in the balance of payments commonly emerged in the wake of the global petroleum crisis of the late 1970s. The populist approach was sustainable only so long as there was either international lending support for the fiscal and balance of payments deficits or an ability to raise revenue internally to pay off those deficits. Few governments proved capable of doing the latter, and when international lending dried up in the early 1980s, the debt crisis ensued (see Stallings and Kaufman, 1989; Dornbusch and Edwards, 1991; Stamos and Pool, 1989). It was the debt crisis that rendered most governments susceptible to pressures for neoliberal reforms.

Most governments avoided the spectacular defiance of the conventional wisdom that characterized Siles Zuazo in Bolivia (1982–1985), García in

Peru (1985–1990), or Ortega in Nicaragua (1985–1990), but most did pursue some variant of populist policy and did resist pressures for neoliberal reforms. Confronted with deficits and hyperinflation and unable to service debts, several governments attempted so-called heterodox shock treatments intended to stop inflation and promote economic growth without all the highly unpopular deflationary measures advocated by the IMF. Good examples are the Austral Plan of Alfonsín in Argentina and a succession of plans adopted by José Sarney and Fernando Collor de Melo in Brazil. In each case, initial success was followed in a few months by a disastrous descent into economic crises even worse than before.

A less radical defense of populist policy—effectively, a policy of strategic retreat—was mounted by countries where the crisis was less acute and where there was considerable investment in welfare state programs and state-owned enterprises. Uruguay and Costa Rica best exemplify this category. In these cases a succession of governments from both major parties have avoided direct confrontation with the IMF and international lenders while implementing only the minimum of neoliberal reforms absolutely necessary to keep international finance flowing. In well-established democracies such as these, unpopular neoliberal measures frequently elicited popular protests, but governments generally stuck to their guns and implemented those policies to which they had committed themselves.

Most governments in the region, confronted with debt and fiscal crises and with hyperinflation, politically unable either to finance social programs or to cut them, responded to neoliberal pressures ad hoc, resisting as long as possible, agreeing to unpopular reforms when absolutely necessary, and failing to implement reforms when internal political pressures grew too intense. Honduras, the Dominican Republic, and Ecuador are typical. In the Dominican case, both the PRD governments (1978–1986) and Balaguer (1986–1996) have maneuvered uncertainly between the extremes of neoliberalism and populism, perhaps cushioned by close economic ties with the United States. Honduras also benefited from U.S. aid during the Reagan administration's (1981–1989) obsession with Central America but has been increasingly on its own since 1989. The governments of Rafael Leonardo Callejas and Carlos Roberto Reina have agreed to reforms when necessary but implemented them without enthusiasm. In Ecuador, a succession of weak rightist and center-left governments, confronting a highly fragmented Congress and an increasingly mobilized public, have needed help from the IMF on a regular basis but have been consistently inconsistent in their economic policies. This pattern culminated in the 1996 election of populist Abdalá Bucaram, who promptly reversed himself and adopted stringent neoliberal reforms, only to face massive popular protests and his removal from power by a congressional vote in February 1997 (Acosta Silva, 1996; Schemo, 1997).

In several cases, incoming presidents have used political blitzkrieg to implement draconian neoliberal shock plans. Major examples include Víctor Paz Estenssoro in Bolivia (1985), Carlos Salinas de Gortari in Mexico (1988), Carlos Andrés Pérez in Venezuela (1989), Carlos Menem in Argentina (1990), Alberto Fujimori in Peru (1992), and Abdalá Bucaram in Ecuador (1996). In each of these cases, presidents made extensive use of discretionary powers and the element of surprise to impose a neoliberal transformation of the national economy. Price controls, tariffs, and subsidies were severely cut, state-owned firms were privatized, state employment was pruned, and major emphasis was placed on controlling inflation by controlling wages. The predictable result was a rise in unemployment and underemployment, an increase in the poverty rate, and a general decline in the standard of living. Pérez's presidency did not survive the shock: bloody popular riots in 1989 and military revolts in 1992 set the context for his impeachment and removal from office in 1993.[3] The successor government of Rafael Caldera has reverted to ad hoc policymaking.[4] Bucaram, with a much less institutionalized party system than Venezuela's, held office only six months before a combination of popular rage and political rivalries swept him away.

Salinas rode out the political crisis and achieved enough economic success to assure the election of his successor, Ernesto Zedillo, in 1994. However, between the election and the inauguration, the Mexican economy came unglued in a major financial panic, a hemorrhage of capital stopped only by a U.S.-backed rescue plan. Unlike Caldera, however, Zedillo has sustained Salinas's commitment to neoliberalism in spite of widespread opposition within Mexico.

In contrast, both Menem and Fujimori proved so popular with their control of inflation that each was able to secure a constitutional amendment permitting immediate reelection and to gain overwhelming reelection victories in 1995. Their political success certainly owes something to an authoritarian propensity in Latin American political culture[5] but is also based on sustained economic stability, even when it has come at the cost of increased poverty and unemployment. By late 1996, both Fujimori and Menem were suffering severe declines in popularity linked to poor economic performance.[6]

In Bolivia, Paz Estenssoro was the first democratically elected president in Latin America to successfully carry out comprehensive neoliberal reforms. His success was facilitated by the strategic defeat of the major labor federation, the Bolivian Workers' Central (COB), and particularly the tin miners' union. Strikes protesting the closure and privatization of the tin mines were forcefully repressed, and the major labor leaders arrested and exiled. After 1986, organized labor ceased to be a threat to the neoliberal agenda of the government. Paz Estenssoro's alliance with the conservative ADN of Hugo Banzer permitted the enactment and implementation of a comprehensive package of neoliberal reforms that, in addition to dismantling the tin industry, privatized other state-owned firms, reduced the state bureaucracy, and cut back on social programs. The hyperinflation of the Siles Zuazo years was quickly ended. The policies of Paz Estenssoro and his minister of economy, Gonzalo Sánchez de Lozada, were so popular that not only Sánchez de Lozada but also his two principal opponents in the elections of 1989 thought it prudent to pledge a continuation of the basic elements of Paz Estenssoro's policy. Although Sánchez de Lozada finished first, he was short of a majority, and Congress ultimately elected the third-place candidate, Jaime Paz Zamora, who had struck a deal with Banzer. Paz Zamora's economic policy did in fact continue the broad outlines of the Paz Estenssoro policy in the period 1989–1993. Sánchez de Lozada was elected president in 1993 and has persisted with neoliberalism. In short, three successive governments, over more than a decade, have maintained neoliberal economic policies in Bolivia (see Gamarra, 1994).

The government of Fernando Henrique Cardoso (1994–1998) in Brazil exemplifies a more moderate version of this blitzkrieg neoliberalism. As economy minister under his predecessor, Itamar Franco, Cardoso had fostered a successful neoliberal program, the Real Plan. On the strength of that success, he was elected president and has continued the plan. As of early 1997, he was moving toward success in getting Congress to approve a constitutional amendment to allow him to run for a second four-year term (Ellison, 1997).

The only country with a consistent record of neoliberalism since the mid-1970s has been Chile.[7] After more than a year of policy incoherence, the Pinochet government became thoroughly committed to neoliberal reform of the Chilean economy after about 1975. The so-called Chicago boys, economists trained by Milton Friedman at the University of Chicago, came to dominate Chilean economic policy. Unchecked by political opposition or popular mobilization, the neoliberal model was systematically implemented. Long-protected industries were gutted by sudden exposure to international competition. Unemployment rose. Real wages fell. State-owned firms were privatized (with the major exception of the copper-mining industry nationalized under Allende in 1971). Public employment was slashed. The result was that Chile experienced two prolonged periods of macroeconomic growth (roughly, 1976–1981 and 1985–1996), punctuated by a serious recession (1982–1985).

Although the recession was auspicious for the first serious campaign of public opposition to Pinochet, the authoritarian regime weathered the crisis. By 1988, Pinochet seemed very secure in power. Most observers were surprised when the Concertación actually defeated him in the referendum of that year and went on to win the general elections of 1989 (see Chapter 3). But the center-left Concertación was at pains to assure voters and business interests that it proposed no substantive change in Pinochet's economic policies. They simply proposed to do more to cushion the negative effects of those policies on the poorest people. In fact, the successive Concertación governments of Patricio Aylwin (1990–1994) and Eduardo Frei (1994–1998) have hewed closely to the neoliberal economic policies set by Pinochet, even as they have taken important steps toward departing from the authoritarian legacy in other respects.[8]

Even Cuba, the only Latin American country that has consistently confronted neoliberalism with a serious alternative model (state-led, centrally planned socialist development), has had to accept and adapt to a degree of economic opening that would have been unimaginable before the crisis of European marxism-leninism removed its principal external support.[9] The Cuban regime has sought, since the mid-1980s, to correct many of the rigidities and weaknesses of the Soviet model, to mobilize internal capital and initiative, to attract external capital and tourism, all the while avoiding a fundamental weakening of the political leadership of the revolution. Whether Cuba can succeed is a big question (see Chapter 4).

How May This Diversity Be Explained?

Potential explanations fall into two broad categories: structural and political. The existence of a global concentration of power in the hands of institutions and governments with strong interests in promoting neoliberal policy reforms is, of course, a structural explanation why no countries and few individual governments have systematically refused to implement such reforms. The diversity of responses to these pressures, however, can itself be explained structurally by referring to the distribution of power within each of the societies. Stephan Haggard and Robert Kaufman (1995), for example, argued that when transitions to democracy have occurred without an economic crisis, the economic policy of the new democratic government will be more constrained by organized parties and interests aligned with the outgoing authoritarian regime. Most clearly in the case of Chile, this pattern helped to guarantee the continuity of neoliberal economic policy. However, there are several cases in which the economic policy of the authoritarian regime was not so consistently neoliberal but still limited the maneuverability of the incoming democratic government if the transition occurred without a severe economic crisis. An example would be Guatemala, where the military regime was distinguished by corruption and repression but lacked a coherent economic strategy. The transition was driven more by U.S. political interests than by economic crisis, but the armed forces and their allies retained strong positions and vested interests in the Guatemalan economy and were capable of frustrating the efforts of successor governments to devise and implement a more coherent economic policy.[10]

Conversely, Haggard and Kaufman argued, when transitions have occurred in a context of economic crisis, the outgoing authoritarian regime and its partisans will be less able to constrain economic policies of the newly elected government. Perhaps the clearest example of this is Argentina, where the regime was pushed into the 1982 Malvinas adventure precisely by its weak economic position; the cost of the war and its loss then exacerbated the economic crisis. The newly elected Alfonsín government was under no pressure to adopt an economic policy congruent with that of the military government and indeed adopted the heterodox Austral Plan.

The Haggard-Kaufman analysis may be extended to include the broader question of whether or not the transition was negotiated with the authoritarian government. As we saw in Chapter 3, in the vast majority of cases the transition was negotiated, and economic policy was usually part of the negotiation. In Uruguay, for example, the adhesion of the Broad Front (FA) to the Naval Club Pact with the military government in 1984 committed the principal party of the Left to an indefinite postponement of radical social and economic reform. That agreement was indispensable to the transition. Even though subsequent negotiations for a social pact failed to bring the major unions on board, the continuing commitment of the FA to democratic stability as a first priority meant that the basic lines of economic policy would continue within the broad neoliberal framework established by the military regime.[11]

Haggard and Kaufman also suggested that the character of party systems shaped the possibility of effective economic policy.

> Fragmented and polarized party systems heighten party rivalries, magnify conflicts among organized interests, and weaken the capacity of the executive to initiate reform. These very failings can increase the incentives for reformist executives to bypass representative institutions and the constitutional process altogether. Even if they succeed in initiating reform, however, the continuity and credibility of policy in such systems is jeopardized by the difficulty of forging stable electoral, legislative, and bureaucratic majorities, by ideological polarization between government and opposition, and by the resulting exacerbation of political business cycles. (Haggard and Kaufman, 1995, pp. 14–15)

In contrast, they argue, effective policy is more likely in cohesive party systems with limited fragmentation and muted polarization. A good example of the former pattern would be Ecuador, whereas the latter may be exemplified by Bolivia. In Ecuador, a succession of weak governments of varying ideological stripe has consistently faced obstructive parliaments and has been consistently inconsistent in economic policy. In Bolivia, the fragmentation and chaos of 1978–1985 has given way to negotiated coalitions bridging ideological gulfs and capable of formulating and carrying out consistent policies (Conaghan and Malloy, 1994).

This Bolivian example illustrates yet again that the distinction between "structural" and "political" explanations is not black and white. To this point we have been discussing structure, that is, distributions of power that fundamentally shape what is possible. A political explanation, in contrast, has to do with choices made by political actors, such as elite settlements. Such choices are in principle undetermined by structure, though structure may set boundaries for choice. The Uruguayan and Bolivian examples we have just considered as illustrating structural effects may as well be used to show the effects of political choices. The decision of the Broad Front to adhere to the Naval Club Pact helped to set the fundamental characteristics of the posttransition party system, a decisive political structure that facilitated the success of the Uruguayan transition. But the Broad Front decision was in no way structurally determined. It was, if anything, a result of political learning, which implies a capacity to transcend and to change structures. Much the same point can be made about the Bolivian example: the historically rooted structures of Bolivian politics could not have produced the transformation of the party system that took place after 1985.

Clearly, then, much of the variation in responses to global neoliberal pressures for reform must be attributed to particular choices made by particular leaders and groups, including mass publics. Why did Paz Estenssoro, Pérez, Fujimori, and Menem all choose to adopt wholly unexpected neoliberal policy departures? It is surely true that they were responding to the structural characteristics of their respective countries, but it is also true that there might have been other responses, as illustrated by Brazil, where neoliberal orthodoxy was consistently evaded until the advent of Fernando Henrique Cardoso as economy minister (1993) and then president (1995).

What Have Been the Results of Neoliberal Policy Reform?

Haggard and Kaufman (1995) summarized the macroeconomic trends for major new democracies in Latin America and Asia (see Table 5.1). The table compares macroeconomic performance (annual averages) of major Latin American and Asian countries that made the transition to democracy during the 1980s, on four dimensions: (1) GDP growth, (2) inflation rate, (3) fiscal deficit as a percentage of GDP, and (4) investment as a percentage of GDP. The cases are divided into two categories, those that made the transition during an economic crisis (mostly Latin American) and those that made it without such a crisis (mostly Asian).[12] Data are provided for the five years before the transition, for the year of the transition, for the first democratically elected government, and for the second such government.

These data illustrate several points. First, the noncrisis countries performed consistently better on each of the four indices than the crisis countries. Second, neither crisis nor noncrisis countries showed

Table 5.1   Macroeconomic Performance in New Democracies

Indices	Five Years Before Transition		Transition Year		First Democratic Government		Second Democratic Government	
	Crisis[a]	Noncrisis[b]	Crisis	Noncrisis	Crisis	Noncrisis	Crisis	Noncrisis
GDP growth	0.6	6.3	0.2	6.2	0.5	7.1	1.5	7.9
Inflation	68.9	17.5	166.8	16.0	896.2	22.3	1062.3	35.4
Fiscal deficit/GDP	−3.7	−2.2	−7.3	−1.1	−7.7	−2.1	−1.8	−0.6
Investment/GDP	19.4	23.0	17.9	23.8	17.8	26.6	16.0	26.1

Source: Haggard and Kaufman (1995), pp. 175–177.

a. Countries that made the transition in a context of economic crisis include Argentina, Bolivia, Brazil, Peru, Uruguay, and the Philippines.

b. Countries that made the transition without a crisis include Chile, Korea, Thailand, and Turkey.

consistent improvement in all indices over the period of the study, though the noncrisis countries did relatively better over time. Third, countries that were in economic crisis at the time of the transition tended to remain in crisis, whereas a noncrisis transition would predict continued avoidance of crisis. Overall, it is obviously better not to have an economic crisis, but the absence of crisis at the time of transition is no guarantee of consistent economic improvement. Neoliberal theory promises such improvement in the long run, but evidently the run used by Haggard and Kaufman is not long enough.

There is ample critical literature concerning the impact and accomplishments of neoliberalism in Latin America and globally. Peter Evans has long been committed to the view that—neoliberal antistatism notwithstanding—development has historically required leadership from a strong and effective state.[13] Recent edited volumes brought a critical perspective to the analysis of the neoliberal challenge.[14] Numerous studies of individual countries also addressed the effect of neoliberal reforms.[15] Luiz Carlos Bresser Pereira, José María Maravall, and Adam Przeworski (1993) offered a very influential social democratic approach to economic reform.

Hard evidence remains inconclusive, but the most common criticisms of neoliberalism center on an alleged increase in inequality, poverty, and unemployment growing from unfettered capitalism and the loss of sovereignty implied in the subordination of state policy to the control of international lenders and transnational and national capital. Carlos Vilas (1995a, pp. 154–155), for example, provided data on income distribution trends during the 1980s in four Latin American countries (see Table 5.2). These data showed that income did indeed become more concentrated in Brazil and especially Guatemala, but somewhat less concentrated in Costa Rica

Table 5.2   Changes in Household Income Polarization, 1980s

	Year	Share of National Income, Household Income Category				Share of the Highest 20% Divided by Lowest 20%
		Lowest 20%	Middle 60%	Top 20%	Top 10%	
Brazil	1983	2.4	35.0	62.6	46.2	26.1
	1989	2.1	30.4	67.5	51.3	32.1
Costa Rica	1986	3.3	42.2	54.5	38.8	16.5
	1989	4.0	45.2	50.8	34.1	12.7
Guatemala	1981	5.5	39.5	55.0	40.8	10.0
	1989	2.1	34.9	63.0	46.6	30.0
Mexico	1984	4.1	40.1	55.9	39.5	13.6
	1989	4.4	42.1	53.5	–	12.1
	1992	5.0	40.8	54.2	38.2	10.8

Source: Vilas (1995a), p. 155. Copyright © 1995 by WestviewPress. Reprinted by permission of WestviewPress.

and Mexico. James Petras and Fernando Ignacio Leiva (1994, pp. 128–129) showed data for Chile that indicated that income distribution did indeed become more unequal in the years before the transition to democracy but may have become slightly less unequal since 1988 (see Table 5.3).

Vilas (1995a, p. 143) also provided data on unemployment trends in Latin America in the 1980s and early 1990s. Between 1980 and 1992, no discernible regional trend emerged, nor did any single country show a steady rise in unemployment over the period (see Table 5.4).[16]

Weeks (1995, p. 121) showed that GDP growth per capita became negative during the 1980s for virtually all of Latin America after being positive everywhere but Nicaragua during the 1970s. At the same time, exports, which supposedly would be promoted by neoliberal policies, in fact grew

Table 5.3   Chile: Changes in Income Distribution, 1978–1990

Quintile	1978[a]	1988	1989	1990
1 (poorest)	4.6	4.2	4.6	4.9
2	9.5	7.5	7.9	8.4
3	14.1	10.9	11.3	11.5
4	19.9	16.9	16.6	17.2
5 (richest)	51.9	60.4	59.6	58.0

Source: Petras and Leiva (1994), p. 129. Copyright © 1994 by WestviewPress. Reprinted by permission of WestviewPress.
    a. May not add to 100 due to rounding.

Table 5.4   Open Urban Unemployment, 1980–1992 (annual average rates)

	1980	1981	1982	1983	1984	1985	1986	1987	1988	1989	1990	1991	1992[a]
Argentina	2.6	4.7	5.3	4.7	4.6	6.1	5.6	5.9	6.3	7.6	7.5	6.5	7.0
Bolivia	7.2	6.1	8.0	8.3	6.7	5.7	7.0	5.7	11.5	9.5	7.3	5.8	6.8
Brazil	6.2	7.9	6.3	6.7	7.1	5.3	3.6	3.7	3.8	3.3	4.3	4.8	4.9
Chile	11.7	9.0	20.0	19.0	18.5	17.0	13.1	11.9	10.0	7.2	6.5	7.3	4.9
Colombia	9.7	8.3	9.1	11.7	13.4	14.1	13.8	11.8	11.2	9.9	10.3	10.0	10.0
Costa Rica	6.0	9.1	9.9	8.5	6.6	6.7	6.7	5.9	6.3	3.7	5.4	6.0	4.3
Ecuador	5.7	6.0	6.3	6.7	10.5	10.4	10.7	7.2	7.4	7.9	6.1	8.5	8.7
El Salvador	–	–	–	–	–	–	–	–	9.4	8.4	10.0	7.1	6.8
Guatemala	2.2	1.5	6.0	9.9	9.1	12.0	14.0	11.4	8.8	6.2	6.4	6.7	6.1
Honduras	8.8	9.0	9.2	9.5	10.7	11.7	12.1	11.4	8.7	7.2	6.9	7.6	–
Mexico	4.5	4.2	4.2	6.6	5.7	4.4	4.3	3.9	3.5	2.9	2.9	2.6	2.9
Panama	10.4	10.7	10.1	11.7	12.4	15.7	12.7	14.1	21.1	20.4	20.0	19.0	18.0
Paraguay	3.9	2.2	5.6	8.3	7.3	5.1	6.1	5.5	4.7	6.1	6.6	5.1	5.3
Peru	7.1	6.8	6.6	9.0	8.9	10.1	5.4	4.8	7.1	7.9	8.3	5.9	–
Uruguay	7.4	6.7	11.9	15.5	14.0	13.1	10.7	9.3	9.1	8.6	9.3	8.9	9.0
Venezuela	6.6	6.8	7.8	11.2	14.3	14.3	12.1	9.9	7.9	9.7	10.5	10.1	8.8
Latin America	6.0	6.4	6.9	8.3	8.7	8.3	7.1	6.4	6.2	5.9	6.2	6.2	6.0

Source: Vilas (1995a), p. 143. Copyright © 1995 by WestviewPress. Reprinted by permission of WestviewPress.

a. Provisional.

more slowly in the 1980s than in the 1970s in all cases save Argentina, Costa Rica, and Venezuela (see Table 5.5). Although performance may have improved in some cases in the 1990s,[17] living standards certainly have a way to go even to regain 1980 levels, and export growth has been disappointing.

We may, at a minimum, conclude from these data that neoliberal economic reforms have been associated with a worsening of economic conditions for the majority, which may or may not prove temporary. The transition to democracy has clearly not shielded people from these consequences, but there is some evidence that democratic governments have at least been able to mitigate the worst effects of neoliberalism. Macroeconomic performance has generally improved, particularly as regards inflation, but improvements have been slow to manifest themselves in daily lives. The "long run" so dear to neoliberal theorists has yet to come.[18]

The issue of the alleged loss of sovereignty is even less susceptible to measurement but is no less significant as a political controversy.[19] Every stabilization plan negotiated with the IMF occasioned embittered criticism from nationalists and leftists upset at the apparent loss of national control over economic policy and indeed over the economy itself. Proposals for privatization of state-owned enterprises (e.g., banks, insurance companies, mines, petroleum) proved particularly neuralgic: even in Chile, paragon of neoliberal virtue, the major copper mines, nationalized by Allende, were

Table 5.5   Annual Growth Rates, GDP per Capita, and Exports (constant 1988 prices)

	GDP per Capita		Exports	
	1971–1980	1981–1990	1971–1980	1981–1990
Argentina	0.8	–2.8	4.8	6.0
Bolivia	1.4	–2.6	2.8	2.0
Brazil	6.3	–0.7	9.9	7.1
Chile	1.1	0.9	10.3	5.6
Colombia	3.1	1.4	6.3	6.0
Costa Rica	2.5	–0.5	5.9	6.6
Dominican Republic	4.3	–0.6	8.1	3.4
Ecuador	5.7	–0.9	14.0	4.6
El Salvador	0.2	–1.9	5.1	–1.5
Guatemala	2.8	–2.0	6.5	–2.1
Honduras	2.2	–1.0	4.6	0.8
Mexico	3.7	–0.7	8.3	7.3
Nicaragua	–3.1	–5.2	1.0	–1.3
Panama	2.6	–1.5	7.0	0.8
Paraguay	5.5	0.0	10.1	6.6
Peru	0.9	–3.2	3.0	–0.8
Uruguay	2.6	–0.3	7.2	4.1
Venezuela	0.8	–2.2	–4.3	2.4
Latin America				
Weighted[a]	3.4	–1.1	4.6	5.0
Unweighted[a]	2.1	–1.1	6.1	3.2

Source: Weeks (1995), p. 121. Copyright © 1995 by WestviewPress. Reprinted by permission of WestviewPress.

a. "Weighted" refers to all countries taken together as a single number for the region. "Unweighted" is the average of country figures.

kept in state hands by Pinochet and his democratically elected successors. There has been some privatization, notably in Argentina under Menem, and some opening of state-owned firms for private investment (e.g., in Bolivia), but on the whole, this has not turned out to be a central feature of the neoliberal reform process. More broadly, the IMF (and indeed, the "Washington consensus") has been widely condemned as allowing the poorest to pay the costs of an adjustment that will primarily benefit the rich and the multinational corporations. By the early 1990s, in fact, the IMF and the World Bank were showing signs of sensitivity to these criticisms, as they promoted programs to soften the impact of structural adjustment programs on the poorest sectors.[20]

The neoliberal demand that state employment and social services be reduced is quite fundamental and has elicited strong resistance. The people affected naturally protested in any way they could. Relatively progressive states such as Costa Rica and Uruguay had achieved enviable levels of human development on such dimensions as life expectancy and literacy, largely on the basis of heavy state investment in social services over many decades. These benefits understandably came to be seen as rights or entitlements, and any state efforts to control their costs elicited resistance. Even in less progressive states, such as Peru, the minimal and miserable social services provided by the state were often vital to the very survival of the poorest and to some semblance of decency for the poor. At the same time, the bureaucracies of the state and state-owned enterprises were everywhere a principal source of employment for the middle class emerging in growing numbers from secondary schools and universities. The prospect that good, secure jobs and a respectable living standard might not continue to be available provoked bitter resistance in most countries from both public employees and students. One result of this resistance is that in most countries, public employment has not been reduced nearly as much as neoliberal reformers would like.

Neoliberalism, in short, has had decidedly mixed results so far. The Latin American economies are now quite different than they were twenty or even ten years ago, but it is not yet demonstrable that they are better off, even at the macroeconomic level. At the microeconomic level of individual citizens, workers, and consumers, the costs of the "lost decade" of the 1980s weigh heavily and have yet to be paid.

How Have Neoliberal Reforms Affected Democracy?

It has been repeatedly shown, with steadily increasing statistical sophistication, that there is a positive association worldwide between economic development and democracy.[21] However, it is quite clear that in the specific context of Latin America in the 1980s and 1990s, this global correlation does not suffice. One problem is that countries across a wide range of economic development have crossed the threshold to democracy more or less simultaneously. A second problem is that democracy in the more developed countries is not necessarily more stable than in less developed Latin American countries (e.g., Bolivian democracy is arguably more stable in the 1990s than Argentine or Brazilian democracy). A third problem (on which this section will focus) is that economic change (e.g., neoliberal reform), even if it promotes economic development, may destabilize political democracy.[22]

Karen Remmer (1990, 1991b, 1993) systematically investigated the political impact of economic crisis in Latin America. She found that democracies on the whole have coped at least as well with economic crises as authoritarian regimes. She concluded that economic crises during the 1980s did undermine support for incumbents and did promote higher levels of electoral volatility, but without fostering political extremism, the exhaustion of elite consensus, or democratic breakdown. Conversely, she found that elections during the 1980s enhanced rather than undermined the capacity of leaders to address macroeconomic problems. In short, Remmer argued that on the whole, democratic regimes are more capable and less fragile than the conventional wisdom allows for. Indeed, the very durability of democratic regimes in contexts of economic crisis and radical neoliberal reform is testimony to the adaptability of this type of regime. Liberal democracy in the Latin America of the 1980s and 1990s is clearly not a hothouse flower.

Nevertheless there is ample cause for concern. These concerns relate on the one hand to the issue of inequality and on the other to the issue of the meaningfulness of popular participation. As we saw in the Introduction, the liberal theory of democracy assumes the equality of all citizens. Clearly, this is a goal that is never fully achieved, but the advent of neoliberal free market reforms poses a particular challenge to the assumption of equality because the unfettered market tends to produce inequality as a result of multiple levels of competition: some win, some lose. And, obviously, economic power enhances political power. Latin America as a region has been characterized by extreme inequalities since the conquest; neoliberal reforms certainly have not diminished that inequality and in most cases have probably made it a bit worse.

Liberal democracy entails a mechanism by which the people, the citizens, can choose those who will govern (Schumpeter, 1950) or choose desired policies (Downs, 1956). The claim of liberal democracy to be democratic rests on the ability of the people to choose their governors or affirm preferred policies, with reasonable assurance that the authorities thus chosen will implement the policies thus approved. However, in the neoliberal era, it has been quite common for newly elected presidents not only to fail to carry out their promises but indeed to carry out policies diametrically opposed to what they promised (O'Donnell, 1994). This was clearly the case with Paz Estenssoro in Bolivia (1985–1989), Menem in Argentina (1989–1998), and Pérez in Venezuela (1989–1993). Interestingly, only in the last case was the president called to account.

One of the most prominent features of neoliberal policymaking poses serious challenges to democracy. Because neoliberal reforms typically damage the immediate well-being of many, it is usually considered necessary to insulate economic policymaking from the democratic political process. This has been particularly evident in Bolivia, Argentina, and Peru, but there is a widespread tendency to put economic technocrats in control of economic policy, on the assumption that the long-term public interest will thereby be better served than by making policy responsive to the will of an allegedly ill-informed public. Now, it is certainly true that the public may be ill-informed, and liberal democratic theory since Madison and Tocqueville has been concerned to provide checks on popular sovereignty for that reason. Still, what is left of democracy when candidates gain election by telling direct falsehoods and then vest policymaking power in officials beyond the reach of the people?

We have seen that liberalism embodies a contradiction between the liberal democratic presupposition of equality and the tendency of economic liberalism to promote inequality. "The real world of democracy" (Macpherson, 1972) is one in which economic power distorts political equality, in which citizens have only minimum and episodic control over government, and in which citizen participation in politics is largely restricted to voting (and may well not even include that). This pathology is characteristic of all liberal democracies, not merely those of Latin America. In Latin America, indeed, the principal political agenda of the last generation has been to secure, to institutionalize liberal democracy; the issue of how to improve it has had a lower priority.

SOCIAL STRUCTURE, CIVIL SOCIETY, AND DEMOCRACY

The structure of a society, including especially its system of classes, is both shaped by and shapes the economic structure. This section will review that relationship, with particular attention to what theorists call "civil society," the organizations and movements through which individuals act to shape their social world.

As was made clear in the Introduction, there is a long-standing body of theory about the relations between social structure and democracy. As far back as Aristotle, it was thought that a strong middle class, neither rich nor poor, was essential for democracy. Rousseau was similarly persuaded of the need to avoid extremes of wealth and poverty. Tocqueville's book *Democracy in America* placed great emphasis on the strength of the smallholding agrarian and trading middle class in the United States as an explanation for the strength of democracy. Marx believed that liberal democracy as it was taking shape in Europe was directly linked to the interests and predispositions of the bourgeoisie, or middle class, and that authentic democracy would have to wait on the economic and political dominance of the working class.

In the twentieth century, similarly, there has continued to be an emphasis on the kind of society that is conducive to democracy. The classic study by Seymour Martin Lipset (1959) again focused attention on the importance of a strong middle class. Barrington Moore (1966) argued that democracy had historically been consolidated in countries with a bourgeoisie that was strong relative to the landed aristocracy.[23] In contrast, Dietrich Rueschemeyer, Evelyne Huber Stephens, and John Stephens (1992) argued that democracy has been strongest in those societies where the working class is strongest and best organized. They argue that democracy has been weaker and less stable in Latin America than in Europe precisely because the working class is consistently weaker in Latin American societies and thus less able to compel the bourgeoisie to accept democratization.

The primary mechanism by which social structure affects the political regime is through organization, or civil society. Larry Diamond (1994, p. 5) defined civil society as

> the *realm of organized social life that is voluntary, self-generating, (largely) self-supporting, autonomous from the state, and bound by a legal order or set of shared rules.* . . . Civil society is an intermediary entity, standing between the private sphere and the state. Thus it excludes individual and family life, inward-looking group activity (e.g., for recreation, entertainment, or spirituality), the profit-making enterprise of individual business firms, and political efforts to take control of the state. (emphasis in original)

An active and pluralistic civil society is essential to the functioning of a healthy liberal democracy, and the question of civil society has thus received considerable attention from students of the transition to democracy.[24] Tocqueville recognized this quality of American democracy, and the most influential shapers of twentieth-century pluralist democratic theory, from Bentley to Truman and Dahl, have worked from the premise that democracy is built on the foundation of widespread political participation through diverse, autonomous organizations that represent the diverse interests and demands of the society.

Perhaps the most systematic and influential recent analysis of civil society is by Sidney Tarrow (1994), who analyzed the phenomenon of national social movements in the West. He argued that such movements have only emerged since the eighteenth century as a result of enhanced communications and the consequently increased capacity to assemble large numbers of people for sustained collective action. Such movements will take shape in response to political opportunities that permit large-scale political mobilization. Social movements' modes of action may initially be "outside the system," but will tend, like strikes, to be absorbed into normal politics. Tarrow raised the question of whether the social movements involved in contemporary democratization processes will similarly be absorbed into politics as usual. His conclusion, in brief, was, "not necessarily."

Within Latin America, corporatism has been an important alternative to pluralism as an approach to civil society. Recall that whereas pluralism posits autonomous organization of civil society, corporatism treats the state as convening, recognizing, and even organizing the entities or corporations that represent society's distinct interests. Whereas pluralism relies on the free interplay of conflicting interests to serve the public good, corporatism vests the protection of the public good in the state. To the extent that the authoritarian regimes of the 1970s and early 1980s sought to do anything other than repress civil society, they largely sought to impose a corporatist structure on it. For example, Paul Drake (1996) analyzed how labor movements in the Southern Cone (Argentina, Chile, and Uruguay) survived authoritarian attempts to either destroy or control them, reemerging with substantial strength in the struggle for a transition to democracy. Taking a longer perspective, Ruth Collier and David Collier (1991) showed how distinct modes of incorporating the working class into politics in major Latin American countries shaped the political arena and hence the prospects of stable democracy. They distinguish four major patterns of incorporation, each of which produced a heritage with major problems. In Brazil and Chile, workers were incorporated using depoliticization and control, and the result has been a polarizing multiparty politics. In Mexico and Venezuela, incorporation took place through radical populism, with the result of integrative party systems that absorbed the workers and limited social conflict. In Uruguay and Colombia, a traditional party mobilized the workers, resulting in a combination of electoral stability and social conflict. Peru and Argentina incorporated the workers through labor populism and produced political stalemate.[25]

Civil society was particularly important during the authoritarian regimes of the 1970s and early 1980s, when political parties opposed to the government were restricted or outlawed.[26] It was during this period in many countries that groups emerged in neighborhoods to organize sectors of the populace in pursuit of common goals such as setting up community kitchens, providing child care, or pressing the authorities for local improvements. These neighborhood associations were often tolerated because they were not overtly political, but they nevertheless provided crucial experience and opportunities for communication.

Perhaps the most spectacular type of civil society organization were those that emerged for aid to victims of human rights violations.[27] Although not avowedly political, these groups were frequently subject to repression because they necessarily attacked and questioned the authorities responsible for the torture, disappearance, and possible death of their loved ones. Certainly the most well-known of the latter type were the Madres de Plaza de Mayo in Argentina, a group of women whose children had disappeared under the dictatorship. Beginning in the late 1970s, these women met weekly in the Plaza de Mayo facing the presidential palace (la Casa Rosada) to march silently with placards demanding that the government tell them where their loved ones were. At a time when murder, torture, and disappearances were still going on, their courage helped to inspire other Argentines to dare to oppose the regime and thereby shaped the climate that led to the transition of 1982–1983. Similar stories can be told of civil society opposition of authoritarian regimes elsewhere.

In addition to these social movements specifically oriented to resisting authoritarian repression, the importance of civil society, in the more traditional sense defined by Diamond previously, was also enhanced during the dictatorships. Organized labor was one of the most important sectors. In the previously cited study by Drake (1996), the labor movements in Argentina, Chile, and Uruguay were certainly adversely affected by authoritarian rule, but they were not wiped out. On the contrary, however weakened and chastened, they nevertheless proved able to mobilize workers against the regimes, thereby providing important nuclei for resistance by other sectors of the population.

Religious organizations also continued to operate under authoritarianism. The progressive wing of the Roman Catholic Church reached the height of its power during the 1970s, in the wake of the Bishops' Conference in Medellín in 1968. That conference, following on the Second Ecumenical Conference in Rome in the early 1960s, committed the Latin American church to the struggle for social justice, the "preferential option for the poor" (Berryman, 1987). From this orientation sprang liberation theology, an interpretation of the Bible as emphatically placing Christ and God the Father on the side of the poor and oppressed. A parallel development at the grass roots was the basic church communities *(comunidades eclesiales de base)*, relatively small groupings of the faithful within parishes devoted to reading the scriptures and interpreting them in terms of everyday social injustices and struggles. Similar tendencies were evident in the mainline Protestant denominations such as the Methodists and within traditionally peace-oriented churches such as the Mennonites.

Religious organizations also provided support for authoritarian rule. Many of the more conservative, fundamentalist Protestants tended toward a strong anticommunism that made them sympathetic to the declared agendas of the authoritarian regimes. Simultaneously, more traditionalist forces within the Catholic Church resisted the implications of liberation theology and struggled, with support from Rome, to reassert control over the hierarchy and the parishes. Traditionalist and conservative bishops and clergy tended to be less politically active and more willing to accept and work with incumbent authoritarian regimes.[28]

Social and economic elites, the business and professional sectors, were of course also organized under the dictatorships, typically not for resistance but rather for collaboration and lobbying. Still, transitions from authoritarian rule were never successful without support and leadership from some elite sectors, whose defection from the regime often marked the beginning of the end. In Brazil, for example, as President João Batista Figueiredo fought to keep control of the election of his successor by blocking the campaign for direct presidential elections, an important faction of the ruling party with strong business connections defected to the opposition Party of the Brazilian Democratic Movement (PMDB). The defectors were rewarded with the PMDB vice-presidential nomination for José Sarney (who then became the first civilian president after the death of president-elect Tancredo Neves). In Chile, the Concertación that campaigned against

Pinochet in 1988 and 1989 drew on significant business support, although perhaps the majority of the business community continued to support the Pinochet regime. In Nicaragua, the ouster of Somoza in 1979 was substantially aided in the final weeks by the emergence of an independent elite coalition ("the Eight"), who demanded Somoza's resignation while maintaining their independence from the Sandinistas.[29]

If civil society was generally a force for democratization of authoritarian regimes, after the transition to liberal democracy the political role of elements of civil society became more complex and problematic.[30] Most sectors of civil society did survive the dictatorships: labor, for example, was largely able to resume legal activity in support of worker demands, including protection of the right to strike. But labor often lacked the power and leverage to achieve its objectives in the context of the global resurgence of neoliberal free trade policy. In general, labor and peasant organizations were able to protest prejudicial economic policies and might occasionally contribute to the defeat of governments but could not normally bring about a basic change in neoliberal economic policies.[31]

However, business and professional organizations were well situated to thrive under the new democratic regimes since those regimes were urgently in need of economic growth, for which they needed collaboration from those with capital to invest. Even more urgently, the new democratic governments needed external credit, and to get it they had little choice but to pursue neoliberal policies likely to be popular with the more globally oriented business sectors.

The politics of religion has generally become less polarized under the new democratic regimes, but liberation theology is by no means finished, and there are still struggles within the church to define its orientation. Again, much the same may be said of the mainline Protestants. The more conservative Protestants are gaining steadily in the number of their adherents but are perhaps a bit less aggressive in their anticommunism since the self-destruction of the Soviet Union. In general, churches and religious people have been less politically prominent since the restoration of democracy, a conclusion that is scarcely surprising given the much wider range of avenues for political expression that are now available.

The indigenous sector of civil society was not prominent under the dictatorships but has become much more active under democracy. Indigenous people naturally have more power in countries where they constitute a large part of the population. For example, in Ecuador, the diverse indigenous groups have formed a very powerful joint organization that has staged several popular protests and strikes and has won important concessions from a succession of democratically elected governments. In Bolivia and Guatemala, indigenous peoples long submerged politically have begun to emerge and to assert themselves in national politics. In Peru and Brazil, as well, indigenous peoples are asserting themselves more strongly and show-ing surprising capacity for operating in the modern global communications system.[32]

Not surprisingly, civil society tends to be more active and inclusive in societies like Argentina, Uruguay, and Costa Rica, which have more literate populations. It is striking, however, that even in poorer societies with less education, such as Bolivia and Ecuador, civil society has shown significant development in the 1980s. As Tarrow pointed out, with modern communi-cations, it is possible even for the poor and humble to organize to defend their interests.

Civil society under democratic rule faces several dilemmas. In many cases, such as Chile and Uruguay, the reemergence of parties has tended to push civil society organizations away from the center of action and to deprive them of some of their ablest activists. Moreover, the mission of such organizations as the Madres de Plaza de Mayo has become more ambiguous as they make demands on popularly elected governments rather than on the authoritarian perpetrators of abuses. A further problem has been that civil society organizations are often susceptible to co-optation by par-ties or the state: either the rank and file demand that the organization deliv-er material benefits (e.g., neighborhood improvements, jobs) from the state, or the leaders seek to use their capability for popular mobilization as a tick-et to personal political advancement. Either way, such organizations can easily move from being part of the solution to part of the problem, from being a force for authentic democracy to being one more component of the clientelist political machinery. Finally, because of its very diversity, civil society cannot in the best of cases be a substitute for a viable, institutional-ized party system. Parties are the mechanism by which a national electoral mandate is generated and carried out, however well or badly. The organiza-tion of civil society is essential to empower people to deal with their own problems and defend their own interests, but without a strong party system civil society cannot approximate a common national purpose.

CONCLUSION

This chapter has treated key aspects of the economic and social environ-ments of politics as those aspects affect the viability of democracy. The interplay of structure and action may be observed throughout the chapter. The economic crisis that was the common lot of the entire region during the 1980s and early 1990s is a classic example of the interplay of external and internal structural factors that severely constrain the options available to Latin American policymakers. Shifting international economic conditions combined with structural weaknesses in Latin American economies to pro-duce insupportable international debt and fiscal crises. Governments then were vulnerable to pressures from abroad and from sectors of their own business communities to adopt neoliberal policy reforms. Those reforms had, as we saw, distinctly mixed results, but in general were prejudicial to the poor majority of Latin America's population.

We also noted that the responses of Latin American governments to the crisis were by no means uniform. This diversity was partly a result of distinct structural conditions in each country but also partly a sign that, despite all of the structural pressures, considerable scope for autonomous action remained to national leaders. Still, at the present writing, the most heterodox of policy responses to the crisis had failed and been discarded. Faced with a universal crisis and a relatively consistent set of policy prescriptions from the world's economic power centers, Latin American leaders might try to act autonomously but in the end were able only to evade compliance temporarily.

Crisis-ridden economic performance certainly constituted a burden on emerging democratic regimes. Worsening income distribution, rising unemployment rates, and declining real incomes all put great stress on governments elected by the very people who were suffering these ill effects. Yet, democratic governments could do little to ameliorate the plight of their constituents. In this grim context, two findings are most surprising. First, democratic governments' economic performance was neither stronger nor weaker than that of their authoritarian counterparts. Second, the stability of democratic governments was not undermined by having to cope with economic crisis and administer neoliberal prescriptions. Nevertheless, we may well be skeptical of the long-term health of democratic regimes that cannot improve the material existence of their people.

How these societies coped with economic crisis and external pressure was shaped substantially by their social structure in general and specifically by how well developed and organized was their civil society. It is through the organizations of civil society that individuals who are not members of elites have their principal opportunity to act in the political process, articulate their interests and demands, and affect policy. As with other political action, that of civil society must be understood in its particular structural context. At the most general level, a relatively nonindustrialized economic structure meant that nowhere would industrial workers have the political weight that they developed in most of western Europe. That, according to Rueschemeyer and his collaborators, largely explains the weakness of democracy in Latin America and its strength in Europe.

One may also see structure at play in variations of patterns of civil society in Latin American countries. The structure of the agricultural economy, for example, will have a decisive effect on patterns of organization among peasants and agricultural workers. The highly industrial relations of production on banana plantations, for example, have promoted militant labor organization among banana workers in several countries, including

Costa Rica and Honduras, while smallholders and sharecroppers tend to be more resistant to organization.

It must still be emphasized that although civil society may be shaped by structures, it is a means of action. The organizations and movements of civil society permit their members to resist and at times to change the structures that bind them. Civil society alone cannot create democracy, but democracy cannot exist without civil society.

NOTES

1. For an overview of the argument and the results in Latin America, see Williamson (1990); Frieden (1991); Borner, Brunetti, and Weder (1995). For critical analyses of prior patterns of economic policy, see de Soto (1989); Dornbusch and Edwards (1991). For a critique of the neoliberal model, see NACLA (1996a).

2. For a comprehensive comparative analysis of the issue of state promotion of development, see Evans (1995). For analyses of the responses of Latin American governments, see Smith, Acuña, and Gamarra (1994a); and Haggard and Kaufman (1995).

3. When finally tried in 1996, he was found guilty on lesser charges, exonerated of the most important, and served only a few more months of house arrest. Subsequently, he has embarked on an attempt to resurrect his political career.

4. On Venezuela since Pérez, see Hellinger (1996); and Romero (1996).

5. For provocative interpretations, see O'Donnell (1994); Mayorga (1994b); McClintock (1994); Borón et al. (1995).

6. On Menem, see Halperín Donghi (1994). On Fujimori, see Stokes (1997).

7. See Haggard and Kaufman (1995); Petras, Leiva, and Veltmeyer (1994); Collins and Lear (1995); Angell and Graham (1995); Kurtz (1995); Boylan (1996).

8. Borner, Brunetti, and Weder (1995) suggested another explanation for Chile's success: the stability of Chilean policies, including the rules about property rights.

9. See Halebsky and Kirk (1992); NACLA (1995b).

10. See Jonas (1991); Handy (1984).

11. See Gillespie (1992).

12. Those that made the transition in a context of economic crisis were Argentina, Bolivia, Brazil, Peru, Uruguay, and the Philippines. Those making the transition without an economic crisis were Chile, Korea, Thailand, and Turkey.

13. See Evans (1979, 1995); Evans, Rueschemeyer, and Skocpol (1987).

14. See Halebsky and Harris (1995); Jonas and McCaughan (1994); Morales and McMahon (1993); Smith, Acuña, and Gamarra (1994b); NACLA (1996c).

15. See, in particular, Petras, Leiva, and Veltmeyer (1994) and Collins and Lear (1995) on Chile; Pizarro and Bejarano (1994) on Colombia; McCoy et al. (1995) and Goodman, et al. (1995), on Venezuela; Espinal (1995) on the Dominican Republic; Malloy (1991) and NACLA (1991) on Bolivia; Sánchez Parga (1993) and Ardaya and Verdesoto (1996) on Ecuador; Acuña (1994) and García Delgado (1994) on Argentina; NACLA (1995a) and Schneider (1996), on Brazil. For a comparison of Argentina and Uruguay, see Blake (1994). For a comparison of Chile and Venezuela, see Angell and Graham (1995). See Conaghan and Malloy (1994) for a comparative study of democracy and neoliberalism in the Central Andes. For a study of Central America, see Stein and Arias Peñate (1992).

16. It is important to remember that neither income distribution data nor

unemployment data for Latin America are particularly reliable. Both are subject to unreliability of reports from individuals and to self-serving manipulation by governments. Moreover, unemployment figures do not account for underemployment (e.g., part-time work, work in the informal sector, work for which one is overqualified, or withdrawal from the labor market because of discouragement). Thus the real state of incomes and employment can only be imperfectly known. But poor data used with caution are better than no data.

17. See Haggard and Kaufman (1995); Calderón and Dos Santos (1995).

18. See Przeworski et al. (1996).

19. See Coraggio and Deere (1987); NACLA (1991); Conaghan and Malloy (1994); Calderón and dos Santos (1995); Collins and Lear (1995).

20. For example, see World Bank (1991), chap. 7; Behrman (1996). Cf. NACLA (1996c).

21. See, for example, Lipset (1959); Lipset, Kyoung-Ryung, and Torres (1993); Abootalebi (1995); Vanhanen (1994).

22. For overviews, see Haggard and Kaufman (1995); Whitehead (1994); Naím (1995); Calderón and dos Santos (1995); Waisman (1992). For critical perspectives on the impact of neoliberal reform, see Chauvin (1995); Halebsky and Harris (1995); Jonas and McCaughan (1994). Relevant case studies are contained in Smith, Acuña, and Gamarra (1994a); Espinal (1995); Blake (1994); Angell and Graham (1995).

23. "Bourgeoisie" and "middle class" are generally used synonymously in this literature.

24. See Tarrow (1994); Levine (1993); Friedheim (1993); Diamond (1994); Keane (1988); Held (1993); Lechner (1991); Vilas (1993); Oxhorn (1995); Cohen and Arato (1992); Hall (1995). Cf. Introduction.

25. Collier and Collier (1991) used a theoretical approach, "critical junctures," quite consistent with that of this book. They postulate that cleavage or crisis in a society may produce a critical juncture wherein fundamental political changes occur. It is the cleavage or crisis that makes change possible by loosening the bonds of preexisting structures. Cf. Almond, Flanagan, and Mundt (1973).

26. The strong role of civil society organizations in resisting authoritarian rule constitutes an implicit critique of the argument (see Chapter 1) that Latin American political culture is incompatible with democracy. For an explicit analysis of this question in light of public opinion data, see Booth and Richard (1996). A good collection is Albala-Bertrand (1992).

27. On civil society and dictatorship, see Eckstein (1989); Corradi, Fagen, and Garretón (1992); Hipsher (1996); Guzmán Bouvard (1994); McManus and Schlabach (1991); Jaquette (1994); Escobar and Alvarez (1992); CIERA (1984); Silva (1996); Drake (1996).

28. On religion and politics in Latin America, see Cleary and Stewart-Gambino (1992); Mainwaring and Wilde (1989); Pottenger (1989); Berryman (1987).

29. On the political role of socioeconomic elites, see Evans (1979); Gil Yepes (1981); NACLA (1996a); Borner, Brunetti, and Weder (1996); de Soto (1989); Grinspun and Cameron (1993); Naim and Francés (1995); Vilas (1995b); Winson (1989) on Costa Rica; Acosta Silva (1996) on Ecuador; Kornblith (1995) on Venezuela; Castillo Ochoa (1996) on Peru; Hagopian (1996) on Brazil.

30. On civil society and democracy, see Levine (1993); Calderón and dos Santos (1995); García Delgado (1994); Albala-Bertrand (1992); Keck (1995); Markoff (1996); NACLA (1996b). For a relevant analysis of civil society in post-communist transitions, see Bernhard (1996).

31. For examples of labor and peasant action, see Avritzer (1995) on Brazil; Aguilar and Ramírez (1989) and Vunderink (1991) on Costa Rica; Espinal (1995) on the Dominican Republic. A comparative historical perspective is provided by Cooper et al. (1993).

32. On indigenous organizations and movements, see NACLA (1996b).

6

The Institutionalization
of Democracy

The task of maintaining liberal democracy implies its institutionalization, that is, the stabilization over some years of critical patterns and channels of political action. In a liberal democracy, political parties are the principal mechanism by which the people are provided with alternative policies and governments, among which they may choose in elections. In a liberal democracy, the people's vote vests authority (the right to rule) in the electoral winners. Liberal democracy is institutionalized to the extent that parties, party systems, elections, and the organization of public authority function in a regular, predictable manner.

The liberal democratic model assumes that the people will, to a large extent, take care of their own local needs without state intervention and will organize themselves to defend their interests before the state authorities. These are the functions of civil society, which operates between the state and the family. An institutionalized liberal democracy, then, will include a vigorous civil society.

The next section will consider at length the issue of how parties and party systems are most central to the institutionalization of liberal democracy.[1] Then, related issues of institutional form will be considered.[2]

PARTIES AND PARTY SYSTEMS

Political parties and party systems were unquestionably central to Latin America's previous democracies of long standing (see Chapter 2) and in their various forms continue to be central to an understanding of democratic politics in contemporary Latin America. Parties and competition among them are essential to the practice of liberal democracy because they process and structure the options to be made available to the electorate, thereby converting millions of votes into a collective decision about who will govern. Scott Mainwaring and Timothy Scully (1995) used several criteria for classifying party systems as either institutionalized or inchoate. The first is regularity of party competition as measured by Mogens N. Pedersen's index of electoral volatility, which measures the net change in the seat or vote shares of all parties from one election to the next (Mainwaring and

Scully, 1995, pp. 6–9). A second criterion is the development by parties of stable roots in society, as indicated by similarity of voting patterns between concurrent legislative and presidential elections, survey and electoral data, party penetration of major social organizations, and party longevity (Mainwaring and Scully, 1995, pp. 9–15). The third criterion is that "citizens and organized interests must perceive that parties and elections are the means of determining who governs, and that the electoral process and parties are accorded legitimacy" (Mainwaring and Scully, 1995, p. 14). This would be best measured by cross-national survey data; lacking that, the authors made informed estimates based on the case studies. The final criterion is that party organizations must be relatively solid. Again, hard data are not systematically available, and the authors resorted to estimates (Mainwaring and Scully, 1995, pp. 15–16). Their measurements and estimates are summarized in Table 6.1.

Two points must be noted about this scheme. First, only the first criterion is based on reliable, quantifiable, and comparable data. The others, to varying degrees, depend on informed estimates. We would thus be ill-advised to impute undue rigor to the classification. Second, the scores represent an average characterization of each party system for the period of the 1980s and 1990s. The scheme thus takes little or no account of the longer history of the party systems. At the same time, it also does not attempt to measure changes in party systems in the course of the last decade and a half. These matching long-term and short-term blind spots mean that the

Table 6.1   Party System Institutionalization in Latin America

Country	Criterion 1	Criterion 2	Criterion 3	Criterion 4	Aggregate
Costa Rica	2.5	3.0	3.0	3.0	11.5
Chile	2.5	3.0	3.0	3.0	11.5
Uruguay	3.0	3.0	3.0	2.5	11.5
Venezuela	2.5	2.5	2.5	3.0	10.5
Colombia	3.0	3.0	2.5	2.0	10.5
Argentina	2.0	2.5	2.5	2.0	9.0
Mexico	1.5	2.5	1.5	3.0	8.5
Paraguay	1.0	2.5	1.0	3.0	7.5
Bolivia	1.0	1.0	2.0	1.0	5.0
Ecuador	1.0	1.0	2.0	1.0	5.0
Brazil	1.0	1.0	2.0	1.0	5.0
Peru	1.0	1.0	1.0	1.5	4.5

Source: Mainwaring and Scully (1995), p. 17. Reprinted from *Building Democratic Institutions: Party Systems in Latin America,* edited by Scott Mainwaring and Timothy R. Scully, with the permission of the publishers, Stanford University Press. © 1995 by the Board of Trustees of the Leland Stanford Junior University.

Note: Criteria are scored as 3.0 = high, 1.0 = low. Criterion 1 is regularity of party competition. Criterion 2 is development of stable roots in society. Criterion 3 is legitimacy of parties and elections. Criterion 4 is solidity of party organizations.

classification, already of debatable rigor in general, may come to quite questionable conclusions about individual cases. As we shall see, for example, long-term patterns in Argentina, combined with recent developments under President Menem, indicate that the Argentine party system is less institutionalized than Mainwaring and Scully suggest. Developments in Venezuela since 1989 may also point to a notable decline in institutionalization. Conversely, Bolivia may be experiencing a significant increase in party system institutionalization. All these caveats notwithstanding, the Mainwaring-Scully classification is an excellent place to start. They classify Venezuela, Costa Rica, Chile, Uruguay, Colombia, and Argentina as institutionalized party systems; Mexico and Paraguay as hegemonic systems in transition (cases I treat in Chapter 4, along with Cuba); and Peru, Brazil, Bolivia, and Ecuador as inchoate party systems. I concur with the classifications except for Argentina and with the proviso that we need to be alert to party system changes. Parties and the party system continue to be strongly institutionalized in Chile, Colombia, Costa Rica, Uruguay, and Venezuela. Most other countries, including most of those not considered by Mainwaring and Scully, display prominent features of inchoate systems.

In Chile, the formerly tripolar party system (right/center/left) has reemerged in the 1980s in the form of a center-left bloc and a right bloc, marginalizing the extreme Left.[3] The successful Concertación that fought the plebiscite of 1988 went on to win the presidency in 1989 (with 55 percent) and 1993 (with 58 percent) and to capture and hold the majority in the Chamber of Deputies after 1989. Surviving authoritarian provisions of the constitution of 1980 (e.g., the provision for eight appointed senators) have prevented the Concertación from achieving all its desired constitutional amendments and policy initiatives, but the transition in Chile must still be judged relatively successful, and that success must be attributed in large part to the old parties (i.e., the Christian Democrats [DC] and the Socialist Party [PS]), a new party (Party for Democracy [PPD], a socialist splinter), and the new party system. Since 1988, these three parties, with several smaller associates, have maintained the only coalition capable of capturing an absolute majority of the vote. Substantively, this coalition is committed to establishing a liberal democracy within the framework of the authoritarian constitution of 1980 and to moving gradually within that constitution to make such changes as may be possible for further democratization. They have been opposed by a right-wing coalition basically committed to maintaining the 1980 constitution with as few changes as possible and by a left-wing coalition that refuses to accept the legitimacy of the constitution as an institutional framework within which to work. These constitutional issues will be more fully discussed in what follows.

The key point here is that a reorganized party system has been critical to the reestablishment of stable democracy in Chile. However, the new party system also poses long-term challenges to democratic stability. Both

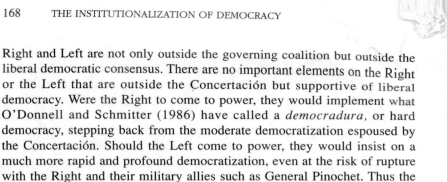

Right and Left are not only outside the governing coalition but outside the liberal democratic consensus. There are no important elements on the Right or the Left that are outside the Concertación but supportive of liberal democracy. Were the Right to come to power, they would implement what O'Donnell and Schmitter (1986) have called a *democradura,* or hard democracy, stepping back from the moderate democratization espoused by the Concertación. Should the Left come to power, they would insist on a much more rapid and profound democratization, even at the risk of rupture with the Right and their military allies such as General Pinochet. Thus the new Chilean party system permits a stable democracy within the gradually receding limits of the 1980 constitution but only by maintaining the Concertación intact and in power. Alternation in power, a normal feature of liberal democracy, cannot happen in Chile without risking the regime itself.

It appears that Chile faces three possible scenarios in the next decade. First, the political dominance of the Concertación could continue, with the Right and Left continuing to be marginalized. In this model, the Right would probably suffer a gradual loss of strength, particularly after the demise of Pinochet. The Left, already much weakened by the defection of the socialists and by the discriminatory effects of the electoral system, would also continue to be marginalized. Chile would evolve toward a dominant party system in which many parties could run for office, but the Concertación would always win national elections.

A second scenario would see part of the Right (most likely National Renewal [RN]) accepting the legitimacy of the Concertación's approach to liberal democracy and becoming a possible coalition partner for the DC. The party system then would offer two alternative governing coalitions, the center-left Concertación and a center-right DC-RN coalition.

A third scenario would have most of the Left (including the communists) agreeing to work within the Concertación's model of liberal democracy and becoming thereby an alternative coalition partner for the socialists. Here again, two alternative coalitions would be possible, Concertación and center-left (socialist-communist). If both the second and third scenarios happened, then virtually the entire political spectrum would be committed to a liberal democratic institutional framework, as has happened in Uruguay. If neither occurred, and if the Concertación could not maintain its electoral dominance, Chile would risk developing a party system in which the only possible governing coalitions were formed by parties disloyal to the democratic regime itself.

In Uruguay, the parties and party system have shown even more continuity with patterns from before the dictatorship.[4] Silvia Dutrénit Bielous (1994) actually used the metaphor of an archipelago (the parties) reemerging after a tidal wave (the dictatorship). However, changes already underway before 1973 have continued, so that by the 1990s it was clear that the long-standing dominance of the two traditional parties (Colorados and

Blancos) was at an end. The leftist Broad Front (FA) already had surpassed 20 percent of the vote in 1971 and reemerged at about that level during the transition in 1985. Subsequently the FA split, and the center-left New Space (NE) emerged. In the 1994 general elections, national results showed a virtual tie among the Colorados (31 percent), the Blancos (29.9 percent), and the FA (29.3 percent), and NE received 4.9 percent (Caetano, 1995, p. 8). Moreover, FA candidate Tabaré Vázquez won the mayoralty of Montevideo with more than 42 percent. Clearly, the Uruguayan Left has made a major step forward and would be well placed to capture the presidency in 1999 under present rules, if they avert major splits.[5] In any case it is clear that the Uruguayan party system now is tripolar; the exclusive dominance of the traditional parties is a thing of the past.

The Uruguayan party system is distinguished from that of Chile in several ways. The Left in Uruguay has become much stronger than its Chilean counterpart, whereas the Uruguayan Right has become weaker.[6] In addition to the rise of the FA and NE, this shift has occurred within the traditional parties, particularly the Colorados, in which the center-left Sanguinetti wing has supplanted the far-right Pacheco wing. Within the National, or Blanco, Party, the center-left Wilson wing lost dominance after the death of its leader and has been supplanted by the more traditionally center-right Lacalle faction. Both traditional parties are now dominated by centrist factions, with minority rightist factions. There are now three parties capable of electing a president in Uruguay, but it is not an ideologically defined tripolar system like that in pre-1973 Chile. Rather, we have a Left that is committed to operating within the institutions of Uruguayan liberal democracy,[7] competing against two centrist traditional parties, each with its semiloyal right wing.[8] This in turn means that electoral alternation is possible without threatening the democratic regime itself, unless the right wing of either major party regained dominance. In such an eventuality, the situation would be similar to that in Chile at the present time, where democratic stability depends on the Concertación remaining united and in control of the government. Though the structure of the two party systems is thus markedly different, both confront a Right that is at best semiloyal to democracy but unable at present to win a national majority. With the advent of a powerful Left in the new Uruguayan party system, it is unlikely that any president could escape the need to negotiate a majority coalition in Congress, but the fragmentation of the major parties under the Ley de Lemas always made such negotiation necessary anyway. If a runoff election were adopted for the presidency, it would not obviate the need for a negotiated congressional majority.[9]

Colombia, Costa Rica, and Venezuela have not had to make transitions to democracy in the last decade, but economic and political problems have subjected them to many of the same strains as those confronting the reestablished democracies of Chile and Uruguay.[10] Each of these countries entered the 1980s with a stable democratic regime based on two-party, or bipolar, party systems and strongly institutionalized parties. Each has faced serious economic dislocations that have challenged the dominant parties. Costa Rica was on the front lines of the Central American political crisis of the 1980s and was subjected to strong external political pressures as a result. Colombia had to deal with chronic guerrilla insurgencies and the burgeoning international drug trade that established important centers in Colombia. Venezuela was also affected by the drug trade, but its crisis was principally economic. Only Costa Rica can still be considered politically stable (and it is not without severe challenges), whereas Colombia's and Venezuela's futures as liberal democracies are more in doubt.

The crisis in Venezuela is discussed in passing in Chapter 5. From 1973 to the late 1980s, Venezuela must be considered one of the most fully developed democratic party systems outside the advanced industrial democracies. The two major parties, Democratic Action (AD) and the social Christian COPEI, received around 85 to 90 percent of the vote in presidential elections and around 75 percent in congressional elections, alternated in the presidency,[11] and predominated in local and state electoral office. The two parties also extensively penetrated and controlled organizations of civil society, turning them to the purpose of supporting the national power of the party and maintaining control through extensive patronage that was ultimately financed by the country's oil wealth and channeled through the state. The center-left Movement Toward Socialism (MAS), led by former guerrillas, became increasingly integrated into the party system, though it never rivaled the two major parties in electoral strength.

It may be argued (see Peeler, 1995a) that this party system was so efficient in mobilizing votes and concentrating them to produce democratically elected governments that worked, that it provoked the very backlash that undermined it. The system became so centralized, so resistant to initiatives from the base or to the rise of alternative political leadership—in a word, *institutionalized*—that it came to be called a "partidocracia," or "partyarchy."[12] In response to widespread demands for reforms that would revitalize democracy by weakening partyarchy, various changes were made during the 1980s to decentralize the state and weaken the grip of the party organizations (see the next section). A new political movement, the center-left, labor-based Causa R, was able to use these new institutional openings to achieve substantial electoral success (see López Maya, 1994).

Although the 1988 presidential and parliamentary elections continued the pattern of AD-COPEI dominance, change was already well advanced below the surface. The winning presidential candidate, former President Carlos Andrés Pérez of AD, was not the choice of the party organization; he won the internal party election on the basis of his personal popularity, having presided over the oil boom of the mid-1970s. At the same time, COPEI turned its back on its founder, former president Rafael Caldera. When

Pérez, acting independently of his party organization, implemented a sweeping neoliberal adjustment plan shortly after his inauguration, the shock waves shredded the party system. Massive urban riots in Caracas and elsewhere led to many deaths and much destruction. Condemnation of the president was almost universal, coming even from AD members of Congress. Demands for Pérez's resignation became a steady drumbeat as he continued to use his presidential powers to impose his reform program. Two military rebellions in 1992 further shook the confidence of Venezuelans in their democracy, but public opinion polls continued to show a preference for democracy even as people expressed rejection of the Pérez government (Myers, 1995). Caldera took the leadership of the opposition to Pérez with an eloquent speech in the Senate after the first military rebellion, in which he flatly condemned government policy and rejected COPEI's qualified support for Pérez in the name of preserving democratic stability.

After Pérez was finally impeached and forced from office in mid-1993, the elections of December 1993 brought Caldera back to the presidency, but this time at the head of a loose ad hoc coalition in opposition to both AD and COPEI. Caldera's winning share of the vote was only 30 percent, whereas candidates for AD, COPEI, and Causa R were virtually tied at between 22 and 23 percent. Moreover, abstention hit a record high of 40 percent, a precipitous decline from 18 percent in 1988 and 13 percent in 1983. AD and COPEI together received only 45 percent of the vote, less than half their 1988 total. The party system is in crisis, and since it has been the keystone of the democratic regime, it follows that the regime is in crisis too.

The general failure of the Caldera government to address the country's economic problems has prolonged the political crisis. Public disillusionment with elections continues; turnout in state and local elections has been very low. This has permitted AD and COPEI, with their superior organizations, to make a partial comeback in governorships and local governments, but popular support for the regime is now weak. A stable new party system in Venezuela will necessarily wait upon re-equilibration of the regime. As Juan Linz (1978) suggested, that may involve an actual change of regime within the democratic genus.

The ancient two-party system of Colombia (Bushnell, 1993) has been under severe strain more or less continuously since the late 1930s, though reports of its demise, to paraphrase Mark Twain, were frequently exaggerated (Peeler, 1976, 1985, 1992, 1995a). Initial strains came from competition between liberals and conservatives to mobilize and incorporate a mass electorate, beginning in the late 1930s. This conflict led, in the late 1940s, to escalating political violence and to dictatorship in the 1950s. The party elites dealt with the problem of competitive mobilization through the adoption in 1958 of the National Front, an arrangement for equal power sharing between the two traditional parties that excluded all other parties (Berry et al., 1980; Dix, 1987; Hartlyn, 1988). However, what had been a pattern of political violence by liberal and conservative partisans against each other was transmuted in the 1960s into guerrilla violence carried out by several marxist or generically leftist forces. The National Front governments were unable to solve the problem of political violence. Every president from 1982 on has made a serious attempt to negotiate an end to the insurgencies, and some groups (most notably the M-19) have laid down their arms and have been incorporated into the legal political process. However, M-19 and other former guerrillas have been subjected to assassination of their leaders and militants by right-wing death squads that function with impunity. Other guerrilla groups have refused to give up the armed struggle, and the Colombian armed forces have been unable to defeat them.[13]

Another challenge to the Colombian system evolved with the rise of the international drug trade (especially in cocaine but also including marijuana and, increasingly, heroin) during the 1980s, for which Colombia became a major center. For present purposes the drug trade posed two problems and a dilemma. The first problem was that the drug trade rendered the preexisting problem of violence all the more severe and complex. This was especially true because of the second problem: corruption. The drug cartels sought systematically to penetrate and corrupt every center of power in Colombian society, including business, the police, the armed forces, the political elite, and the guerrillas; they had substantial success in all arenas. Among major institutions, only the church proved largely immune. By the mid-1990s, the political system was convulsed by credible accusations that President Ernesto Samper himself had knowingly accepted political contributions from the Cali cartel.[14]

The dilemma posed by the drug trade was that it evidently provided a subsidy of unknown magnitude for the Colombian economy. It was not by chance that Colombia avoided the worst dislocations of the economic crisis of the 1980s and was under less pressure to conform to neoliberal policy strictures.[15] Thus Colombian policymakers had to know that any success in bringing the drug trade under control would likely have negative macroeconomic consequences. Yet they had no choice but to try to control it, given the threat the drug trade posed to their control of the country and the intense pressure imposed on Colombia by the United States.

The Colombian political elite responded to this array of challenges in a characteristic manner, with moderate political reforms that made it substantially easier for new parties to win elections and that devolved considerable authority to elected local officials. The election of mayors was an innovation of the mid-1980s, for example. President Virgilio Barco's attempt to push significant constitutional changes through Congress failed in late 1989. A popular mobilization in early 1990, led by university students, gathered petitions to place the question of a constituent assembly on the ballot of the 1990 legislative elections. An overwhelmingly positive vote (but with low turnout) led to a second positive vote coinciding with the presidential elections later that year. By decree of newly elected President César Gaviria Trujillo, the special Constituent Assembly was elected in December 1990 (with the astonishingly low turnout of 16 percent) and met for five months in early 1991. The election rules guaranteed representation to insurgent groups such as M-19 that had laid down their arms and to indigenous and black ethnic minorities. In fact, M-19 had over one-fourth of the delegates, second only to the liberals, whereas the fragmented conservatives were well behind. The composition of the Assembly appeared to foreshadow a new party system, but the low turnout must be kept in mind.

The debates of the Constituent Assembly were the object of close national attention and organized pressure, and public political discourse was dominated by constitutional issues for over a year. The prominence of the unexpectedly large M-19 delegation was especially notable as representing a potential break with the power monopoly of the traditional parties. There was widespread expectation that adoption of a new constitution could mark a major turning point in the development of Colombian democracy.

The new constitution contains several initiatives designed to enhance political democracy, including ballot and electoral reform, approval of referenda and plebiscites as valid channels of law making and constitutional amendment, restriction of presidential emergency powers, prohibition of presidential reelection, congressional power to force the resignation of ministers by a vote of censure in both chambers, and the establishment of a Constitutional Court separate from the Supreme Court. The armed forces retain their autonomy but are restricted from trying civilians in military courts. Social policies oriented to protecting the poorest parts of the population are also enshrined in the constitution.[16]

In spite of the hints of change in the Constituent Assembly and the new constitution, the electoral dominance of the liberals, in particular, was reasserted in the 1994 elections and in subsequent local and congressional elections. However, as the 1998 elections approached, fragmentation of both Liberal and Conservative Parties seemed to augur continued instability in the party system. Paradoxically, the Colombian party system is both unstable and resistant to change, even as the state's capacity to control the territory and population are under severe challenge.

Of the three surviving older democracies, the oldest, Costa Rica, has also weathered the storm of the 1980s and 1990s with the least damage. Since the 1940s, Costa Rica developed a relatively active state with a strong commitment to social democratic programs such as health care, social security, and education and a correspondingly large state sector that included state monopolies in insurance and banking. The advent of the debt crisis put severe pressure on a succession of governments to prune back the bureaucracy and reduce the state's role in the economy, in order to meet IMF criteria for fiscal soundness and openness to international trade. Simultaneously, Central America was subjected to a prolonged political and military crisis occasioned by the Sandinista revolution in Nicaragua, insurgencies in El Salvador and Guatemala, and the U.S. response to these challenges to regional hegemony. Costa Rica came under intense U.S. pressure to allow counterrevolutionary insurgents (contras) to operate from its territory while intervening in Nicaragua. The Monge government (1982–1986) largely succumbed to these pressures, however tacitly and covertly. The succeeding government of Oscar Arias was less amenable and in fact took the lead in forging a Central American peace settlement that went against U.S. policy (Rojas and Solís, 1988). Overall, Costa Rica benefited economically from the Central American crisis because the United States channeled much more aid to the region between 1980 and 1990 than before or since. Most aid went to El Salvador and Honduras, but Costa Rica got its share. That certainly eased the impact of the debt crisis on Costa Rica, though the decade was still characterized by little or no economic growth (see Table 5.5).

Whereas the party systems of Colombia and especially Venezuela were showing significant signs of change or even breakdown in the 1990s, that of Costa Rica has, if anything, become more institutionalized since the beginning of the 1980s. What was previously a bipolar system, with one strong party (National Liberation Party, or PLN) and a shifting series of ad hoc opposition coalitions (cf. Peeler, 1985, table 5, p. 100), has become a stable two-party system (albeit with some continuing parliamentary representation for leftist and regional parties. See Mora, 1994). The two major parties, PLN and the Social Christian Unity Party (PUSC) regularly receive over 95 percent of the presidential vote, over 85 percent of the legislative vote, 55 of 57 legislative seats, and a great majority of local elected positions (Yashar, 1995; Chalker, 1995). PUSC held the presidency and a congressional majority from 1990 to 1994, and a general tendency toward alternation of PLN and PUSC in power appears firmly entrenched. In spite of popular protests, resistance from organized labor, and the emergence of locally based social movements, the regime remains basically quite capable of responding to demands in a manner sufficient to keep political pressures manageable.[17] Abstention rates in national elections continue to be in the range of 15–20 percent, the same level that has been consistently present since compulsory voting was implemented in the late 1950s.

Having now considered the strongly institutionalized party systems of Chile, Uruguay, Colombia, Venezuela, and Costa Rica, we turn to the category that Mainwaring and Scully (1995) called "inchoate" party systems. Included here are virtually all of the other Latin American countries (save Cuba, Mexico, and Paraguay, considered in Chapter 4), and it will become obvious that the category is residual (i.e., noninstitutionalized party systems) and that our understanding will be better served by asking additional questions, such as how close they come to institutionalization, how they are changing, and whether the party systems facilitate or retard democratization.

We begin with the special case of Argentina.[18] Mainwaring and Scully (1995) included Argentina among institutionalized party systems, but I have not. Although the Peronists and the radicals have long been central to the Argentine party system, it has not been a true two-party system but instead a series of unsuccessful attempts to impose a single-party hegemony. James McGuire (1995) made this clear in his contribution to the Mainwaring-Scully volume. In Argentina we have two major parties that are highly institutionalized, but the party system is not. That is, the relationship between the major parties continues to be subject to major changes with each shift in party control of the presidency. It is by no means clear that the party system is stable, or institutionalized, in its present form, even · though the two principal parties are clearly quite well institutionalized.

The radicals successfully displaced the conservative hegemony after 1916 but were themselves displaced from their hegemony by the conservative coup of 1930. Juan Perón established the hegemony of his own movement after 1946 but was displaced by the coup of 1955. Successive military and civilian governments from 1955 to 1973 failed to disperse the popular base of Peronism, and the party won control of the government again in 1973. The Peronists were ousted again in 1976 by the last and most savage of the military regimes. To the surprise of almost everyone, the post-Malvinas elections of 1983 brought a radical victory over the Peronists; for a while, among radicals, there was talk of a new era of radical hegemony, but that ended with the economic meltdown of 1988–1989. Carlos Menem's victory in 1989 reawakened Peronist dreams of hegemony as well, dreams that were fed by Menem's political success in getting the constitution amended to permit reelection and then getting himself reelected by an overwhelming margin in 1995. In short, competition and alternation have been taking place since 1983, for the first time in Argentine history, but leaders and activists have not yet accepted their legitimacy and normality.

A major attempt to break the mold of two-party dominance came in the early 1990s from the National Solidarity Front (FREPASO), which achieved substantial success in the federal capital and Buenos Aires with a centrist, anticorruption program and posed a significant threat in particular to the radicals in the federal capital. However, in early 1996, the gravitational pull of the two major parties tore FREPASO apart, as some of its most important leaders sought to use it as a tool to affect the struggle for control of the Peronist Party. The split seemed likely to permit the radicals successfully to reassert themselves as the principal opposition to the Peronists.

Carlos Menem's politically successful imposition of a sweeping program of neoliberal reforms has put great stress on the Peronist political coalition, with its strong base among the industrial working class and the poor. A principal example of Guillermo O'Donnell's (1994) model of "delegative democracy," Menem came to office in 1989 on the basis of a classic Peronist campaign in favor of social justice for workers and then by 1991 gravitated to a neoliberal policy that would mean a severe increase in unemployment as the principal price for achieving low inflation. It is striking that large numbers of Peronist voters have evidently continued to support Menem through the constitutional referendum of 1994 and the presidential elections of 1995.[19] Now that he is in his second term and unable to succeed himself without another constitutional amendment (desired by some backers, but highly unlikely to command enough support), a major power struggle is taking place within the Peronist Party.

A basic obstacle to the institutionalization of a competitive party system in Argentina is that leaders and activists in both parties (and especially the Peronists) have tended to regard themselves as *movements* rather than *parties,* that is, they have implicitly or explicitly assumed that they speak, potentially, for the whole nation. The very idea of a party is that it represents *part of the nation,* whereas a movement may purport to represent everyone. If one movement represents the whole people, then there is no necessary or legitimate role for other parties. Competition becomes no more than a tactical necessity. It remains to be seen whether the two major Argentine parties have moved definitively away from this perspective (cf. McGuire, 1995).

Brazil is as puzzling a case as Argentina.[20] By far the largest and most populous Latin American country, it has also long been a regional leader in industrial development and stands relatively high on most measures of economic development. Most of Brazil's history has been marked by elected governments, though a true liberal democracy existed only from 1945 to 1964 and 1985 to the present. Whereas Argentina's parties have persisted through many regime changes (even if the party *system* is judged not to be institutionalized), in Brazil both the parties and the party system have been transformed with each regime change. The party system of the empire did not last into the Old Republic. The party system fostered by Getulio Vargas did not survive the coup of 1964. The party system promoted by the military regime transformed itself in the course of the transition and continues to be in flux. In the 1990s, there is only one party, the Workers Party (PT), that has moved considerably beyond personalism, institutionalized its organization, and developed a national capability for mass political mobilization (Keck, 1992). As such, the PT has posed a major challenge to other parties; the national campaigns of 1989 and 1994 both placed PT leader "Lula" da Silva in the presidential runoff against opponents backed by coalitions of centrist and rightist parties. In both cases, Lula lost to the center-right candidate (Collor in 1989, Cardoso in 1994), but the party system remains characterized by high volatility and low institutionalization.

None of the other countries to be considered here have parties as thoroughly institutionalized as Argentina's, and of course none have institutionalized party systems. A key question involves levels of mass political mobilization by parties. In most countries with inchoate party systems, there is nevertheless a significant history of mass political mobilization by at least one party. This would certainly be true of Bolivia, Peru, and perhaps Ecuador, Panama, and the Dominican Republic.[21] In each of the first two cases, at least one party has not only been institutionalized but has developed a true mass base that goes beyond a mere clientelistic search for jobs and favors. In Bolivia, that party is the Nationalist Revolutionary Movement (MNR), principal party of the 1952 revolution and still a principal player in national politics. In Peru, it is the American Popular Revolutionary Alliance (APRA) and, to a much lesser extent, Popular Action (AP). Yet as in Argentina, the presence of institutionalized parties with mass bases has not meant an institutionalized party system. A principal cause has been personal ambition of competing leaders who can gain more (e.g., congressional seats for themselves and their supporters) by splitting off than by remaining with a party they do not control. The MNR failed in its initial project of a Mexican-style single party hegemony and proved highly prone to fragmentation. President Siles Zuazo (1982–1985), for example, was a founding leader of MNR who broke away in the 1960s. The Bolivian party system as it has evolved since 1978 includes, in addition to the MNR and its splinters, the conservative National Democratic Alliance (ADN) founded and led by General Banzer and various leftist or formerly leftist parties such as the Revolutionary Left Movement (MIR) and the Free Bolivia Movement (MBL). There is some sign that Bolivia may be moving toward a more institutionalized party system whose most distinguishing mark is the negotiation of electoral and governing coalitions among competing party leaders, with MNR, MIR, and ADN as the principal players. However, the system continues to generate important new "outsiders" as well, such as beer magnate Max Fernández or radio and television personality Carlos Palenque.

In Peru, an institutionalized party system built around APRA and AP might have emerged after 1980 but was nullified by the successive economic failures of the Fernando Belaúnde (AP) and García (APRA) presidencies. As a consequence, by the 1990 election there was no doubt that "outsiders" would prevail over the established parties. Though it first appeared that well-known novelist Mario Vargas Llosa would win, he was ultimately overtaken by the virtually unknown Alberto Fujimori. Both were antiparty candidates. In light of the current political dominance of Fujimori and the weakness of the old parties, the emergence of a wholly new party system seems likely, perhaps initially turning on support for or opposition to Fujimori.

In several other countries there have been popularly supported parties or movements of some durability, but always highly personalistic rather than institutionalized. Ecuadoran politics long orbited around populist leaders such as José María Velasco Ibarra and later, Abdalá Bucaram; today, in the absence of any such overpowering personalist leader, Ecuadoran parties continue to be highly personalist and prone to fragmentation. Much the same can be said about Panama, where populist caudillo Arnulfo Arias was succeeded by strongmen Omar Torrijos and Manuel Noriega. Dominican politics since the assassination of Trujillo in 1961 have revolved around two caudillos, the conservative Trujillo collaborator Joaquín Balaguer and the nationalist reformer Juan Bosch.[22] In these cases, an institutionalized party system waits upon institutionalized parties.

Most of the other countries classified as having inchoate party systems (El Salvador, Nicaragua, Guatemala, Haiti, Honduras) have little history of popular mobilization by parties. In some of these cases, formerly stable elitist party systems are being rendered inchoate by the emergence for the first time of genuinely popular parties or movements.[23] This is most clearly the case in Nicaragua and Haiti, where the Sandinista Front for National Liberation (FSLN) and the Lavalas movement, respectively, mobilized majorities of the national populations for the first time in their countries' history. Preexisting elitist parties were not equipped to confront such a challenge save by use of force and fraud. In this they were aided by U.S. administrations deeply mistrustful of the popular movements.

The stories of the two countries differ in many ways. In Nicaragua, the Sandinistas took power by force in 1979 and attempted a revolutionary transformation of society. By 1980, the United States was openly supporting their opponents; under Ronald Reagan (1981–1989) the United States was in a state of undeclared war with the Sandinista regime. Nevertheless, the Sandinistas probably expected that their organization and popular support would keep them in power indefinitely, but they lost free elections in 1990, in an environment of economic crisis and externally supported civil war. Subsequently, under president Chamorro, the party system and political system have continued in flux through the 1996 elections (Vargas, 1995). There may be some tendency toward a bipolar party system pitting the Sandinistas against all opponents, but the latter sector has yet to show durable cohesion, even though an overwhelming majority of anti-Sandinista voters in both 1990 and 1996 coalesced around one candidate (Chamorro and Alemán, respectively).[24]

In Haiti, Lavalas leader Jean-Bertrand Aristide led a nonviolent popular movement that was critical in forcing Jean-Claude Duvalier from power in 1986 and that finally brought about Aristide's election to the presidency in 1990. Overthrown nine months later by a military coup, Aristide was finally reinstated by the U.S.-led, U.N.-sponsored intervention of 1994. In late 1995, the Lavalas movement won the presidency with René Preval and control of Congress with an overwhelming majority in the first truly honest elections in the country's history.

In both these cases, the emergence of movements that could effectively mobilize mass support threw the old, elitist party systems into terminal chaos. However, as during the post-Trujillo crisis in the Dominican Republic in the 1960s, the hegemonic presence of the United States provided the old elites with the opportunity and the resources with which to attempt a reconstitution and reorganization of their vested interests as the opposition to the newly dominant popular movements. In Nicaragua, the anti-Sandinista elites are showing some signs of having developed the mass mobilization capability critical to their political survival: without it, they could not have defeated the Sandinistas in 1990, even with the massive U.S. support they enjoyed. In Haiti, the old elites, having miscalculated U.S. policy when they overthrew Aristide, are either in exile or politically marginalized. But certainly some attempt will be made in the next few years to constitute a viable, popularly supported opposition to Lavalas, and such a party or movement will probably enjoy at least tacit support from the United States, where both the Bush and Clinton administrations have been deeply ambivalent about Aristide.

The remaining Central American cases (Honduras, El Salvador, and Guatemala) have not seen such a clear-cut emergence of movements with a new capability for mass mobilization. The Farabundo Martí Front for National Liberation (FMLN) in El Salvador certainly aspired to be such a movement, and it did develop the capacity to occupy and govern a substantial part of Salvadoran territory during the 1980s. It posed a genuinely revolutionary threat to the old order in which the armed forces ruled in alliance with the economic elite; it might have won power if the United States, in the wake of the fall of Somoza in Nicaragua, had not intervened to prop up and reform the old regime. But in fact the Salvadoran regime was renovated and did negotiate a peaceful settlement with the FMLN in 1990. The latter, competing in elections for the first time, was much weaker than the ruling National Renewal Alliance (ARENA), but the Left did emerge as the country's second political force. The very emergence of ARENA as a mass-based right-wing party must be seen as a direct response to the threat of the FMLN.

Guatemala was also subjected to the rule of a succession of reactionary military governments (since the U.S.-sponsored coup in 1954) and also fought a serious insurgency, the Guatemalan National Revolutionary Union (URNG), during the 1980s. But the insurgency never seriously threatened to take power, U.S. aid and intervention was much less prominent, and no new conservative party emerged with a strong mass-mobilization capability. Instead, a personalist movement was built around former dictator Efraín Ríos Montt (1982–1983), the Guatemalan Republican Front (FRG), which did indeed show substantial popular support, particularly in rural areas. However, the FRG cannot yet be considered a true party, and the only other serious party, the Christian Democratic Party, was deeply discredited by the corrupt Cerezo government (1985–1990). Personalism and party fragmentation, in short, continue to prevail in the inchoate Guatemalan party system.

Finally, the Honduran party system has been less affected by the Central American turmoil of the 1980s than any other Central American country save Costa Rica. It is perhaps the last country in Latin America that could be construed as having a traditional party system as it existed before mass mobilization. The Liberal and National Parties have their roots in the nineteenth century, like their counterparts elsewhere, and have long taken the form of rival elite coalitions with relatively minor ideological differences, weak organizational structures, and minimal capacity for mass mobilization beyond a very simple clientelism (i.e., "I am your patron. Vote for me and my party, and we will take care of you."). For decades up to the 1980s, Honduran politics consisted of successive party hegemonies achieved by alliances with the army, which permitted one of the two parties to perpetuate itself in power until the other party could wean the army away. Some mass political mobilization by labor unions, but not by parties, has occasionally occurred. The pattern has changed since the early 1980s, as the United States, anxious to legitimize its Central American allies in the struggle with the Sandinistas, pushed the army to end its most recent dictatorship and to permit honest political competition. In this new environment, some new parties have emerged, but no party or movement developed the mass mobilization capability to challenge the traditional parties. The Liberal and National Parties continue to dominate elections. Now, however, elections are relatively free, and both parties have held the presidency. The Liberal Party's Azcona gave way to the National Party's Callejas in 1990; Callejas gave way to the liberal Reina in 1994. Reina, in particular, has had some success in imposing civilian control over the army. Honduras, in short, retains an institutionalized party system, but only because it has not yet confronted the challenge of mass political mobilization. In the absence of such a challenge, we may expect the traditional two-party system to persist. However, because of low levels of mass mobilization, Honduras clearly does not fit in the same category as the other institutionalized party systems.

Samuel Huntington (1968) distinguished between "civic" and "praetorian" polities primarily on the basis of whether political institutions (especially parties) were strong enough (i.e., institutionalized) to organize and channel the level of political participation existing in the society. Civic polities are stable because their parties and other institutions are adequate to the political participation they confront. If participation is low, institutions do not have to be as strong in order to achieve stability. Instability is characteristic of periods when participation is on the increase and institutions are adapting, periods that are also likely to display strong economic change. The case of the Honduran party system brings us back to Huntington, reminding us that institutionalization does not simply rise with political development; rather, inchoate systems are a consequence of political change. Table 6.2 summarizes this perspective by situating the democratic regimes of Latin America in 1995 in terms of three variables: (1) level of mass political mobilization; (2) high or low levels of party system institutionalization; and (3) trends in party system institutionalization, from higher to lower. This table, it must be noted, is no more than a summary of impressions: it is even less precise than the original Mainwaring and Scully classification presented in Table 6.1. But it presents a more complex picture by adding the element of trends in institutionalization. Thus the countries in the upper left part of the table (Uruguay, Chile, and Costa Rica) not only have highly institutionalized party systems at high levels of mass mobilization, but their party systems are either stable or moving toward a higher level of institutionalization. These countries have the best prospects for continued stable democracy. Conversely, countries in the lower right corner (Guatemala, Ecuador, Panama, and Peru) have poorly institutionalized party systems at low levels of mass political mobilization, and institutionalization is either stable or deteriorating. The basis for stable democracy in these cases is very weak.

INSTITUTIONAL STRUCTURE AND DEMOCRATIC STABILITY

If political parties and party systems are central to the process of institutionalizing democracy, other factors are independently important. One such

Table 6.2   Party System Institutionalization and Levels of Mass Mobilization

| | Party System Institutionalization | | | | | |
| | High Institutionalization Trends | | | Low Institutionalization Trends | | |
Mass Mobilization	Higher	Stable	Lower	Higher	Stable	Lower
High	Uruguay Chile	Costa Rica	Venezuela Colombia	Argentina Bolivia Dominican Republic El Salvador	Ecuador Guatemala	Brazil Nicaragua Haiti Peru Panama
Low		Honduras				

concerns authority patterns, that is, the principles and procedures by which the right to rule is gained. In Chapter 1 we reviewed the historical importance of legalism and constitutionalism as bases for democracy in Latin America, and in the era of democratization they are more important than ever. In this section we consider the main elements of debates about such institutions as presidential versus parliamentary governments, electoral systems, staggered versus coinciding terms for president and legislature, centralism versus federalism, presidential reelection, and the survival of authoritarian features in democratic constitutions.

A principal focus of constitutional debate across much of the region in recent years has been the relative merits of presidential versus parliamentary systems of government.[25] Since independence, of course, Latin America has almost universally hewed to variations on the presidential system of the United States, with its independent, separately elected president and Congress that relate to each other through a variety of constitutional checks and balances tending to assure that neither branch can acquire absolute power. Many scholars (but few politicians or generals) have argued that the presidential system works against political stability in the Latin American context. For example, it is typical that congresses are elected by some variation on proportional representation (leading to representation of many small parties), whereas presidents are either elected with a plurality well below an absolute majority or by means of a runoff second round. In either case, the newly elected president will be inaugurated without assurance of a working majority in the Congress.

In contrast, advocates of a parliamentary system point out that the chief executive holds office only so long as he or she has a majority in parliament, either through a single majority party or a negotiated governing coalition. Governmental gridlock common in presidential systems is thus avoided by vesting unambiguous authority in a government that depends on parliament for its tenure.

Advocates of presidentialism typically emphasize its consistency with Latin American culture and tradition and point to the high levels of party fragmentation present in most Latin American parliaments. The likely result of parliamentary government, they argue, would be short-lived governments and frequent crises during which caretaker cabinets would have to administer public affairs in the absence of a majority mandate. It is far better, they say, to stay with the presidential system in which one person with extensive powers and discretion has a mandate to govern for a fixed term, independent of the vagaries of legislative politics. Mark Jones (1995) argued that presidential regimes can be stable and effective if electoral systems generate majority or near-majority legislative support.

In recent years, democratically elected presidents (e.g., Fujimori in Peru, Paz Estenssoro in Bolivia, and Menem in Argentina) have fed the arguments of both sides as, acting by both constitutional and extraconstitutional means, they have implemented sweeping programs of economic reform without either congressional action or popular consent.[26] Presidentialists often point out that such bold initiatives would be far less likely in a parliamentary system because of the need to consult the members and hold the majority together. Parliamentarists see such arbitrary actions as inherently contrary to democratic principles and hold that a parliamentary system would tend to restrict such initiatives.

The only Latin American country to have recently given formal consideration to parliamentarism is Brazil. Under its new constitution, a referendum was mandated to allow the voters to make two choices: (1) between monarchy and republic and (2) between presidential and parliamentary governmental systems. The referendum took place in 1993, and the electorate decisively opted for the status quo: a presidential republic.[27] The issue of presidential versus parliamentary government is of considerable theoretical interest, but it seems clear that no major Latin American country is on the verge of a shift to a parliamentary system.[28]

René Antonio Mayorga (1995b) argued that Bolivia's newfound stability is in considerable measure attributable to "parliamentarized presidentialism," a practice whereby presidents are normally elected by Congress but only after they are able to negotiate majority coalitions. Such coalitions, moreover, are then renegotiated periodically for purposes of governing. Mayorga argued that without forswearing its presidential system, Bolivia has gained most of the benefits of a parliamentary system. But should the country adopt a runoff system for presidential elections in place of the congressional election when no candidate gains an absolute majority, then stability will be adversely affected because the need for such coalitions would diminish. The contrast with Ecuador is instructive here: Ecuadoran presidents are elected by runoff, typically lack congressional majorities, and are usually confronted by gridlock, whereas Bolivian presidents since 1985 have consistently had governing majorities based on negotiated coalitions (cf. Gamarra and Malloy, 1995, and Conaghan, 1995). In this case, the system of presidential elections, there is substantial variation.

Most Latin American countries now provide for a runoff popular election in the event that no candidate receives an absolute majority (or sometimes, some specified plurality such as 40 percent). And except where one party (Mexico) or two parties (Colombia, Honduras) are overwhelmingly dominant, a runoff is commonly needed. The Ecuadoran pattern described in the previous paragraph is thus not uncommon in the region. In recent years, presidents have lacked a reliable congressional majority in Brazil, the Dominican Republic, Nicaragua, and Guatemala.

Other countries, notably Colombia, Costa Rica, and Venezuela, provide for no runoff, simply electing the candidate receiving the most votes. This has worked satisfactorily in these countries because of their highly institutionalized bipolar party systems. However, as the Venezuelan party system has shown signs of decay, the most recent election, in 1993, saw the victory of Rafael Caldera with under 30 percent of the vote. His coalition gained an even smaller proportion of seats in the Congress, and as a result he has lacked a reliable majority.

Systems for electing the legislature are the other component of this great dilemma of presidential governance. The majority of Latin American legislatures are elected through proportional representation (PR), which in most cases has led to representation of several small parties (certainly good in itself) but has also often meant seating a legislature without a clear majority. The few cases of stable and strongly bipolar party systems have generally produced majorities in spite of PR, but any decay in party dominance is likely to release the fragmenting tendencies of PR. In the heyday of Venezuelan democracy in the 1970s, AD was able to gain a majority even under PR, but in the crisis-ridden elections of 1993, no party was even close to a majority.

Even as PR is criticized for impeding effective governance by obstructing the formation of legislative majorities, other reformers have criticized it for vesting too much power in national party elites and thereby weakening the link between representatives and their constituents. Consequently, a principal initiative of Venezuelan state reformers since the late 1980s has been the implementation of single-member districts for members of Congress. The goal is to counteract excessive party dominance, but it might well have the opposite effect, in view of the well-known tendency of single-member, plurality election systems to discriminate against small parties and thereby manufacture legislative majorities by granting disproportionate numbers of seats to the two largest parties (cf. Duverger, 1962; Lijphart, 1994).

There have been similar arguments across the region on several other issues of how formal governmental structure may affect democracy. Proposals to separate presidential from congressional and local elections are motivated by a desire to reduce the concentration of power but inevitably would also have the effect of further reducing the possibility of cooperation between president and Congress.

Also notable are proposals in several countries to make government more responsive by enhancing the autonomy and authority of state, provincial, and local governments. In view of long-standing patterns of clientelism in many local and regional governments, it may be that the main beneficiaries of such a reform would be local political elites—if the reforms really were to give them control of significant new resources.

Most of these proposed reforms in state institutions are inspired by a fundamentally liberal spirit of restricting the concentration of power. Within this perspective, the efficacy of the government would be distinctly secondary because, in Jefferson's words, "That government is best which governs least." It might be argued that adopting a parliamentary system would serve both efficacy and liberty by restricting presidential power and giving more power to the people's representatives; most of the other reforms would primarily restrict the concentration of power.

Two other types of institutional reform, however, are emphatically oriented toward increasing governmental efficacy by means of concentrating power. Although prohibitions on presidential reelection are traditionally widespread in the region, several presidents at the peak of their popularity have succeeded in pushing through constitutional reforms permitting their reelection. The major cases are Menem in Argentina, Fujimori in Peru, and possibly Cardoso in Brazil.

Last, but very important, many ostensibly democratic constitutions contain major authoritarian features, sometimes dating from the nineteenth century (e.g., giving the president the authority to declare a state of siege or emergency and thereby rule by decree) and sometimes having been mandated by the outgoing authoritarian regime (as in Chile's "bionic senators," or Brazil's continuing recognition of the tutelary role of the armed forces in its new constitution, cf. Loveman, 1993).

All these issues of formal governmental structure are important for the fate of democracy. They define the rules of the political game, the boundaries within which actors do politics. That is precisely why one of the main preoccupations of political actors is the shaping of those formal structures. Again we come to our central theme: structures matter because they constrain action, but structures are also constituted and changed by action.

CONCLUSION

The institutionalization of liberal democracy means that its mechanisms function smoothly to produce a popularly elected government that is able to govern, an organized civil society capable of a wide range of self-government, with well-established lines of communication between the two levels provided by parties and interest groups. Institutionalization, however, does not imply immunity from problems or challenges. Indeed, by its very nature, liberal democracy continually confronts the need to perfect itself in order to maintain its legitimacy and assure its survival. It is to this question that we turn in the last chapter.

NOTES

1. See especially Mainwaring and Scully (1995). See also Seligson and Booth (1995); Goodman, LeoGrande, and Forman (1992); Perelli, Picado, and Zovatto (1995); Chalmers, Campello de Souza, and Borón (1992); Torres Rivas (1993).

2. See Stepan and Skach (1993, 1994); Linz and Valenzuela (1994); Diamond and Plattner (1993).

3. See Scully (1995); Baño (1995); Garretón (1993a, 1995); Godoy Arcaya (1993); Munck (1994); Wolter (1993); Moulián (1995); Carey (1994); Saffirio (1994).

4. See González (1995); Dutrénit Bielous (1994); Mieres (1994a, 1994b); Caetano and Rilla (1995); De Riz and Smulovitz (1992).

5. However, these two provisos may be hard to meet. The FA has been notoriously prone to schisms, the most recent of which occurred in February 1996 over the terms of a change in the electoral law negotiated by FA leader Liber Seregni. His agreement with the Colorado and Blanco leaders would eliminate the long-standing "Ley de Lemas" that even survived the dictatorship. That law has permitted the parties to run many competing lists for the presidency and congress, with the presidential winner being the leading candidate of the party with the most votes. The winner of the presidential election was not necessarily the candidate with the most votes. The Ley de Lemas worked against the FA and other nontraditional parties, because they usually ran only one candidate, whereas the traditional parties would have several, with distinct positions and electoral bases. Seregni put a high priority on eliminating the Ley de Lemas, accepting in return the principle of a runoff presidential election if no candidate received an absolute majority. However, the left wing of the FA, fearing that the runoff would deny the FA the presidency, refused to support the reform, and Seregni resigned. At this writing, the FA looks likely to continue as a major force. The future of the proposed electoral law is uncertain.

6. Note the remarkable reversal from the pre-1973 democracies, when the Chilean Left could elect a president, whereas in Uruguay the Left was just emerging as a serious electoral force. See Chapter 2.

7. Even the former Tupamaro guerrillas, whose insurgency provoked and provided excuses for the authoritarian regime, have renounced violence and joined the FA.

8. For the concept of a semiloyal opposition, see Linz (1978), pp. 27ff.

9. But recall that the inability of the right-wing Colorado government of Bordaberry to command a majority in Congress ultimately provoked the closure of Congress and the inauguration of the authoritarian regime in 1973.

10. See Peeler (1985, 1992). On Colombia, see Archer (1995); Martz (1992). On Costa Rica, see Yashar (1995); Sojo (1995a, 1995b); Rojas Bolaños and Sojo (1995); Vega Carballo (1992); Fernández (1994); Rovira Mas (1994). On Venezuela, see Kornblith and Levine (1995); Goodman et al. (1995); McCoy et al. (1995); Coppedge (1993, 1994a, 1994b); Crisp (1994); Ellner (1993–1994); Salamanca (1994). For a comparison of the crises in Colombia and Venezuela, see Peeler (1995a).

11. AD held the office most of the time, but COPEI held it twice, 1969–1974 and 1979–1984.

12. See Coppedge (1993, 1994a, 1994b); Brewer-Carías (1988); Martz (1994).

13. On the Colombian party system, see Martz (1997); Archer (1995); Cárdenas and Delgado (1996).

14. On the political significance of the drug trade in general, see Thoumi (1995).

15. To give due credit to Colombian policymakers, however, see Pizarro and Bejarano (1994).

16. On the new constitution, see Pastrana Borrero (1991); Restrepo (1992); Hartlyn (1994b).

17. See, for example, Sojo (1995a, 1995b); Mora (1992); Salom (1996).

18. See McGuire (1995); Cavarozzi (1986, 1992); Munck (1992); De Riz

(1993); Fraga (1995); Cabrera and Murillo (1994); Novaro (1994a, 1994b); Borón et al. (1995); Labourdette (1991); Paz (1995); Remmer (1984).

19. Fraga (1995), p. 34.

20. On the Brazilian party system, see Hagopian (1996); Mainwaring (1995); Schneider (1996).

21. On party systems: For Bolivia, see Gamarra and Malloy (1995); Campero (1996); Mayorga (1995a, 1995b). For Peru, see Cotler (1995a, 1995b); Rudolph (1992); Mauceri (1995); Velarde (1995); Amat et al. (1992); Guerra García (1995); Sagasti and Hernández (1993–1994); Schmidt (1996). For Ecuador, see Acosta Silva (1996); Conaghan (1995); Cabezas Castillo (1995); Conaghan and Espinal (1990); Echeverría (1994). For Panama, see Ropp (1997); R. Leis (1996); O. Pérez (1995); McDonald and Ruhl (1989); Smith (1992). For the Dominican Republic, see Betances and Spalding (1995); Rosario Adames (1996a, 1996b); Hartlyn (1994a); Lozano (1994); Espinal (1987); Conaghan and Espinal (1990); McDonald and Ruhl (1989).

22. Both Panama and the Dominican Republic have also suffered the effects of U.S. intervention, which has certainly worked against an institutionalized party system in Panama, although it may have aided such a development in the Dominican case by supporting the emergence of the Dominican Revolutionary Party (more conservative after the defection of Bosch) as a viable alternative to Balaguer after 1978.

23. On party systems: For Honduras, see Ruhl (1997); Salomón (1996); Rosenberg (1995); Paz Aguilar (1992). For El Salvador, see Montgomery (1997, 1995); Baloyra-Herp (1995); Eguizábal (1995); Murgialday (1996). For Guatemala, see Holiday (1997); Rohter (1996c); Jonas (1995); Rosada Granados (1992); Gálvez Borrell (1996). For Nicaragua, see McCoy and McConnell (1997); Anderson (1995); Richard and Booth (1995); Godoy Reyes (1992); LeoGrande (1992); Williams (1994); Prevost (1991); Weaver and Barnes (1991); Lara and Herrera (1996). For Central America in general, see Booth and Richard (1996); Rovira Mas (1992, 1994); Rojas Bolaños and Sojo (1995). For Haiti, see Mintz (1995); NACLA (1994a).

24. *La Nación* (Costa Rica), 5 de diciembre 1996, Internet edition.

25. See Linz and Valenzuela (1994); Linz and Stepan (1996a, 1996b); Lijphart (1994); Lijphart and Waisman (1996); Lijphart (1992); von Mettenheim (1997); Domínguez (1997); O'Donnell (1996); Huntington (1996); Horowitz (1990); Lipset (1990); Stepan and Skach (1993); Mainwaring and Shugart (1994); Mainwaring (1993); Thibaut (1993); Gamarra (1992); Mayorga (1992); Andrade (1992); dos Santos (1992); Cintra (1992); Lehoucq (1996); Ensalaco (1994). For a theoretical overview of broader questions of institutionalism, see Polity Forum (1995).

26. This pattern has been analyzed in detail by O'Donnell (1994) under the term "delegative democracy." He argued that popular election is construed to provide a mandate to the leader, as delegate of the people, to take whatever action he deems appropriate in the interests of the people, whether or not it accords with campaign promises or indeed falls with the law.

27. See Lamounier (1994a, 1994b); Schneider (1996).

28. The new Haitian constitution does have a prime minister responsible to the legislature, but that body is so much weaker than the president that the prime minister remains effectively responsible to the president.

7

Conclusion

Twenty years ago, no observer of Latin American politics would have predicted the massive wave of transitions to democracy that would shortly break upon the region. What the next twenty years will bring is similarly uncertain. We know now—this book has pulled together much evidence—that liberal democracy is feasible in Latin America and that it is widely desired as a good in itself by Latin Americans across the political spectrum. We also know how precarious are these liberal democratic regimes. We do not know whether some deeper form of democracy is feasible.

SOME CONCLUDING PROPOSITIONS

1. Liberal democracy is the best system yet invented for protecting people from abuse by their government. It is certainly not perfectly effective in doing this, but no other system does it better over a sustained period. This is the principal basis for the desirability of liberal democracy over other regime types. The institution of individual rights of citizens, not to be violated by rulers, is the major contribution of liberalism to political philosophy. Whether those rights are based in natural law, contract, or utility, their recognition by an increasing number of governments around the world has made people's lives much less "nasty, brutish, and short" (in Hobbes's phrase [1991]) than they used to be. The very newsworthiness at present of egregious violations of human rights by outlaw governments is a sign of how universal the aspiration for inviolable rights has become.

This is what liberal democracy can do well, while also providing mechanisms for pursuit of the common good; this is why Latin Americans increasingly demand it. If liberal democracy is attainable, it no longer appears inevitable that the persons and lives of citizens will be subject to violation at will by rulers. Surely, if the twentieth century—this epoch of global insanity, inhumanity, and carnage—is to have any positive political legacy, the spreading affirmation of human rights and liberal democracy will be a large part of it.

2. Liberal democracy is attainable in Latin America. The widespread establishment of such regimes, and their persistence through adverse conditions, refutes definitively the arguments of those who said democracy was impossible in the region because of culture, history, or class structure.

189

Given appropriate internal and external structures, it was possible in the most unlikely places to establish and maintain credible liberal democracies. By the late 1990s, liberal democracy was so much the rule in Latin America that countries that did not meet the criteria (Paraguay, Mexico, and Cuba) had to be treated as special cases.

Once these regimes have been established, a key problem is of course to ensure that they fulfill their aspirations with regard to respect for citizen rights. It has not been uncommon for elected presidents to use their popularity as a weapon to intimidate opponents and manipulate elections under cover of a popular mandate. The formal presence of a liberal democracy is no assurance of its vitality. Conversely, citizen rights are rarely, if ever, better protected in the formal absence of liberal democracy. In any given setting, some people, both elites and nonelites, may prefer a nondemocratic system if they are unsatisfied with the results of a democracy. It is increasingly true that most Latin Americans state a preference for democracy, at least in the abstract.

3. The establishment of liberal democracy is fundamentally a matter of elite action. This is contrary to the rhetoric of democracy, of course, but everything we know about the practice of liberal democracy, even in advanced industrial countries, confirms that power remains in the hands of elites. In the United States, for example, the argument between pluralists and elitists is over how cohesive the elites are, not over whether elites rule. Joseph Schumpeter's formulation still captures the essence of liberal democracy: it is a system wherein the people have regular opportunities, through competitive elections, to choose their rulers.

Grand structures such as class do matter in setting boundaries: a society with a very weak working class and middle class and very strong landowners is (as suggested by Rueschemeyer, Huber Stephens, and Stephens, 1992) most unlikely to establish a democracy. A shift of the international environment to a pattern less conducive to democracy would surely lead to numerous breakdowns of democratic regimes in the countries least likely to succeed at democracy. Nevertheless, in late-twentieth-century Latin America even the least likely countries have been establishing liberal democratic regimes. To some extent this is attributable to international pressures (e.g., in Haiti), but it must also be attributed to a will on the part of competing elites to contain their contestation within the bounds of liberal democracy. Often, this has occurred as a direct reaction to the oppression suffered under the preceding authoritarian regime.

We have observed considerable variation in the kinds of elite action that have led—or not led—to the establishment of liberal democracies. One thing that must happen at the elite level is that groups formerly willing to use any method—force or fraud—to get or keep power must begin to compete for power within the confines of liberal democratic rules. When elites representing all sectors of society with the power to disrupt the political process are committed to competing within liberal democratic rules, a stable liberal democracy becomes possible. Liberal democracies can be established on a narrower elite base, with significant elites left out, but the risks to stability are greater. If the regime is successful, the elites left out may later join (in Burton, Gunther, and Higley's "elite convergence"). This happened in Costa Rica during the 1950s after the establishment of the regime in 1949 on a relatively narrow base (see Chapter 2).

Left-out elites may also successfully undermine a regime by continuing to use force and to reject the legitimacy of elections and elite pacts within the regime. The clearest example of this came during the 1950s and 1960s in Argentina (see Chapters 2 and 3), when two successive attempts were made to establish liberal democracies that excluded the Peronist elite. Because the Peronist elite was consistently able to mobilize the movement's mass base in the labor unions, both democratic regimes were effectively stillborn and were replaced by military governments. Indeed, in general, a key part of the power of elites is derived from their mass base.

Elites forming a liberal democracy may do so via explicit pacts defining the terms of cooperation and competition or may operate ad hoc, guided in part by constitutional rules and electoral laws. In the latter case, the risk is higher of a degeneration into ungovernability, as each successive government finds itself unable to hold together a legislative coalition because each major leader will be running for president as soon as the last election is over. Without pacts, Ecuador has tended toward ungovernability, whereas Bolivian elites have achieved an unprecedented stability as they have learned to make good use of pacts (see Chapters 3 and 6).

Some of the smaller countries of the Caribbean and Central America have made progress toward stable democracy in spite of the absence of pacts because the United States has in recent years played the role of a moderator favoring liberal democracy. This has been most clearly the case in the Dominican Republic, Honduras, and Panama (see Chapter 3).

Where a ruling elite retains overwhelming dominance over the combined opposition, there are no incentives for negotiating a transition from authoritarian rule. The most that can be expected in the short run is a controlled liberalization, with the possibility that liberalization could get out of control and lead to democratization as opposition elites gain more room for maneuver and popular mobilization. In Chile, Brazil, and Uruguay, the military regimes attempted such controlled liberalizations, but unexpectedly lost elections and were compelled to accept a genuine transition to democracy (see Chapter 3).

4. Liberal democracies are neither more nor less capable than authoritarian regimes of dealing successfully with economic stress and adjustment. Substantial investigations concluded that, contrary to many predictions, democratic regimes have at least as good a record on economic policy and performance and are just as capable of carrying out unpopular policies (see Chapter 5).

5. *Party systems that are institutionalized and characterized by moderate pluralism are most conducive to liberal democratic stability.* The countries with the most success in establishing and maintaining liberal democracies have been those whose party systems show less volatility between elections and have parties with substantial roots in the population. A stable set of two to four major parties suffices to represent major sectors of society in the legislature and the government. Conversely, a party system with a proliferation of short-lived parties representing only ambitious elites and with few popular roots is a recipe for ungovernability (see Chapter 6).

6. *Presidentialism may be a source of instability, but it is unlikely to be supplanted on a large scale in Latin America.* The divided government that is an inherent characteristic of presidential constitutions has probably had negative effects on governability and political stability in Latin America. It is the norm that elected presidents either lack a legislative majority from the beginning or lose their majority in short order after their inauguration. Rival political leaders, rather than supporting the incumbent president, find it more useful to maneuver with a view to winning the next presidential election. The prohibition on immediate reelection, common in Latin America as a means of retarding the concentration of power in the hands of the executive, also works to render an incumbent too weak to govern. Correspondingly, popular presidents, frustrated by congressional intransigence, are tempted to resort to states of emergency or siege, arbitrary actions, plebiscitory appeals to the populace, or constitutional amendments to permit reelection. All of these possibilities tend to weaken the legitimacy and effectiveness of democracy. Notwithstanding these disadvantages, there is little to indicate that either elites or voters are ready to experiment with parliamentarism. The reluctance may be partially due to the widespread contempt in which parliamentarians are held (see Chapter 6).

7. *The role of nonelites in liberal democracy is relatively marginal.* Liberal democracy is superior to nondemocracies in that all citizens have the right to choose public officials in periodic, competitive elections. Moreover, the citizen's rights protected by liberal democracy include freedom of speech and the right to try to influence government actions. But the people do not rule in liberal democracy. Accountability and responsiveness are legitimate goals for a liberal democracy, but even if they are less than complete, liberal democracy will still function. In fact, stable liberal democracies are those in which elites have the most control over mass political behavior. That control need not be coercive: it could consist simply in channeling citizen energies into two centrist parties that do not threaten vested elite interests.

8. *The role of nonelites in regime change is more important but not*

decisive. Regime changes in general, including transitions to democracy, often involve some kind of mass political breakthrough whereby citizens previously under elite control temporarily break out and act autonomously. Most clearly this was the case in the popular insurrection against Somoza in Nicaragua in 1978–1979; it may also be seen in the Venezuelan uprisings of 1989 that helped to bring down President Pérez and put the Venezuelan democratic regime in crisis and in the Argentine demonstrations of 1982 that protested the defeat in the Malvinas/Falklands War and forced the military to agree to a transition (see Chapters 2 and 3).

Other regime changes may involve successful mobilization of mass publics by opposition elites. The credibility of the opposition elites as potential negotiators with the government depends substantially on their ability to mobilize and guide a mass of their followers. This was, again, most clearly the case in the transitions of Brazil, Chile, and Uruguay (see Chapter 3).

Because even in the best of cases individuals and local communities have little impact on national politics and the national government (except in the occasional mass breakthrough as described above), people develop survival strategies that permit them as much as possible to control their own personal and local situations. For individuals, this could be as simple as trying to avoid paying taxes. For local communities, it often takes the form of organizing community organizations and social movements, which often try to do what is in their power to deal with local problems. In the later stages of authoritarian regimes, social movements also briefly took on national significance in many countries as parties were outlawed or harassed. But once parties resumed center stage in national democratic politics, there has been less room for social movements. Much of the energy of political activists in Chile, for example, shifted from social movements to parties after 1988. Another common problem with social movements is a tendency to slide into a clientelistic logic wherein the purpose of the organization ceases to be self-help and instead becomes seeking help from the government (see Chapter 5).

Social movements and community organizations are nevertheless quite significant in showing the potentiality of a more genuine democracy, where there is little difference between leaders and followers and where participation is needed from most of the members most of the time. Small-scale participatory democracy of this kind must surely be part of any plan for deepening democracy.

9. Liberal democracy, given conducive structural conditions, can probably achieve stability in Latin America. Although it is true that at the philosophical-level liberal democracy lies uneasily in the procrustean bed of liberal economics, and although it suffers many practical problems such as government inefficiency and elite corruption, these diseases are not necessarily fatal. Whatever practical problems liberal democracies have are no worse than those posed by alternative forms, and liberal democracy has at least an orderly and peaceful mechanism for "throwing the rascals out" periodically. The philosophical difficulty may have limited practical effect, since citizens may in practice have broad tolerance for both economic and political inequality. The occasional adoption of modest reforms will usually suffice to keep popular protest from threatening political stability. People who believe their situation could be worse will be loathe to rock the boat. Within Latin America, Costa Rica provides a particularly good example of a country whose successive political elites, over generations, have been intelligent about ameliorating the worst social and economic injustices and have thereby consolidated the liberal democratic regime. It is no accident that Costa Rica is the senior democracy in the region and still one of the most stable.

Nevertheless, the continuing application of uncompromising neoliberal economic reforms without regard to short- and long-term social costs might well undermine liberal democratic stability, particularly when most of the population come to believe that they have been betrayed by their political leaders. Carlos Menem and Alberto Fujimori were able to get away with such a reversal of course and consolidated their power at the expense of parliament and opposition parties. Carlos Andrés Pérez did not get away with it, and the Venezuelan democracy has yet to regain its stability (see Chapters 2 and 5).

10. The need to deepen democracy is an ethical imperative but not a practical necessity. Liberal democracies need to be somewhat responsive to the felt needs of the people to maintain the legitimacy of their authority, but they will often be able to maintain stability even with significant unresponsiveness and injustice. A democracy based on a more egalitarian economy and a more participatory polity would have a stronger base of legitimacy— but only if the egalitarian economy were also productive enough to meet expectations.

We ought to favor a deepening of democracy because it is the right thing to do, the just thing to do. Democratic theory (including liberal democracy) assumes the equality of all citizens and the competence of every citizen to judge her or his own interest. Every citizen ought to have equal opportunity to develop her or his potential because if everyone is equal, no one has a right to claim more. Indeed, none of us can achieve our full potential as human beings, and society cannot achieve its full potential without seeing to it that all of us have that opportunity.

DEEPENING DEMOCRACY

The remainder of this concluding chapter will more fully develop an approach to deepening democracy. The question of strengthening democracy implies a reexamination of the radical approach to democracy exemplified by Rousseau and Marx and by a broad range of contemporary theorists (see the Introduction and Chapter 6). The point is not to negate liberal democracy, whose achievements are important; rather, the point is to build on it, to "take its declared principles literally and force liberal democratic societies to be accountable for their professed ideals" (Mouffe, 1992, p. 2).

I have pointed out that although liberalism emphasizes citizen rights and limited government, radical approaches to democracy tend to emphasize popular sovereignty and equality. Chantal Mouffe (1992, preface) quite rightly pointed out that liberal democracy involves an articulation of these two currents that are in conflict on fundamental principles. The principles of equality and liberty do not always fit together easily. She argued that a radical approach to democracy, rather than trying to resolve this tension, should protect and enhance it.

> Between the democratic logic of identity and equivalence and the liberal logic of pluralism and difference, the experience of a radical and plural democracy can only consist in the recognition of the multiplicity of social logics and the necessity of their articulation. But this articulation should always be recreated and renegotiated, and there is no hope of a final reconciliation. This is why radical democracy also means the radical impossibility of a fully achieved democracy. (p. 14)

That is, liberalism promotes a vision of society as composed of unique individuals who should have maximum liberty to develop themselves. Democracy presupposes that fundamentally, all human beings are equal and are equal parts of a community. The two perspectives converge in that liberalism also demands equality, at least in the sense of equal opportunity, whereas democracy demands liberty, at least in the sense that there should be no restrictions imposed by any authority other than the people. Yet the tension remains and must remain: liberalism makes no provision for community except in the narrow sense of temporary and contingent shared interests; democracy vests sovereignty precisely in a community that has a right to restrict the liberties of nonconforming members. If liberty is primary, the people cannot, finally, rule. If popular sovereignty is primary, liberty is contingent on the popular will.

This basic contradiction is rooted in contrasting liberal and radical approaches to truth itself. Liberalism (e.g., John Stuart Mill) promotes pluralism because liberals believe that truth can never be finally known and can best be approached by leaving every person free to express her or his thoughts. Radicalism (e.g., Jean-Jacques Rousseau) affirms that the people, collectively, can know the truth (if they are not poisoned by thoughts of their individual self-interest) and have the right to enforce it on nonconformists. Rousseau's idealization of the whole people is truly sovereign, but they keep their right to rule only so long as they think only of the common good, not of any particular good.

Rousseau resurrects the classical ideal of the citizen as active participant in the affairs of the community, as indeed an integral part of the community. For Rousseau, difference and pluralism are mortal threats to the integrity of the community. However, as we saw in the Introduction, his vision of how a whole people could rule is so riven by contradictions as to be useless as a guide to practice. It can serve only, as here, as a conceivable but unattainable alternative to liberal democracy.

How can a radical perspective on democracy be reformulated to pose a practical means of enriching and deepening liberal democracy? This is fundamentally a question of coming to terms with the meaning of citizenship in a world in which conventional territorial states—democratic or not—are too small to deal with a globalized economy and too large to be meaningfully governed by the people.[1]

To be a citizen is to be a member, a part, a participant in a political community. In its original classical meaning, the citizens were the demos, the people of a polis. The ancient Greeks certainly assumed that citizenship implied direct and extensive involvement in the collective choices made by the polity. For Plato as well as Aristotle, one could only be fully human as a member of a polis, as a citizen.

Citizenship in this classical sense has been in crisis, not just since the dawn of the modern nation-state but since the advent of the Roman Empire. The old notion of the citizenry collectively ruling themselves simply cannot have the same meaning in polities of tens of millions of people and hundreds of thousands of square miles. Liberal democracy attempts to adapt citizenship by adding the element of representation but loses the element of direct and intense involvement. Liberalism, moreover, also loses the classical sense of community as prior to the citizen. The liberal political order, instead, is built on a foundation of egoistic individuals pursuing their unique self-interests. Thus liberal democratic citizenship is a poor copy indeed of the classical ideal. Perhaps, though, classical citizenship is not even an ideal worth holding, since modern industrial society is inherently and deeply pluralistic, whereas the classical polis was, in principle, unified. The diversity that liberalism recognizes and encourages would have been highly problematic to the ancient Greeks.

But how is even liberal democratic citizenship possible in a world where economic power is so concentrated—nationally and globally—as to negate the equality of citizens? Capitalism has always been a global (or at least supranational) economy that thrived on being able to foster rivalries between competing territorial states (Wallerstein, 1974), but until recently even the largest corporations were firmly rooted in one country and were thus subject to some regulation and control by political authorities. That is now becoming steadily less true as the major corporations operate more and more transnationally to drive down wages and reduce costs. Even the most powerful states have difficulty in resisting threats to close factories and move operations to some other country with lower wages and costs. What can it mean to have a democracy when the citizens have no control over such decisions? Has the contradiction between liberal economics and liberal politics reached the point of rupture?

The line of least resistance in resolving this contradiction is simply to adapt liberal democracy to liberal economics by accepting that property yields political power, that policy must serve the interests of the capitalist system, and that popular participation and decisionmaking must be kept within limits that do not threaten these interests. This has certainly been the position of the U.S. government and the major international lenders and has been largely accepted by Latin American governments. It is not unreasonable in these times to begin with the assumption that it is necessary to adapt to capitalism. There is no other extant system of economic organization that is more efficient for the allocation of resources on a global level.[2] Furthermore, as Lindblom (1977) pointed out, if you have a capitalist system, then a healthy economy requires policies that will induce capitalists to invest.

Just what is a "healthy" economy? High rates of growth in GDP or even GDP per capita are not to be scorned, but what if they conceal growing unemployment and stagnating or falling real wages? The global neoliberal offensive in economic policy over the last twenty years has yielded very high profits for some firms and individuals while creating an ever-growing number of losers worldwide. Neoliberal economic theory has faith that "in the long run" free markets will make everyone better off, but it is at least as plausible to expect a global economic crisis when not enough people with good jobs are left to pay for all the products made by low-wage workers who cannot buy what they produce.

How can capitalism be saved from its worst excesses and how can democracy thereby be rendered more meaningful, richer, or deeper? How can we utilize the unparalleled productivity of capitalism while restricting its destructive tendencies? The most important task must be to demystify the neoliberal religion of the free market, that is, the myth that the free market will inevitably serve the general interest over the long run. This is a kind of microeconomic romanticism, a belief that rational, self-seeking individuals and firms, left to themselves, will unknowingly serve the common interest as well as their own.[3] The fact is that the past fifteen years of neoliberal orthodoxy on a global scale have produced massive economic instability and insecurity provoked by the rapid migration of capital and jobs in search of the highest profits. A few transnational corporations have monopolized most of the gains. On a global scale, neoliberal capitalism is fulfilling Marx's prophecy at long last: production of goods and services is ever more efficient, while the real disposable income of workers/consumers stagnates or falls.

The control of capitalist excess is thus a necessity not only for the well-being of the workers but also for the capitalist system itself. The present unchecked cycle of competition threatens to undermine the security and well-being of most of the world's population. At any given time, some will win and more will lose, but the winners will have little security: decisions made thousands of miles away and beyond their control could make them losers tomorrow. The problem may be construed as political: unchecked abuse of authority by the owners of capital.[4] The problem being thus conceived, the remedy is economic democracy.

The attack on the problem should come from the bottom and from the top. From the bottom, it is indispensable that workers gain control of their firms. Employee ownership will not eliminate the need for a firm to operate efficiently and compete in the market. It will, however, place the issue of job security higher on the agenda. Investors and managers have no interest in preserving jobs: it is often easier and cheaper to close a plant and move the operation abroad than to invest in upgrading machinery or retraining workers. Worker-owners, in contrast, are much more likely to do what they must in order to keep a shop open. In short, a widespread movement toward worker ownership would drastically reduce the mobility of capital and increase the security and well-being of workers, without actually destroying capitalism. The very insecurity under which many workers now labor would provide a strong impetus for the national and international political organizing that would be necessary to create a political climate friendly to worker ownership. It is important that the movement be global, not merely national, for otherwise a move toward worker ownership in one or a few countries would simply constitute one more reason for companies to move elsewhere.

This brings us to the corresponding attack from the top. Governments around the world must break away from the free market mythology and forge a global consensus on achieving minimal, sustainable living standards for people everywhere, thereby reducing and controlling the destructive competition for investments that has led to the bidding down of wages, working conditions, and environmental protection. Global regulation of this kind would also protect businesses by setting up a level playing field. There is, moreover, nothing out of the ordinary about governments cooperating to set common rules to regulate the global economy. That is what the gold standard was; that is what the General Agreement on Tariffs and Trade (GATT) was; that is what the World Trade Organization is. There is no reason in principle why the world's governments, whose laws create, regulate, and protect capitalist property, should not take common global regulatory action that serves the common interest of humanity. Since capitalism is global, policy must be global.

Some such two-pronged local and global economic reorientation would both grow from and in turn encourage broader and deeper political participation, laying the foundation for a deepening of democracy by establishing more economic equality. The enhanced economic autonomy growing from worker ownership would in turn help to create an environment for a flowering of social pluralism outside the workplace, as sectors formerly deficient in resources and autonomy find themselves newly able to shape their environments. Citizenship, in short, could be enriched and deepened in the pluralism of civil society at the local level.

If the deepening of democracy depends fundamentally on changes at the microeconomic and global levels, what is there to say about the state? As was noted above, conventional large territorial states are too small to deal with global economic forces and too big to be democratic except in the most minimal sense. But the state is still needed because many problems transcend local or firm capabilities. At the same time, there is not—probably there cannot be and perhaps there should not be—a global government. The world is too complicated to be centrally administered, even when we need to agree on common global policies. We still need states, and they ought to be as democratic as possible so that they will be responsive to their people. Here we are really considering only reforms in liberal democracy. Deeper democracy, radical democracy, can happen only on a smaller scale (firm or neighborhood, perhaps a town), but it requires reinforcing changes at the national as well as the global level. What does democracy require at the level of the state?

A democratic state must, minimally, be responsive to the people's will. That implies, first, that it creates channels and mechanisms of communication to inform the leaders of the state of what the people want. Elections and a competitive party system are the principal means by which the populace sends binding messages to the state. Second, responsiveness means an ability to act. Once a popular mandate is clear, a responsive state is able and has the resources to accomplish what is expected of it, able to make decisions and carry them out in a timely manner. Responsiveness is partly a result of strong organization, but only if the organization is led by elites with a will to be responsive to the populace.

DEEPENING DEMOCRACY IN LATIN AMERICA

It may be tempting to argue that concerns of deepening democracy are more appropriate to the well-institutionalized liberal democracies of the North Atlantic area. However, the agenda of deepening democracy may lack urgency and broad appeal in those countries precisely because liberal democracy has worked adequately for a long time and has even adapted itself to certain concessions to egalitarianism in the form of social democracy. By contrast, in Latin America, even though liberal democracy is now generally held to be better than the alternatives, few are satisfied with it. It has blatantly failed to address the long-standing problems of social injustice and has failed even to prevent a worsening of social conditions as a result of neoliberal reforms. Moreover, Latin American liberal democracies have done no better than their North Atlantic counterparts in performing their core mission: providing a meaningful link between the popular will expressed in elections and the policies of the government thus elected. Latin American elections, like those in the United States, tend to have a plebiscitory tone, where the issue is the expression of confidence in a ruler, not the communication of a popular will regarding policy. To a great extent, of course, national elections are necessarily blunt instruments that serve better to select rulers than to make policy decisions.

Because problems of social and economic injustice are more acute in Latin America, we may expect more Latin Americans to be receptive to the kind of radical democratic reforms we have been discussing. At the base, diverse social movements have already shown substantial vitality and have had significant effects on national politics. Such revitalization of popular participation at the community and neighborhood level can make nationally elected governments more responsive. National governments must be induced to open the way, politically and legally, to more worker ownership. Such democratization of the economy is even more critical in Latin America than in the North Atlantic area, because Latin Americans have even less control over decisions about opening and closing plants and are already burdened by wages at or below subsistence.

Latin American governments also have a key role to play at the global level. Forging the new global economic consensus around minimal levels of human well-being will of course require the agreement of the advanced industrial countries, but it must also have the active commitment of Latin American and other Third World governments. These governments will have good reason to pursue such a new consensus, since it promises to substantially raise the standards of living of their own populations and to break out of the old vicious cycle of having to keep wages down in order to compete for investment. In sum, radical democratic reforms at local, national, and global levels would more easily engage elite as well as nonelite interests in Latin American societies than in advanced liberal democracies such as the United States.

Some radical democratic reforms, however, are particularly important and particularly difficult for Latin America. If it is important that neoliberalism be surmounted, it is equally important to leave behind populism. Populism in Latin America has adapted the state to clientelism in the age of democracy. Throughout the region, politicians appeal for support on the basis of promises of benefits, and this is what the voters have come to expect. A populist state, however, normally has more commitments than resources, so the state satisfies those constituencies with the best connections. Clientelism enshrines private interest as the engine of public policy, and populism democratizes clientelism. The neoliberal political economic offensive proposed precisely to challenge the clientelization of economic policy and to rectify the fiscal penury of the populist state. But neither neoliberalism nor populism is the answer. A strong and responsive state must live within its means if it is to be able to promote the public interest in radical economic reform. Correspondingly, the population, the citizenry, must cease to look to the state for their material salvation. Organization and self-help at the base (especially including worker ownership) are critical to deepening democracy.

Latin America thus has an opportunity to make a major contribution to the political theory and practice of democracy by pushing forward with a vision of radical democratic reform at a time when the stable democracies of the north seem unable to move. Such a democracy will include the economic sphere and will provide citizens with greatly expanded opportunities for participating in social decisions. Reduction of economic inequality will permit more citizens to have real access to the benefits of liberty and political participation. Possession of more resources will permit citizens to develop their capacities by acting in the political arena and in civil society. A deeper democracy will thus surpass liberal democracy without negating it. It will still include political liberties, competition for power through elections, and an autonomous civil society—in short, all the democratic achievements of liberal democracy. It will add a commitment to more economic equality and to a pluralism of the whole people rather than only of well-off, well-organized minorities (Dahl, 1982, 1985, 1989; Mouffe, 1992; cf. the vision for Haiti proposed by Aristide, 1997).

*   *   *

The task is huge, and the prospects, it must be admitted, are not good. But democracy is, at bottom, an ethical commitment that calls upon us always to look to how we can move toward the ideal. As Chantal Mouffe said in the passage previously quoted, "radical democracy also means the radical impossibility of a fully achieved democracy." Meaning lies in moving toward the goal, not only in getting there. Liberal democracies in Latin America probably can, in many cases, persist without radical reform, even though they rest upon deeply unjust societies. But the democratic ideal they ambivalently embody clamors for realization, for those who have ears to hear.

NOTES

1. In addition to Mouffe (1992), previously cited, major sources include Gould (1988); Warren (1992, 1996); Trend (1996); H. Leis (1996); Cabrero Mendoza (1996); Castro Silva and Keinert (1996). See the Introduction for further background and bibliography.

2. This remains true even though capitalism promotes shameful waste of human and material resources, serious environmental damage, and an unjust concentration of resources. The point is that capitalism still works better than any other economic system in the history of the world.

3. Marxism-Leninism embodied a corresponding *macroeconomic* romanticism: that a national or even global economy could be rationally and efficiently administered from the center.

4. Notwithstanding the contract theorists' supposed "natural right" to property, in practice governments create and regulate property by law and grant authority to property owners as to how they may and may not dispose of their property.

References

Abente, Diego. 1995. "A Party System in Transition: The Case of Paraguay," in Scott Mainwaring and Timothy Scully, eds., *Building Democratic Institutions: Party Systems in Latin America* (Stanford: Stanford University Press), pp. 298–320.

Abente, Diego, ed. 1993. *Paraguay en transición* (Caracas: Nueva Sociedad).

Abootalebi, Ali R. 1995. "Democratization in Developing Countries, 1980–1989," *Journal of Developing Areas* 29: 507–530.

Acosta Silva, Adrián, et al. 1995. "El fin del sistema político mexicano," *Nexos* 18 (208): 40–53 (April).

Acosta Silva, Alberto. 1996. "Ecuador: El Bucaramismo en el poder," *Nueva Sociedad* 146: 16–28.

Acuña, Carlos H. 1994. "Politics and Economics in the Argentina of the Nineties (Or, Why the Future No Longer Is What It Used to Be)," in William C. Smith, Carlos H. Acuña, and Eduardo A. Gamarra, eds., *Democracy, Markets, and Structural Reform in Latin America* (New Brunswick, N.J.: Transaction), pp. 30–73.

Aguilar, Marielos, and Victoria Ramírez. 1989. "Crisis económica y acción sindical en Costa Rica," *Ciencias Sociales* 44: 49–68 (June).

Aguilar Bulgarelli, Oscar. 1980. *Costa Rica y sus hechos políticos de 1948* (San José: EDUCA).

Alba, Victor. 1967. *The Mexicans: The Making of a Nation* (New York: Praeger).

Albala-Bertrand, Luis, coord. 1992. *Democratic Culture and Governance* (New York: UNESCO).

Allison, Graham T., and Robert P. Beschel. 1992. "Can the United States Promote Democracy?" *Political Science Quarterly* 107: 81–98.

Almond, Gabriel. 1973. "Approaches to Developmental Causation," in Gabriel Almond, Scott Flanagan, and Robert Mundt, eds., *Crisis, Choice, and Change: Historical Studies of Political Development* (Boston: Little, Brown), pp. 1–42.

Almond, Gabriel, and James Coleman, eds. 1960. *The Politics of the Developing Areas* (Princeton: Princeton University Press).

Almond, Gabriel, Scott Flanagan, and Robert Mundt, eds. 1973. *Crisis, Choice, and Change: Historical Studies of Political Development* (Boston: Little, Brown).

Almond, Gabriel, and G. Bingham Powell. 1966. *Comparative Politics: A Developmental Approach* (Boston: Little, Brown).

Amat, Carlos, et al. 1992. "Democracia y participación," *Debate* 15 (69): 44–52 (June–August).

Ameringer, Charles. 1982. *Democracy in Costa Rica* (New York: Praeger).

Anderson, Leslie. 1995. "Elections and Public Opinion in the Development of Nicaraguan Democracy," in Mitchell A. Seligson and John A. Booth, eds., *Elections and Democracy in Central America Revisited* (Chapel Hill: University of North Carolina Press), pp. 84–102.

Anderson, Terry. 1995. *The Movement and the Sixties* (New York: Oxford University Press).

Andrade, Régis de Castro. 1992. "Presidencialismo e reforma eleitoral no Brasil," in Hélgio Trindade, org., *Reforma eleitoral e representação política* (Porto Alegre: Ed. da Universidade), pp. 74–88.

Angell, Alan. 1993. "The Transition to Democracy in Chile: A Model or an Exceptional Case?" *Parliamentary Affairs* 46: 563–578.

Angell, Alan, and Carol Graham. 1995. "Can Social Sector Reform Make Adjustment Sustainable and Equitable? Lessons from Chile and Venezuela," *Journal of Latin American Studies* 27: 189–219.

Aquinas, Thomas. 1952. *The Summa Theologica* (Chicago: Encyclopaedia Britannica).

Archer, Ronald. 1995. "Party Strength and Weakness in Colombia's Besieged Democracy," in Scott Mainwaring and Timothy Scully, eds., *Building Democratic Institutions: Party Systems in Latin America* (Stanford: Stanford University Press), pp. 164–199.

Ardaya, Gloria, and Luis Verdesoto. 1996. "Ecuador: De la expectativa por la nación a una sociedad sin expectativas," *Nueva Sociedad* 142: 16–21 (March–April).

Arendt, Hannah. 1951. *The Origins of Totalitarianism* (New York: Harcourt, Brace).

Aristide, Jean-Bertrand. 1997. "Democratize Democracy," *Latinamerica Press*, 23 January, p. 3.

Aristotle. 1960. *Politics*. Ernest Barker, trans. (Oxford: Oxford University Press).

Arriagada, Genaro. 1988. *Pinochet: The Politics of Power* (Boston: Unwin Hyman).

Arroyo Talavera, Eduardo. 1988. *Elecciones y negociaciones: Los límites de la democracia en Venezuela* (Caracas: Fondo Editorial CONICIT).

Augustine. 1948. *The City of God*. Marcus Dods, trans. (New York: Hafner).

Avritzer, Leonardo. 1995. "Transition to Democracy and Political Culture: An Analysis of the Conflict Between Civil and Political Society in Post-Authoritarian Brazil," *Constellations* 2 (2): 242–267.

Aziz Nassif, Alberto. 1995. "¿Como acabar con el sistema de partido del Estado sin acabar con el país?" *Nueva Sociedad* 137: 24–30 (May–June).

Bachrach, Peter. 1967. *The Theory of Democratic Elitism* (Boston: Little, Brown).

Backer, James. 1975. *La iglesia y el sindicalismo en Costa Rica* (San José: Ed. Costa Rica).

Balbi, Carmen Rosa. 1992. "Perú: El golpe y los problemas de la transición a la democracia," *Nueva Sociedad* 121: 4–10 (September–October).

Balladares, José Emilio, ed. 1987. *Sobre el contrato social* (San José: Libro Libre).

Baloyra, Enrique, ed. 1987. *Comparing New Democracies: Transition and Consolidation in Mediterranean Europe and the Southern Cone* (Boulder: Westview).

Baloyra-Herp, Enrique. 1995. "Elections, Civil War, and Transition in El Salvador, 1982–1994," in Mitchell A. Seligson and John A. Booth, eds., *Elections and Democracy in Central America Revisited* (Chapel Hill: University of North Carolina Press), pp. 45–65.

Baño, Rodrigo. 1993. "Coaliciones políticas y representación en Chile," in Manuel Antonio Garretón, ed., *Los partidos y la transformación política de América Latina* (Santiago: FLACSO), pp. 87–94.

Baracho, José Alfredo de Oliveira. 1985. "Teoria geral das constituções escritas," *Revista Brasileira de Estudos Politicos*, 60–61 (January–July), pp. 25–98.

Barber, Benjamin. 1984. *Strong Democracy: Participatory Politics for a New Age* (Berkeley: University of California Press).

Barker, Ernest. 1947. *Social Contract: Essays by Locke, Hume and Rousseau* (Oxford: Oxford University Press).

Basañez, Miguel. 1994. "Encuestas y resultados de la elección de 1994," *Este País*, October, pp. 13–21.

Behrman, Jere. 1996. *Human Resources in Latin America and the Caribbean* (Baltimore: Johns Hopkins University Press and Inter-American Development Bank).

Beiner, Ronald, ed. 1995. *Theorizing Citizenship* (Albany: State University of New York Press).

Bengelsdorf, Carollee. 1994. *The Problem of Democracy in Cuba: Between Vision and Reality* (New York: Oxford University Press).

Bentham, Jeremy. 1988. *The Principles of Morals and Legislation* (Buffalo: Prometheus).

Berhard, Michael. 1996. "Civil Society After the First Transition." *Communist and Post-Communist Studies* 29: 309–330 (September).

Bernstein, Eduard. 1961. *Evolutionary Socialism* (New York: Schocken).

Berry, R. Albert, et al., eds. 1980. *Politics of Compromise: Coalition Goverment in Colombia* (New Brunswick, N.J.: Transaction).

Berryman, Phillip. 1987. *Liberation Theology* (New York: Pantheon).

Betances, Emelio, and Hobart Spalding, Jr., eds. 1995. "The Dominican Republic: Social Change and Political Stagnation," *Latin American Perspectives* 22 (3): 3–130.

Bethell, Leslie, ed. 1987a. *Colonial Brazil* (Cambridge: Cambridge University Press).

———. 1987b. *Colonial Spanish America* (Cambridge: Cambridge University Press).

———. 1987c. *The Independence of Latin America* (Cambridge: Cambridge University Press).

———. 1987d. *Spanish America After Independence* (Cambridge: Cambridge University Press).

———. 1993. *Chile Since Independence* (Cambridge: Cambridge University Press).

Black, Jan Knippers. 1986. *The Dominican Republic: Politics and Development in an Unsovereign State* (Winchester, Mass.: Allen and Unwin).

———. 1993. "Almost Free, Almost Fair: Paraguay's Ambiguous Election," *NACLA Report on the Americas* 27 (2): 26–28 (September–October).

Blake, Charles. 1994. "Social Pacts and Inflation Control in New Democracies: The Impact of 'Wildcat Cooperation' in Argentina and Uruguay," *Comparative Political Studies* 27: 381–401.

Blakemore, Harold. 1993. "From the War of the Pacific to 1930," in Leslie Bethell, ed., *Chile Since Independence* (Cambridge: Cambridge University Press).

Blanco, Juan Antonio. 1995. *Tercer milenio: Una visión alternativa de la Posmodernidad*, 2d ed. (Havana: Centro Félix Varela).

Blanco, Juan Antonio, and Medea Benjamin. 1993. *Cuba: Talking About Revolution* (San Francisco: Global Exchange).

Blank, David Eugene. 1984. *Venezuela: Politics in a Petroleum Republic* (New York: Praeger).

Booth, John A. 1985. *The End and the Beginning*, 2d ed. (Boulder: Westview).

Booth, John A., and Patricia Bayer Richard. 1996. "Repression, Participation, and Democratic Norms in Urban Central America," *American Journal of Political Science* 40: 1205–1232.

Booth, John A., and Mitchell A. Seligson, eds. 1989. *Elections and Democracy in Central America* (Chapel Hill: University of North Carolina Press).

Borner, Silvio, Aymo Brunetti, and Beatrice Weder. 1995. *Political Credibility and Economic Development* (New York: St. Martin's).

Borón, Atilio, et al. 1995. *Peronismo y Menemismo: Avatares del populism en la Argentina* (Buenos Aires: Ed. El Cielo por Asalto).

Boylan, Delia. 1996. "Taxation and Transition: The Politics of the 1990 Chilean Tax Reform," *Latin American Research Review* 31: 7–32.

Bracey, John, August Meier, and Elliott Rudwick, eds. 1970. *Black Nationalism in America* (Indianapolis: Bobbs Merrill).

Bradford, James, ed. 1993. *Crucible of Empire: The Spanish American War and Its Aftermath* (Annapolis: Naval Institute Press).

Brading, D. A. 1987. "Bourbon Spain and Its American Empire," in Leslie Bethell, ed., *Colonial Spanish America* (Cambridge: Cambridge University Press).

Brandenburg, Frank. 1964. *The Making of Modern Mexico* (Englewood Cliffs, N.J.: Prentice-Hall).

Bresser Pereira, Luiz Carlos, José María Maravall, and Adam Przeworski. 1993. *Economic Reforms in New Democracies: A Social Democratic Approach* (New York: Cambridge University Press).

Brewer-Carías, Allan R. 1988. *Problemas del estado de partidos* (Caracas: Editorial Jurídica Venezolana).

Bruneau, Thomas. 1992. "Brazil's Political Transition," in John Higley and Richard Gunther, eds. *Elites and Democratic Consolidation in Latin America and Southern Europe* (Cambridge: Cambridge University Press), pp. 257–281.

Burns, E. Bradford. 1980. *The Poverty of Progress: Latin America in the Nineteenth Century* (Berkeley: University of California Press).

———. 1986. *Latin America: A Concise Interpretive History*, 4th ed. (Englewood Cliffs, N.J.: Prentice-Hall).

———. 1993. *A History of Brazil*, 3d ed. (New York: Columbia University Press).

Burton, Michael, Richard Gunther, and John Higley. 1992. "Introduction: Elite Transformations and Democratic Regimes," in John Higley and Richard Gunther, eds. *Elites and Democratic Consolidation in Latin America and Southern Europe* (Cambridge: Cambridge University Press), pp. 1–37.

Bushnell, David. 1993. *The Making of Modern Colombia: A Nation in Spite of Itself* (Berkeley: University of California Press).

Bushnell, David, and Neill Macaulay. 1994. *The Emergence of Latin America in the Nineteenth Century*, 2d ed. (New York: Oxford University Press).

Caballero, Esteban. 1995. "Wasmosy: A tientas en un mundo hostil," *Nueva Sociedad* 137: 10–16 (May–June).

Cabezas Castillo, Tito. 1995. "Partidos y organismos electorales, una relación que debe mejorarse: El caso of Ecuador," in Carina Perelli et al., eds. *Partidos y clase política en América Latina en los 90* (San José: IIDH/CAPEL), pp. 455–473.

Cabrera, Ernesto, and María Victoria Murillo. 1994. "The 1993 Argentine Elections," *Electoral Studies* 13: 150–156.

Cabrero Mendoza, Enrique. 1996. "Las políticas descentralizadoras en el ámbito internacional: Retos y experiencias," *Nueva Sociedad* 142: 72–95 (March–April).

Caetano, Gerardo. 1995. "Uruguay: La encrucijada política del fin de siglo," *Nueva Sociedad* 138: 80–82.

Caetano, Gerardo, and José Rilla. 1995. *Historia contemporánea del Uruguay* (Montevideo: Colección CLAEH).

Caetano, Gerardo, José Rilla, and Romeo Pérez. 1987. "La partidocracia uruguaya," *Cuadernos del CLAEH* 44: 37–62.

Calderón, Fernando, and Mario R. dos Santos. 1995. *Sociedades sin atajos: Cultura, política, y reestructuración en América Latina* (Buenos Aires: Paidós).

Calvert, Peter. 1985. *Guatemala: A Nation in Turmoil* (Boulder: Westview).

Camacho G., Alvaro. 1986. *La Colombia de hoy* (Bogotá: Fondo Editorial CEREC).

Camp, Roderic Ai. 1995. "Battling for the Voter: Mexico's Path to Democracy," *Mexican Studies/Estudios Mexicanos* 11 (1): 131–136 (Winter).

Camp, Roderic Ai, ed. 1996a. *Democracy in Latin America: Patterns and Cycles* (Wilmington, Del.: Scholarly Resources).

Camp, Roderic Ai. 1996b. *Politics in Mexico*, 2d ed. (New York: Oxford University Press).

Campero, Ana María. 1996. "Bolivia: Carrera contra el tiempo," *Nueva Sociedad* 141: 6–10 (January–February).

Cansino, César. 1995. "Mexico: The Challenge of Democracy," *Government and Opposition* 30 (1): 60–73.

Cárdenas, Miguel Eduardo, and Oscar Delgado. 1996. "Reconstrucción de la esfera pública y voto cívico independiente en Colombia," *Nueva Sociedad* 141: 54–67 (January–February).

Carey, John M. 1994. "Los efectos del ciclo electoral sobre el sistema de partidos y el respaldo parlamentario al ejecutivo," *Estudios Públicos* 5 (55): 305–313 (Winter).

Carrera Damas, Germán. 1988. *La necesaria reforma democrática del Estado* (Caracas: Grijalbo).

Carrigan, Ana. 1995. "Chiapas: The First Post-Modern Revolution," *Fletcher Forum of World Affairs* 19: 71–98 (Winter–Spring).

Casper, Gretchen, and Michelle Taylor. 1996. *Negotiating Democracy: Transitions from Authoritarian Rule* (Pittsburgh: University of Pittsburgh Press).

Castro, Fidel. 1976. *History Will Absolve Me* (Havana: Book Institute).

Castro Silva, Claudete de, and Tania Margarete Keinert. 1996. "Globalización, estado nacional e instancias locales de poder en América Latina," *Nueva Sociedad* 142: 96–107 (March–April).

Cavarozzi, Marcelo. 1983. *Autoritarismo y democracia (1955–1983)* (Buenos Aires: Centro Editor de America Latina).

———. 1986. "Political Cycles in Argentina Since 1955," in Guillermo O'Donnell, Philippe Schmitter, and Laurence Whitehead, eds., *Transitions from Authoritarian Rule: Latin America* (Baltimore: Johns Hopkins University Press), pp. 19–48.

———. 1992. "Patterns of Elite Negotiation and Confrontation in Argentina and Chile," in John Higley and Richard Gunther, eds. *Elites and Democratic Consolidation in Latin America and Southern Europe* (Cambridge: Cambridge University Press), pp. 208–236.

Caviedes, César N. 1991. *Elections in Chile* (Boulder: Lynne Rienner).

Cerdas Cruz, Rodolfo. 1985. *Formación del estado en Costa Rica (1821–1842)* (San José: Ed. Universidad de Costa Rica).

———. 1992. "Colonial Heritage, External Domination, and Political Systems in Central America," in Louis W. Goodman, William Leo Grande, and Johanna Mendelson Forman, eds. *Political Parties and Democracy in Central America* (Boulder: Westview), pp. 17–32.

Chalker, Cynthia. 1995. "Elections and Democracy in Costa Rica," in Mitchell A. Seligson and John A. Booth, eds., *Elections and Democracy in Central America Revisited* (Chapel Hill: University of North Carolina Press), pp. 103–122.

Chalmers, Douglas, Maria do Carmo Campello de Souza, and Atilio Borón, eds. 1992. *The Right and Democracy in Latin America* (New York: Praeger).

Chauvin, Lucien. 1995. "Latin American Democracy: Paradise Postponed," *Latinamerica Press* 27 (48): 1–2.

CIERA (Centro de Investigaciones y Estudios de la Reforma Agraria). 1984. *La democracia participativa en Nicaragua* (Managua: CIERA).

Cintra, António Octávio. 1992. "Reforma eleitoral, representação e política," in Hélgio Trindade, org., *Reforma eleitoral e representação política* (Porto Alegre: Ed. da Universidade), pp. 96–105.

Cleary, Edward, and Hannah Stewart-Gambino, eds. 1992. *Conflict and Competition: The Latin American Church in a Changing Environment* (Boulder: Lynne Rienner).

Close, David, ed. 1995. *Legislatures and the New Democracies in Latin America* (Boulder: Lynne Rienner).

Cnudde, Charles, and Deane Neubauer, eds. 1969. *Empirical Democratic Theory* (Chicago: Markham).

Cohen, Jean, and Andrew Arato. 1992. *Civil Society and Political Theory* (Cambridge: Massachusetts Institute of Technology Press).

Collier, David, ed. 1979. *The New Authoritarianism in Latin America* (Princeton: Princeton University Press).

Collier, Ruth Berins, and David Collier 1991. *Shaping the Political Arena* (Princeton: Princeton University Press).

Collier, Simon. 1993. "From Independence to the War of the Pacific," in Leslie Bethell, ed., *Chile Since Independence* (Cambridge: Cambridge University Press).

Collins, Joseph, and John Lear. 1995. *Chile's Free-Market Miracle: A Second Look* (San Francisco: Institute for Food and Development Policy).

Comisión de Estudios sobre la Violencia. 1988. *Colombia: Violencia y democracia* (Bogotá: Universidad Nacional de Colombia).

Conaghan, Catherine M. 1995. "Politicians Against Parties: Discord and Disconnection in Ecuador's Party System," in Scott Mainwaring and Timothy Scully, eds. *Building Democratic Institutions: Party Systems in Latin America* (Stanford: Stanford University Press), pp. 434–458.

Conaghan, Catherine M., and Rosario Espinal. 1990. "Unlikely Transitions to Uncertain Regimes? Democracy Without Compromise in the Dominican Republic and Ecuador," *Journal of Latin American Studies* 22: 553–574.

Conaghan, Catherine M., and James M. Malloy. 1994. *Unsettling Statecraft: Democracy and Neoliberalism in the Central Andes* (Pittsburgh: University of Pittsburgh Press).

Cooper, Frederick, et al. 1993. *Confronting Historical Paradigms* (Madison: University of Wisconsin Press).

Coppedge, Michael. 1993. "Parties and Society in Mexico and Venezuela: Why Competition Matters," *Comparative Politics* 25: 253–274.

———. 1994a. "Prospects for Democratic Governability in Venezuela," *Journal of Inter-American Studies and World Affairs* 36 (2): 39–65.

———. 1994b. *Strong Parties and Lame Ducks: Presidential Partyarchy and Factionalism in Venezuela* (Stanford: Stanford University Press).

Coraggio, José Luis. 1986. *Nicaragua: Revolution and Democracy* (Winchester, Mass.: Allen & Unwin).

Coraggio, José Luis, and Carmen Diana Deere, coords. 1987. *La transición difícil: La autodeterminación de los pequeños países periféricos* (Managua: Vanguardia).

Cordera, Rolando, and Adolfo Sánchez Rebolledo. 1995. "La transición mexicana: La política y la reforma social," in Carina Perelli et al., eds. *Partidos y clase política en América Latina en los 90* (San José: IIDH/CAPEL), pp. 437–454.

Cornelius, Wayne A. 1973. "Nation-Building, Participation, and Distribution: The Politics of Social Reform Under Cárdenas," in Gabriel Almond, Scott Flanagan, and Robert Mundt, eds., *Crisis, Choice, and Change: Historical Studies of Political Development* (Boston: Little, Brown), pp. 392–498.

———. 1996. *Mexican Politics in Transition: The Breakdown of a One-Party-Dominant Regime* (San Diego: Center for U.S.-Mexican Studies, University of California).

Corradi, Juan E., Patricia Weiss Fagen, and Manuel Antonio Garretón, eds. 1992. *Fear at the Edge: State Terror and Resistance in Latin America* (Berkeley: University of California Press).

Cotler, Julio. 1995a. "Crisis política, outsiders y democraduras: El 'Fujimorismo,'" in Carina Perelli et al., eds., *Partidos y clase política en América Latina en los 90* (San José: IIDH/CAPEL), pp. 117–141.

———. 1995b. "Political Parties and the Problems of Democratic Consolidation in Peru," in Scott Mainwaring and Timothy Scully, eds., *Building Democratic Institutions: Party Systems in Latin America* (Stanford: Stanford University Press), pp. 323–353.

Couffignal, Georges, comp. 1994. *Democracias posibles: El desafío latinoamericano* (Buenos Aires: Fondo de Cultura Económica).

Craig, Ann L., and Wayne A. Cornelius. 1995. "Houses Divided: Parties and Political Reform in Mexico," in Scott Mainwaring and Timothy Scully, eds., *Building Democratic Institutions* (Stanford: Stanford University Press), pp. 249–299.

Crespo Martínez, Ismael. 1991. "Brasil: El Debate sobre la Reforma Constitucional," *Cuadernos del CLAEH* 57: 19–36 (September).

Crisp, Brian. 1994. "Limitations to Democracy in Developing Capitalist Societies: The Case of Venezuela," *World Development* 22: 1491–1509.

Cross, Peter. 1995. "Cuba's Socialist Revolution: Last Rites or Rejuvenation?" in Barry Gills and Shahid Qadir, eds., *Regimes in Crisis: The Post-Soviet Era and the Implications for Development* (London: Zed), pp. 243–285.

Cruz, Rafael de la. 1988. *Venezuela en busca de un nuevo pacto social* (Caracas: Alfadil).

Cumberland, Charles. 1968. *Mexico: The Struggle for Modernity* (New York: Oxford University Press).

Dahl, Robert. 1956. *A Preface to Democratic Theory* (Chicago: University of Chicago Press).

———. 1961. *Who Governs?* (New Haven: Yale University Press).

———. 1970. *After the Revolution?* (New Haven: Yale University Press).

———. 1971. *Polyarchy: Participation and Opposition* (New Haven: Yale University Press).

———. 1982. *Dilemmas of Pluralist Democracy* (New Haven: Yale University Press).

———. 1985. *A Preface to Economic Democracy* (Berkeley: University of California Press).

———. 1989. *Democracy and Its Critics* (New Haven: Yale University Press).

Davis, Diane E. 1994. "Failed Democratic Reform in Contemporary Mexico: From Social Movements to the State and Back Again," *Journal of Latin American Studies* 26 (2): 375–408 (May).

Davis, Harold Eugene. 1972. *Latin American Thought: A Historical Introduction* (Baton Rouge: Louisiana State University Press).

Dealy, Glen Candill. 1992. *The Latin Americans: Spirit and Ethos* (Boulder: Westview).

De Riz, Liliana. 1993. "Los partidos políticos y el gobierno de la crisis en

Argentina," in Manuel Antonio Garretón, ed., *Los partidos y la transformación política de América Latina* (Santiago: FLACSO), pp. 37–54.

De Riz, Liliana, and Catalina Smulovitz. 1992. "Instauración democrática y reforma política en Argentina y Uruguay: Un análisis comparado," *Ibero-Amerikanisches Archiv* 18: 181–224.

De Soto, Hernando. 1989. *The Other Path: The Invisible Revolution in the Third World* (New York: Harper and Row).

Del Aguila, Juan M. 1994. *Cuba: Dilemmas of a Revolution,* 3d ed. (Boulder: Westview).

Diamond, Larry. 1994. "Rethinking Civil Society: Toward Democratic Consolidation," *Journal of Democracy* 5 (3): 4–17.

Diamond, Larry, Juan J. Linz, and Seymour Martin Lipset, eds. 1989. *Democracy in Developing Countries,* Vol. Four: *Latin America* (Boulder: Lynne Rienner).

———, eds. 1995. *Politics in Developing Countries,* 2d ed. (Boulder: Lynne Rienner).

Diamond, Larry, and Marc Plattner. 1993. *The Global Resurgence of Democracy* (Baltimore: Johns Hopkins University Press).

Dietz, Gunther. 1995. "Zapatismo y movimientos étnico-regionales en México," *Nueva Sociedad* 140: 33–50 (November–December).

Dix, Robert H. 1987. *The Politics of Colombia* (New York: Praeger).

Domínguez, Jorge. 1997. "Latin America's Crisis of Representation," *Foreign Affairs* 76 (1): 100–113.

Dornbusch, Rudiger, and Sebastian Edwards, eds. 1991. *The Macroeconomics of Populism in Latin America* (Chicago: University of Chicago Press).

dos Santos, Wanderley Guilherme. 1992. "Reforma eleitoral, cidadania e cultura cívica," in Hélgio Trindade, org., *Reforma eleitoral e representação política* (Porto Alegre: Ed. da Universidade), pp. 89–95.

Downs, Anthony. 1957. *An Economic Theory of Democracy* (New York: Harper).

Drake, Paul. 1993. "Chile, 1930–1958," in Leslie Bethell, ed. *Chile Since Independence* (Cambridge: Cambridge University Press).

———. 1996. *Labor Movements and Dictatorships: The Southern Cone in Comparative Perspective* (Baltimore: Johns Hopkins University Press).

Drake, Paul, and Iván Jaksic, eds. 1991. *The Struggle for Democracy in Chile, 1982–1990* (Lincoln: University of Nebraska Press).

Drake, Paul, and Eduardo Silva, eds. 1986. *Elections and Democratization in Latin America, 1980–1985* (San Diego: Center for Iberian and Latin American Studies).

Dresser, Denise. 1997. "Mexico: Uneasy, Uncertain, Unpredictable," *Current History* 96 (607): 49–54.

Dulles, John W. F. 1972. *Yesterday in Mexico: A Chronicle of the Revolution, 1919–1936* (Austin: University of Texas Press).

Dunkerley, James. 1984. *Rebellion in the Veins: Political Struggle in Bolivia, 1952–1982* (London: Verso).

Durkheim, Emile. 1986. *Durkheim on Politics and the State,* Anthony Giddens, ed. (Stanford: Stanford University Press).

Dutrénit Bielous, Silvia. 1994. *El maremoto militar y el arquipiélago partidario: Testimonios para la historia reciente de los partidos políticos uruguayos* (Montevideo: Instituto Mora).

Duverger, Maurice. 1962. *Political Parties: Their Organization and Activity in the Modern State* (New York: Wiley).

Easton, David. 1953. *The Political System* (New York: Knopf).

———. 1965. *A Systems Analysis of Political Life* (New York: Wiley).

————. 1990. *The Analysis of Political Structure* (New York: Routledge).

Echeverría, Julio. 1994. "La construcción social de la política: Notas sobre la crisis del sistema de partidos en el Ecuador," *Nueva Sociedad* 134: 130–141 (November–December).

Eckstein, Susan. 1994. *Back from the Future: Cuba Under Castro* (Princeton: Princeton University Press).

————, ed. 1989. *Power and Popular Protest: Latin American Social Movements* (Berkeley: University of California Press).

Edelstein, Joel, et al. 1995. "The Future of Democracy in Cuba," including responses and a rejoinder, *Latin American Perspectives* 22 (4): 7–42 (Fall).

Eguizábal, Cristina. 1992. "Parties, Programs, and Politics in El Salvador," in Louis W. Goodman, William LeoGrande, and Johanna Mendelson Forman, eds., *Political Parties and Democracy in Central America* (Boulder: Westview), pp. 135–160.

Ellison, Katherine. 1997. "Congress Clears Cardoso's Path," *Miami Herald,* Internet edition, 29 January.

Ellner, Steve. 1993–1994. "The Deepening of Democracy in a Crisis Setting: Political Reform and the Electoral Process in Venezuela," *Journal of Inter-American Studies and World Affairs* 35 (4): 1–42.

Ensalaco, Mark. 1994. "In with the New, Out with the Old? The Democratising Impact of Constitutional Reform in Chile," *Journal of Latin American Studies* 26: 409–429.

Escobar, Arturo, and Sonia Alvarez, eds. 1992. *The Making of Social Movements in Latin America* (Boulder: Westview).

Espinal, Rosario. 1987. *Autoritarismo y democracia en la política dominicana* (San José: Centro Interamericano de Asesoría y Promoción Electoral/Instituto Interamericano de Derechos Humanos).

————. 1995. "Economic Restructuring, Social Protest, and Democratization in the Dominican Republic," *Latin American Perspectives* 22 (3): 63–79.

Etzioni, Amitai, ed. 1995. *New Communitarian Thinking: Persons, Virtues, Institutions, and Communities* (Charlottesville: University Press of Virginia).

Evans, Peter. 1979. *Dependent Development: The Alliance of Multinational, State, and Local Capital in Brazil* (Princeton: Princeton University Press).

————. 1995. *Embedded Autonomy: States and Industrial Transformation* (Princeton: Princeton University Press).

Evans, Peter, Dietrich Rueschemeyer, and Theda Skocpol, eds. 1987. *Bringing the State Back In* (New York: Cambridge University Press).

Ferguson, Ann. 1991. *Sexual Democracy: Women, Oppression, and Revolution* (Boulder: Westview).

Fernández, Oscar. 1994. "Costa Rica: La reafirmación del bipartidismo," *Nueva Sociedad* 131: 4–10 (May–June).

Finch, M.H.J. 1981. *A Political Economy of Uruguay Since 1870* (London: Macmillan).

Finley, M. I. 1980. *Ancient Slavery and Modern Ideology* (New York: Viking).

————. 1983. *Politics in the Ancient World* (Cambridge: Cambridge University Press).

————. 1985. *Democracy Ancient and Modern* (New Brunswick: Rutgers University Press).

Fisher, Lillian. 1966. *The Last Inca Revolt, 1780–1783* (Norman: University of Oklahoma Press).

Fitzgerald, Frank T. 1994. *The Cuban Revolution in Crisis* (New York: Monthly Review).

Fleischer, David. 1986. "Brazil at the Crossroads: The Elections of 1982 and 1985," in Paul Drake and Eduardo Silva, eds. *Elections and Democratization in Latin America, 1980–1985* (San Diego: Center for Iberian and Latin American Studies), pp. 299–328.

Fox, Jonathan. 1994. "The Difficult Transition from Clientelism to Citizenship: Lessons from Mexico," *World Politics* 46 (2): 151–184.

Fraga, Rosendo. 1995. *Argentina en las urnas, 1916–1994* (Buenos Aires: Centro de Estudios Unión para la Nueva Mayoría).

Frieden, Jeffrey. 1991. *Debt, Development, and Democracy: Modern Political Economy and Latin America, 1965–1985* (Princeton: Princeton University Press).

Friedheim, Daniel. 1993. "Bringing Society Back into Democratic Transition Theory After 1989: Pact Making and Regime Collapse," *East European Politics and Societies* 7: 482–512.

Friedrich, Carl, and Zbigniew Brzezinski. 1965. *Totalitarian Dictatorship and Autocracy,* 2d ed. (Cambridge: Harvard University Press).

Gager, John. 1975. *Kingdom and Community: The Social World of Early Christianity* (Englewood Cliffs, N.J.: Prentice-Hall).

Gálvez Borrell, Víctor. 1996. "Guatemala: Nueva derecha y viejos problemas," *Nueva Sociedad* 142: 6–11 (March–April).

Gamarra, Eduardo A. 1992. "Presidencialismo híbrido y democratización," in René Antonio Mayorga, coord., *Democracia y gobernabilidad: América Latina* (Caracas: Nueva Sociedad), pp. 21–40.

———. 1994. "Crafting Political Support for Stabilization: Political Pacts and the New Economic Policy in Bolivia," in William C. Smith, Carlos H. Acuña, and Eduardo A. Gamarra, eds., *Democracy, Markets, and Structural Reform in Latin America: Argentina, Bolivia, Brazil, Chile, and Mexico* (New Brunswick, N.J.: Transaction), pp. 105–127.

Gamarra, Eduardo A., and James M. Malloy. 1995. "The Patrimonial Dynamics of Party Politics in Bolivia," in Scott Mainwaring and Timothy Scully, eds., *Building Democratic Institutions: Party Systems in Latin America* (Stanford: Stanford University Press), pp. 399–433.

García de León, Antonio. 1995. "Chiapas and the Mexican Crisis," *NACLA Report on the Americas* 29 (1): 10–13 (July–August).

García Delgado, Daniel. 1994. *Estado & sociedad: La nueva relación a partir del cambio estructural* (Santiago: FLACSO).

Garretón, Manuel Antonio. 1989. *The Chilean Political Process* (Boston: Unwin Hyman).

———. 1993a. "Coaliciones políticas y procesos de democratización: El caso chileno," in Manuel Antonio Garretón, ed., *Los partidos y la transformación política de América Latina* (Santiago: FLACSO), pp. 95–103.

———, ed. 1993b. *Los partidos y la transformación política de América Latina* (Santiago: FLACSO).

———. 1995. *Hacia una nueva era política: Estudio sobre las democratizaciones* (Santiago: Fondo de Cultura Económica).

Garvin, Glenn. 1996. "Guatemala, Rebels Sign Peace Accord," *Miami Herald,* Internet edition, 30 December.

Gil, Federico. 1966. *The Political System of Chile* (Boston: Houghton Mifflin).

Gil Yepes, José Antonio. 1981. *The Challenge of Venezuelan Democracy* (New Brunswick, N.J.: Transaction).

Gillespie, Charles. 1986. "Uruguay's Transition from Collegial Military-Technocratic Rule," in Guillermo O'Donnell, Philippe Schmitter, and Laurence

Whitehead, eds., *Transitions from Authoritarian Rule: Latin America* (Baltimore: Johns Hopkins University Press), pp. 173–195.

———. 1991. *Negotiating Democracy: Politicians and Generals in Uruguay* (Cambridge: Cambridge University Press).

———. 1992. "The Role of Civil-Military Pacts in Elite Settlements and Elite Convergence: Democratic Consolidation in Uruguay," in John Higley and Richard Gunther, eds., *Elites and Democratic Consolidation in Latin America and Southern Europe* (Cambridge: Cambridge University Press), pp. 178–207.

Gillespie, Charles, and Luis Eduardo González. 1989. "Uruguay: The Survival of Old and Autonomous Institutions," in Larry Diamond, Juan J. Linz, and Seymour Martin Lipset, eds., *Democracy in Developing Countries,* Vol. Four: *Latin America* (Boulder: Lynne Rienner), pp. 207–246.

Gills, Barry, and Shahid Qadir, eds. *Regimes in Crisis: The Post-Soviet Era and the Implications for Development* (London: Zed).

Gilmore, Robert L. 1965. *Caudillism and Militarism in Venezuela, 1830–1910* (Athens: Ohio University Press).

Godoy Arcaya, Oscar. 1994. "Las elecciones de 1993," *Estudios Públicos* 54: 301–337.

Godoy Reyes, Virgilio. 1992. "Nicaragua 1944–84: Political Parties and Electoral Processes," in Louis W. Goodman, William LeoGrande, and Johanna Mendelson Forman, eds., *Political Parties and Democracy in Central America* (Boulder: Westview), pp. 175–186.

Gómez, Leopoldo, and John Bailey. 1990. "La transición política y los dilemas del PRI," *Foro Internacional* 31: 57–87 (July–September).

González, Luis Eduardo. 1991. *Political Structures and Democracy in Uruguay* (Notre Dame: University of Notre Dame Press).

———. 1995. "Continuity and Change in the Uruguayan Party System," in Scott Mainwaring and Timothy Scully, eds., *Building Democratic Institutions: Party Systems in Latin America* (Stanford: Stanford University Press), pp. 138–163.

González Casanova, Pablo. 1970. *Democracy in Mexico* (New York: Oxford University Press).

Goodin, Robert. 1995. *Utilitarianism as a Public Philosophy* (Cambridge: Cambridge University Press).

Goodman, Louis W., William LeoGrande, and Johanna Mendelson Forman, eds. 1992. *Political Parties and Democracy in Central America* (Boulder: Westview).

Goodman, Louis W., Johanna Mendelson Forman, Moisés Naím, Joseph Tulchin, and Gary Bland. 1995. *Lessons of the Venezuelan Experience* (Baltimore: Johns Hopkins University Press).

Gosman, Eleonora. 1997. "El empresariado ya saborea una reelección de Cardoso," *Clarín,* Internet edition, 30 January.

Gould, Carol. 1988. *Rethinking Democracy: Freedom and Social Cooperation in Politics, Economy, and Society* (Cambridge: Cambridge University Press).

Gramsci, Antonio. 1971. *Selections from the Prison Notebooks* (New York: International).

Grinspun, Ricardo, and Maxwell Cameron, eds. 1993. *The Political Economy of North American Free Trade* (New York: St. Martin's).

Gudmundsen, Lowell, and Héctor Lindo-Fuentes. 1995. *Central America, 1821–1871: Liberalism Before Liberal Reform* (Tuscaloosa: University of Alabama Press).

Guerra García, Francisco, et al. 1995. "Análisis de una victoria," *Debate* 17 (82): 14–23 (May–June).

Guerrero, Andrés. 1996. "El levantamiento indígena de 1994: Discurso y representación política en Ecuador," *Nueva Sociedad* 142: 32–43 (March–April).

Guillén, Abraham. 1973. *Philosophy of the Urban Guerrilla: The Revolutionary Writings of Abraham Guillén* (New York: William Morrow).

Guillén Martínez, Fernando. 1979. *El poder político en Colombia* (Bogotá: Ponta de Lanza).

Guzmán Bouvard, Marguerite. 1994. *Revolutionizing Motherhood: The Mothers of the Plaza de Mayo* (Wilmington, Del.: Scholarly Resources).

Guzmán Campos, Germán, et al. 1980. *La violencia en Colombia*, 2 vols. 9th ed. (Bogotá: Carlos Valencia).

Haggard, Stephan, and Robert R. Kaufman. 1995. *The Political Economy of Democratic Transitions* (Princeton: Princeton University Press).

Hagopian, Frances. 1996. *Traditional Politics and Regime Change in Brazil* (New York: Cambridge University Press).

Halebsky, Sandor, and Richard Harris, eds. 1995. *Capital, Power, and Inequality in Latin America* (Boulder: Westview).

Halebsky, Sandor, and John Kirk, eds. 1992. *Cuba in Transition: Crisis and Transformation* (Boulder: Westview).

Hall, John A., ed. 1995. *Civil Society: Theory, History, Comparison* (Cambridge: Polity Press).

Halperín Donghi, Tulio. 1993. *The Contemporary History of Latin America* (Durham, N.C.: Duke University Press).

———. 1994. *La larga agonía de la Argentina peronista* (Buenos Aires: Ariel).

Handy, Jim. 1984. *Gift of the Devil: A History of Guatemala* (Boston: South End Press).

Hartlyn, Jonathan. 1988. *The Politics of Coalition Rule in Colombia* (Cambridge: Cambridge University Press).

———. 1994a. "Crisis-Ridden Elections (Again) in the Dominican Republic: Neopatrimonialism, Presidentialism, and Weak Electoral Oversight," *Journal of Inter-American Studies and World Affairs* 36 (4): 91–144.

———. 1994b. "Presidentialism and Colombian Politics," in Juan Linz and Arturo Valenzuela, eds. *The Failure of Presidential Democracy* (Baltimore: Johns Hopkins University Press), pp. 294–327.

Hartlyn, Jonathan, Lars Schoultz, and Augusto Varas, eds. 1992. *The United States and Latin America in the 1990s: Beyond the Cold War* (Chapel Hill: University of North Carolina Press).

Held, David, ed. 1993. *Prospects for Democracy* (Stanford: Stanford University Press).

Hellinger, Daniel, ed. 1996. "Post-Bonanza Venezuela," *Latin American Perspectives* 23 (3): 3–158.

Hellman, Judith Adler. 1983. *Mexico in Crisis,* 2d ed. (New York: Holmes and Meier).

———. 1994. "Mexican Popular Movements, Clientelism, and the Process of Democratization," *Latin American Perspectives* 21 (2): 124–142 (Spring).

Hengel, Martin. 1974. *Property and Riches in the Early Church: Aspects of a Social History of Early Christianity* (Philadelphia: Fortress).

Hernández, Luis. 1994. "Mexico: The New Mayan War," *NACLA Report on the Americas* 27 (5): 6–10 (March–April).

Higley, John, and Michael Burton. 1989. "The Elite Variable in Democratic Transitions and Breakdowns," *American Sociological Review* 54: 17–32.

Higley, John, and Richard Gunther, eds. 1992. *Elites and Democratic Consolidation in Latin America and Southern Europe* (Cambridge: Cambridge University Press).

Hill, Bennett, ed. 1970. *Church and State in the Middle Ages* (New York: Wiley).
Hill, Christopher. 1965. *The Intellectual Origins of the English Revolution* (Oxford: Clarendon).
———. 1972. *The World Turned Upside Down: Radical Ideas During the English Revolution* (New York: Viking).
———. 1980. *The Century of Revolution, 1603–1714* (New York: Norton).
Hipsher, Patricia. 1996. "Democratization and the Decline of Urban Social Movements in Chile and Spain," *Comparative Politics* 28: 273–298 (April).
Hirschman, Albert O. 1970. *Exit, Voice, and Loyalty: Responses to Decline in Firms, Organizations, and States* (Cambridge: Harvard University Press).
Hobbes, Thomas. 1991. *Leviathan* (Cambridge: Cambridge University Press).
Holiday, David. 1997. "Guatemala's Long Road to Peace," *Current History* 96 (607): 68–74.
Hollinger, Robert. 1996. *The Dark Side of Liberalism: Elitism vs. Democracy* (Westport, Conn.: Praeger).
Holmes, Stephen. 1995. *Passions and Constraint: On the Theory of Liberal Democracy* (Chicago: University of Chicago Press).
Horowitz, Donald L. 1990. "Presidents vs. Parliaments: Comparing Democratic Systems," *Journal of Democracy* 1 (4): 74–79.
Hunter, Floyd. 1953. *Community Power Structure: A Study of Decision-Makers* (Chapel Hill: University of North Carolina Press).
Huntington, Samuel. 1968. *Political Order in Changing Societies* (New Haven: Yale University Press).
———. 1991. *The Third Wave: Democratization in the Late Twentieth Century* (Norman: University of Oklahoma Press).
———. 1996. "Democracy for the Long Haul," *Journal of Democracy* 7 (2): 3–13.
Immerman, Richard. 1982. *The CIA in Guatemala* (Austin: University of Texas Press).
Isaacs, Anita. 1993. *Military Rule and Transition in Ecuador, 1972–92* (Pittsburgh: University of Pittsburgh Press).
Jaquette, Jane S. 1994. *The Women's Movement in Latin America*, 2d ed. (Boulder: Westview).
Jefferson, Thomas. 1974. *The Portable Thomas Jefferson,* Merrill Peterson, ed. (New York: Viking).
Jeffrey, Paul. 1996. "Arzú Takes Over in Guatemala," *Latinamerica Press* 28 (1): 1, 8 (18 January).
Jelin, Elizabeth. 1994. "The Politics of Memory: The Human Rights Movement and the Construction of Democracy in Argentina," *Latin American Perspectives* 21 (2): 38–58.
Jonas, Susanne. 1989. "Elections and Transitions: The Guatemalan and Nicaraguan Cases," in John A. Booth and Mitchell A. Seligson, eds., *Elections and Democracy in Central America* (Chapel Hill: University of North Carolina Press), pp. 126–157.
———. 1991. *The Battle for Guatemala: Rebels, Death Squads, and U.S. Power* (Boulder: Westview).
———. 1995. "Electoral Problems and the Democratic Project in Guatemala," in Mitchell A. Seligson and John A. Booth, eds., *Elections and Democracy in Central America Revisited* (Chapel Hill: University of North Carolina Press), pp. 25–44.
Jonas, Susanne, and Edward McCaughan, eds. 1994. *Latin America Faces the Twenty-First Century: Reconstructing a Social Justice Agenda* (Boulder: Westview).

Jonas, Susanne, and Nancy Stein, eds. 1990. *Democracy in Latin America: Visions and Realities* (New York: Bergin and Garvey).

Jones, Mark P. 1995. *Electoral Laws and the Survival of Presidential Democracies* (Notre Dame, Ind.: University of Notre Dame Press).

Jorrín, Miguel, and John Martz. 1970. *Latin American Political Thought and Ideology* (Chapel Hill: University of North Carolina Press).

Karl, Terry. 1987. "Petroleum and Political Pacts: The Transition to Democracy in Venezuela," *Latin American Research Review* 22: 63–94.

Kaufman, Edy. 1979. *Uruguay in Transition* (New Brunswick, N.J.: Transaction).

Keane, John. 1988. *Democracy and Civil Society* (London: Verso).

Keck, Margaret E. 1992. *The Workers' Party and Democratization in Brazil* (New Haven: Yale University Press).

————. 1995. "Social Equity and Environmental Politics in Brazil: Lessons from the Rubber Tappers of Acre," *Comparative Politics* 27: 409–424.

Keen, Benjamin, and Mark Wasserman. 1988. *A History of Latin America*, 3d ed. (Boston: Houghton Mifflin).

Kelley, Jonathan, and Herbert S. Klein. 1981. *Revolution and the Rebirth of Inequality: A Theory Applied to the National Revolution in Bolivia* (Berkeley: University of California Press).

Kinsbruner, Jay. 1973. *Chile: A Historical Interpretation* (New York: Harper and Row).

Kirkpatrick, Jeane. 1982. *Dictatorships and Double Standards* (New York: Simon and Schuster).

————. 1990. *The Withering Away of the Totalitarian State . . . and Other Surprises* (Washington, D.C.: American Enterprise Institute AEI Press).

Klein, Herbert S. 1992. *Bolivia: The Evolution of a Multi-Ethnic Society*, 2d ed. (New York: Oxford University Press).

Klesner, Joseph L. 1995. "The 1994 Mexican Elections: Manifestation of a Divided Society?" *Mexican Studies/Estudios Mexicanos* 11 (1): 137–149 (Winter).

Knight, Alan. 1986. *The Mexican Revolution* (Cambridge: Cambridge University Press).

————. 1992. "Mexico's Elite Settlement: Conjuncture and Consequences," in John Higley and Richard Gunther, eds., *Elites and Democratic Consolidation in Latin America and Southern Europe* (Cambridge: Cambridge University Press), pp. 113–145.

————. 1994. "Cardenismo: Juggernaut or Jalopy?" *Journal of Latin American Studies* 26 (1): 73–107.

Kornblith, Miriam. 1995. "Public Sector and Private Sector: New Rules of the Game," in Jennifer McCoy, Andrés Serbin, William C. Smith, and Andrés Stambouli, eds., *Venezuelan Democracy Under Stress* (New Brunswick, N.J.: Transaction), pp. 77–105.

Kornblith, Miriam, and Daniel Levine. 1995. "Venezuela: The Life and Times of the Party System," in Scott Mainwaring and Timothy Scully, eds., *Building Democratic Institutions: Party Systems in Latin America* (Stanford: Stanford University Press), pp. 37–71.

Kristeller, Paul. 1961. *Renaissance Thought: The Classic, Scholastic, and Humanistic Strains* (New York: Harper).

Kryzanek, Michael J. 1996. "The Dominican Republic: The Challenge of Preserving a Fragile Democracy," in Howard Wiarda and Harvey Kline, eds., *Latin American Politics and Development*, 4th ed. (Boulder: Westview), pp. 490–505.

Kurtz, Marcus. 1995. "Urban Participation and Rural Exclusion: Neo-Liberal

Transformation and Democratic Transition in Chile," paper presented at the American Political Science Association meeting, Chicago.

LaBotz, Dan. 1995. *Democracy in Mexico: Peasant Rebellion and Political Reform* (Boston: South End Press).

Labourdette, Sergio D. 1991. *El menemismo y el poder* (Buenos Aires: Quirón).

Ladman, Jerry R., ed. 1982. *Bolivia: Legacy of the Revolution and Prospects for the Future* (Tempe: Center for Latin American Studies, Arizona State University).

Lamounier, Bolívar. 1994a. "Brazil at an Impasse," *Journal of Democracy* 5 (3): 72–87.

———. 1994b. "Brazil: Toward Parliamentarism?" in Juan Linz and Arturo Valenzuela, eds., *The Failure of Presidential Democracy* (Baltimore: Johns Hopkins University Press), pp. 253–293.

Lara, Xochitl, and René Herrera. 1996. *La pacificación en Nicaragua* (San José: FLACSO).

LaRamée, Pierre. 1995. "Differences of Opinion: Interviews with Sandinistas," *NACLA Report on the Americas* 27 (5), pp. 11–14.

Las Casas, Bartolomé de. 1992. *The Devastation of the Indies,* trans. Erma Briffault (Baltimore: Johns Hopkins University Press).

Lechner, Norberto. 1991. "The Search for Lost Community: Challenges to Democracy in Latin America," *Journal of Developing Areas* 129: 541–553.

Lehoucq, Fabrice Edouard. 1996. "The Institutional Foundations of Democratic Cooperation in Costa Rica," *Journal of Latin American Studies* 28 (2): 329–356.

Leis, Héctor Ricardo. 1996. "Globalización y democracia en los 90: ¿Hacia un espacio público transnacional?" *Nueva Sociedad* 142: 44–54 (March–April).

Leis, Raúl. 1996. "Panamá: Entre el asedio y la esperanza," *Nueva Sociedad* 141: 14–18 (January–February).

Lenin, Vladimir. 1963. *What Is to Be Done?* (London: Clarendon).

LeoGrande, William. 1992. "Political Parties and Postrevolutionary Politics in Nicaragua," in Louis W. Goodman, William LeoGrande, and Johanna Mendelson Forman, eds., *Political Parties and Democracy in Central America* (Boulder: Westview), pp. 187–202.

Levine, Daniel H. 1989. "Venezuela: The Nature, Sources, and Future Prospects of Democracy," in Larry Diamond, Juan J. Linz, and Seymour Martin Lipset, eds., *Democracy in Developing Countries,* Vol. Four: *Latin America* (Boulder: Lynne Rienner), pp. 247–290.

———. 1993. "Constructing Culture and Power," in Daniel Levine, ed., *Constructing Culture and Power in Latin America* (Ann Arbor: University of Michigan Press), pp. 1–39.

———, ed. 1993. *Constructing Culture and Power in Latin America* (Ann Arbor: University of Michigan Press).

Lewis, Paul. 1982. *Socialism, Liberalism, and Dictatorship in Paraguay* (New York: Praeger).

———. 1993a. *Paraguay Under Stroessner* (Chapel Hill: University of North Carolina Press).

———. 1993b. *Political Parties and Generations in Paraguay's Liberal Era* (Chapel Hill: University of North Carolina Press).

Lijphart, Arend. 1994. *Electoral Systems and Party Systems* (Oxford: Oxford University Press).

———, ed. 1992. *Parliamentary Versus Presidential Government* (Oxford: Oxford University Press).

Lijphart, Arend, and Carlos Waisman, eds. 1996. *Institutional Design in New Democracies: Eastern Europe and Latin America* (Boulder: Westview).

Lindblom, Charles. 1977. *Politics and Markets* (New York: Basic Books).

Linz, Juan. 1975. "Totalitarian and Authoritarian Regimes," in Fred Greenstein, ed., *Handbook of Political Science,* vol. 3 (Reading, Mass.: Addison-Wesley), pp. 175ff.

Linz, Juan. 1978. *Crisis, Breakdown, and Equilibrium,* vol. 1 of Linz and Alfred Stepan, eds. *The Breakdown of Democratic Regimes* (Baltimore: Johns Hopkins University Press).

Linz, Juan, and Alfred Stepan. 1996a. *Problems of Democratic Transition and Consolidation* (Baltimore: Johns Hopkins University Press).

————. 1996b. "Toward Consolidated Democracies," *Journal of Democracy* 7 (2): 14–33.

————, eds. 1978. *The Breakdown of Democratic Regimes* (Baltimore: Johns Hopkins University Press).

Linz, Juan, and Arturo Valenzuela, eds. 1994. *The Failure of Presidential Democracy* (Baltimore: Johns Hopkins University Press).

Lipset, Seymour Martin. 1959. "Some Social Requisites of Democracy: Economic Development and Political Legitimacy," *American Political Science Review* 53: 69–105.

————. 1990. "Presidents vs. Parliaments: The Centrality of Political Culture," *Journal of Democracy* 1 (4): 80–83.

Lipset, Seymour Martin, Kyoung-Ryung Seong, and John Charles Torres. 1993. "A Comparative Analysis of the Social Requisites of Democracy," *International Social Science Journal* 136: 155–175.

Liss, Sheldon. 1994. *Fidel! Castro's Political and Social Thought* (Boulder: Westview).

Lockhart, James, and Stuart Schwartz. 1983. *Early Latin America: A History of Colonial Spanish America and Brazil* (Cambridge: Cambridge University Press).

Lombardi, John V. 1982. *Venezuela: The Search for Order, the Dream of Progress* (New York: Oxford University Press).

Longley, Kyle. 1997. *The Sparrow and the Hawk: Costa Rica and the United States During the Rise of José Figueres* (Tuscaloosa: University of Alabama Press).

López, Alexander. 1996. "Understanding Costa Rica's Political Stability," *Journal of Theoretical Politics* 8: 115–120.

López Maya, Margarita. 1994. "The Rise of Causa R: A Workers' Party Shakes Up the Old Politics," *NACLA* 27 (5): 29–34 (March–April).

López Maya, Margarita, and Luis Gómez Calcaño. 1989. "Desarrollo y hegemonía en la sociedad venezolana: 1958 a 1985," in Margarita López Maya et al., *De Punto Fijo al Pacto Social* (Caracas: Fondo Editorial Acta Científica Venezolana), pp. 15–125.

López Maya, Margarita, Luis Gómez Calcaño, and Thaís Maingón. 1989. *De punto fijo al Pacto Social: Desarrollo y hegemonía en Venezuela (1958–1985)* (Caracas: Fondo Editorial Acta Científica Venezolana).

Loveman, Brian. 1988. *Chile: The Legacy of Hispanic Capitalism,* 2d ed. (New York: Oxford University Press).

————. 1993. *The Constitution of Tyranny: Regimes of Exception in Spanish America* (Pittsburgh: University of Pittsburgh Press).

Loveman, Brian, and Thomas Davies, eds. 1997. *The Politics of Antipolitics: The Military in Latin America,* revised and updated (Wilmington, Del.: Scholarly Resources).

Lozano, Wilfredo. 1994. "República Dominicana: El fin de los caudillos," *Nueva Sociedad* 134: 11–16 (November–December).

Machiavelli, Niccolo. 1995. *The Prince* (New York: Humanities).

Macpherson, C. B. 1972. *The Real World of Democracy* (Oxford: Oxford University Press).

———. 1973. *Democratic Theory: Essays in Retrieval* (Oxford: Oxford University Press).

———. 1977. *The Life and Times of Liberal Democracy* (Oxford: Oxford University Press).

Madison, James, Alexander Hamilton, and John Jay. 1987. *The Federalist Papers* (New York: Viking Penguin).

Mainwaring, Scott. 1993. "Presidentialism, Multipartism, and Democracy: The Difficult Combination," *Comparative Political Studies* 26: 198–228 (July).

———. 1995. "Brazil: Weak Parties, Feckless Democracy," in Scott Mainwaring and Timothy Scully, eds., *Building Democratic Institutions: Party Systems in Latin America* (Stanford: Stanford University Press), pp. 354–398.

Mainwaring, Scott, and Timothy Scully, eds. 1995. *Building Democratic Institutions: Party Systems in Latin America* (Stanford: Stanford University Press).

Mainwaring, Scott, and Matthew Shugart. 1994. "Juan J. Linz: Presidencialismo y democracia: Una revisión crítica," *Desarrollo Económico* 34 (135): 397–418 (October–December).

Mainwaring, Scott, and Alexander Wilde, eds. 1989. *The Progressive Church in Latin America* (Notre Dame: University of Notre Dame Press).

Malloy, James M. 1991. "Democracy, Economic Crisis, and the Problem of Governance: The Case of Bolivia," *Studies in Comparative International Development* 26 (2): 37–57.

Malloy, James M., and Eduardo Gamarra. 1987. "The Transition to Democracy in Bolivia," in Malloy and Mitchell Seligson, eds., *Authoritarians and Democrats: Regime Transition in Latin America* (Pittsburgh: University of Pittsburgh Press), pp. 93–120.

———. 1988. *Revolution and Reaction: Bolivia, 1964–1985* (New Brunswick: Transaction).

Malloy, James M., and Mitchell Seligson, eds. 1977. *Authoritarianism and Corporatism in Latin America* (Pittsburgh: University of Pittsburgh Press).

———, eds. 1987. *Authoritarians and Democrats: Regime Transition in Latin America* (Pittsburgh: University of Pittsburgh Press).

Markoff, John. 1996. *Waves of Democracy: Social Movements and Political Change* (Thousand Oaks, Calif.: Pine Forge Press).

Marks, Gary, and Larry Diamond, eds. 1992. *Reexamining Democracy* (Newbury Park, Calif.: Sage).

Martins, Luciano. 1986. "The 'Liberalization' of Authoritarian Rule in Brazil," in Guillermo O'Donnell, Philippe Schmitter, and Laurence Whitehead, eds., *Transitions from Authoritarian Rule: Latin America* (Baltimore: Johns Hopkins University Press), pp. 72–94.

Martz, John D. 1966. *Acción Democrática: Evolution of a Modern Political Party in Venezuela* (Princeton: Princeton University Press).

———. 1987. *Politics and Petroleum in Ecuador* (New Brunswick, N.J.: Transaction).

———. 1992. "Party Elites and Leadership in Colombia and Venezuela" *Journal of Latin American Studies* 24: 87–121.

———. 1994. "Technological Elites and Political Parties: The Venezuelan Professional Community," *Latin American Research Review* 29 (1): 7–27.

———. 1997. *The Politics of Clientelism: Democracy and the State in Colombia* (New Brunswick, N.J.: Transaction).

Martz, John D., and David J. Myers, eds. 1986. *Venezuela: The Democratic Experience*, rev. ed. (New York: Praeger).

Mauceri, Philip. 1995. "State Reform, Coalitions, and the Neoliberal *Autogolpe* in Peru," *Latin American Research Review* 30 (1): 7–38.

Mayorga, René Antonio. 1991. *¿De la autonomía política al orden democrático?* (La Paz: CEBEM).

―――. 1992. "Gobernabilidad en entredicho: Conflictos institucionales y sistema presidencialista," in René Antonio Mayorga, coord. 1992 *Democracia y gobernabilidad: América Latina* (Caracas: Nueva Sociedad), pp. 41–62.

―――. 1994a. "Gobernabilidad y reforma política: La experiencia de Bolivia," *América Latina Hoy: Revista de Ciencias Sociales* (Universidad Complutense de Madrid), no. 8, pp. 35–60.

―――. 1994b. "Neopopulist Actors and Democracy in Latin America: A Comparative Analysis of Peru, Brazil, and Bolivia," paper presented at the Vienna Dialogue on Democracy, Vienna.

―――. 1995a. "Outsiders y Kataristas en el sistema de partidos, la política de pactos y la gobernabilidad en Bolivia," in Carina Perelli et al., eds., *Partidos y clase política en América Latina en los 90* (San José: IIDH/CAPEL), pp. 219–264.

―――. 1995b. "Parliamentarized Presidentialism, Moderate Multiparty System and State Transformation: The Case of Bolivia," paper presented at the Seminar "L'Etat en Amérique Latine: Privatisation ou Redéfinition?" Institut des Hautes Études de l'Amérique Latine, Paris.

―――, coord. 1992. *Democracia y gobernabilidad: América Latina* (Caracas: Nueva Sociedad).

McCaughan, Michael. 1994. "An Interview with *Subcomandante* Marcos," *NACLA Report on the Americas* 28 (1): 35–37 (July–August).

McClintock, Cynthia. 1994. "The Breakdown of Constitutional Democracy in Peru," paper presented at the Latin American Studies Association meeting, Atlanta.

McClintock, Cynthia, and Abraham Lowenthal, eds. 1983. *The Peruvian Experiment Reconsidered* (Princeton: Princeton University Press).

McClintock, Michael. 1992. *Instruments of Statecraft: U.S. Guerrilla Warfare, Counterinsurgency, and Counter-Terrorism, 1940–1990* (New York: Pantheon Books).

McCoy, Jennifer, and Shelley McConnell. 1997. "Nicaragua: Beyond the Revolution," *Current History* 96 (607): 75–80.

McCoy, Jennifer, Andrés Serbin, William C. Smith, and Andrés Stambouli, eds. 1995. *Venezuelan Democracy Under Stress* (New Brunswick, N.J.: Transaction).

McDonald, Ronald H., and J. Mark Ruhl. 1989. *Party Politics and Elections in Latin America* (Boulder: Westview).

McGuire, James W. 1995. "Political Parties and Democracy in Argentina," in Scott Mainwaring and Timothy Scully, eds., *Building Democratic Institutions: Party Systems in Latin America* (Stanford: Stanford University Press), pp. 200–246.

McManus, Philip, and Gerald Schlabach, eds. 1991. *Relentless Persistence: Nonviolent Action in Latin America* (Philadelphia: New Society).

Melo, Artemio L. 1995. *El gobierno de Alfonsín: La instauración democrática argentina (1983–1989)* (Buenos Aires: Homo Sapiens Ediciones).

Meyer, Lorenzo. 1981. *Historia de la Revolución Mexicana* (México: Colegio de México).

Meyer, Michael, and William Sherman. 1991. *The Course of Mexican History*, 4th ed. (New York: Oxford University Press).

Michels, Robert. 1949. *Political Parties: A Sociological Study of the Oligarchical Tendencies of Modern Democracy* (Glencoe: Free Press).

Mieres, Pablo. 1994a. *Desobediencia y lealtad: El voto en el Uruguay de fin de siglo* (Montevideo: CLAEH).

————. 1994b. "Uruguay: Un escenario competitivo," *Nueva Sociedad* 133: 4–12 (September–October).

Mill, James. 1992. *Political Writings* (Cambridge: Cambridge University Press).

Mill, John Stuart. 1975. *Three Essays: On Liberty, Representative Government, The Subjection of Women* (London: Oxford University Press).

————. 1994. *Principles of Political Economy* (Oxford: Oxford University Press).

Miller, John. 1990. *Absolutism in Seventeenth Century Europe* (New York: St. Martin's).

Mills, C. Wright. 1956. *The Power Elite* (New York: Oxford University Press).

Mintz, Sidney W. 1995 "Can Haiti Change?" *Foreign Affairs* 74 (1): 73–86.

Miranda, Carlos R. 1990. *The Stroessner Era: Authoritarian Rule in Paraguay* (Boulder: Westview).

Monge Alfaro, Carlos. 1980. *Historia de Costa Rica*, 16th ed. (San José: Trejos).

Montesquieu, Charles Louis de Secondat, Baron. 1952. *The Spirit of the Laws* (Chicago: Encyclopaedia Britannica).

Montgomery, Tommie Sue. 1995. *Revolution in El Salvador: From Civil Strife to Civil Peace*, 2d ed. (Boulder: Westview).

————. 1997. "Constructing Democracy in El Salvador," *Current History* 96 (607): 61–67.

Moore, Barrington. 1966. *Social Origins of Dictatorship and Democracy* (Boston: Beacon).

Mora, Jorge. 1992. "Movimientos campesinos en Costa Rica," *Cuadernos de Ciencias Sociales* 53 (San José: FLACSO).

————. 1994. "Costa Rica: Economic Aperture and Changes in the Electorate Options and in the Political Representation of Rural Family Householders," paper presented at the Thirteenth World Congress of Sociology meeting, Bielefeld, Germany.

Mora Mérida, José Luis. 1981. *Paraguay y Uruguay contemporáneos* (Sevilla: Escuela de Estudios Hispano-Americanos).

Morales, Juan Antonio, and Gary McMahon, eds. 1993. *La política económica en la transición a la democracia* (Santiago: CIEPLAN).

Morris, James A. 1984. *Honduras: Caudillo Politics and Military Rulers* (Boulder: Westview).

Morris, Stephen D. 1995. *Political Reformism in Mexico: An Overview of Contemporary Mexican Politics* (Boulder: Lynne Rienner).

Mosca, Gaetano. 1939. *The Ruling Class* (New York: McGraw-Hill).

Mouffe, Chantal, ed. 1992. *Dimensions of Radical Democracy* (London: Verso).

Moulián, Tomás. 1995. "Chile: Las condiciones de la democracia," *Nueva Sociedad* 140: 4–11 (November–December).

Munck, Gerardo. 1994. "Democratic Stability and Its Limits: An Analyis of Chile's 1993 Elections," *Journal of Inter-American Studies and World Affairs* 36 (2): 1–37.

Munck, Ronaldo. 1989. *Latin America: The Transition to Democracy* (London: Zed).

————. 1992. "The Democratic Decade: Argentina Since Malvinas," *Bulletin of Latin American Research* 11: 205–216.

Muñoz Guillén, Mercedes. 1990. *El estado y la abolición del ejército, 1914–1949* (San José: Ed. Porvenir).

Muñoz Patraca, Víctor Manuel. 1994. "Transición a la democracia en México," *Revista Mexicana de Ciencias Políticas y Sociales* 39 (157): 9–23 (July–September).

Murgialday, Clara. 1996. "Mujeres, transición democrática y elecciones: El Salvador en tiempos de posguerra," *Nueva Sociedad* 141: 34–42 (January–February).

Myers, David J. 1986. "The Venezuelan Party System: Regime Maintenance Under Stress," in John D. Martz and David J. Myers, eds., *Venezuela: The Democratic Experience,* rev. ed. (New York: Praeger), pp. 109–147.

———. 1995. "Perceptions of a Stressed Democracy: Inevitable Decay or Foundation for Rebirth?" in Jennifer McCoy, Andrés Serbin, William C. Smith, and Andrés Stambouli, eds. *Venezuelan Democracy Under Stress* (New Brunswick, N.J.: Transaction), pp. 107–138.

NACLA (North American Congress on Latin America). 1982. "Dominican Republic: The Launching of Democracy?" *Report on the Americas* 16 (6): 2–35 (November–December).

———. 1987. "Haiti: Plus ça Change . . ." *Report on the Americas* 21 (3): 14–39 (May–June).

———. 1991. "Bolivia: The Poverty of Progress," *Report on the Americas* 25 (1): 10–38 (July).

———. 1994a. "Haiti: Dangerous Crossroads," *Report on the Americas* 27 (4): 15–53 (January–February).

———. 1994b. "Mexico Out of Balance," *Report on the Americas* 28 (1): 17–51 (July–August).

———. 1995a. "Brazil: The Persistence of Inequality," *Report on the Americas* 28 (6): 16–45 (May–June).

———. 1995b. "Cuba Adapting to a Post-Soviet Word," *Report on the Americas* 29 (2): 6–48 (September–October).

———. 1996a. "In Pursuit of Profit: A Primer on the New Transnational Investment," *Report on the Americas* 29 (4): 10–41 (January–February).

———. 1996b. "Gaining Ground: The Indigenous Movement in Latin America," *Report on the Americas* 29 (5): 14–43 (March–April) .

———. 1996c. "Rhetoric and Reality: The World Bank's New Concern for the Poor," *Report on the Americas* 29 (6): 15–43 (May–June).

———. 1996d. "Privilege and Power in Fujimori's Peru," *Report on the Americas* 30 (1): 15–43 (July–August).

———. 1997. "Contesting Mexico," *Report on the Americas* 30 (4): 13–40 (January–February).

Naím, Moisés. 1995. "Latin America the Morning After," *Foreign Affairs* 74 (4): 45–61.

Naím, Moisés, and Antonio Francés. 1995. "The Venezuelan Private Sector: From Courting the State to Courting the Market," in Louis W. Goodman, Johanna Mendelson Forman, Moisés Naím, Joseph Tulchin, and Gary Bland, eds., *Lessons of the Venezuelan Experience* (Baltimore: Johns Hopkins University Press).

Nash, June. 1995. "The Reassertion of Indigenous Identity: Mayan Responses to State Intervention in Chiapas," *Latin American Research Review* 30 (3): 7–42.

Needler, Martin C. 1987. *The Problem of Democracy in Latin America* (Lexington, Mass.: Heath).

Nef, Jorge, and Nibaldo Galleguillos. 1995. "Legislatures and Democratic Transitions in Latin America: The Chilean Case," in David Close, ed., *Legislatures and the New Democracies in Latin America* (Boulder: Lynne Rienner), pp. 113–136.

Novaro, Marcos. 1994a. "Menemismo y peronismo: Viejo y nuevo populismo," *Cuadernos del CLAEH* 71: 55–78.

―――. 1994b. *Pilotos de tormentas: Crisis de representación y personalización de la política en Argentina (1989–1993)* (Buenos Aires: Letra Buena).

Nunn, Frederick. 1976. *The Military in Chilean History* (Albuquerque: University of New Mexico Press).

Oconitrillo, Eduardo. 1982. *Un siglo de política costarricense* (San José: Ed. Universidad Estatal a Distancia).

O'Donnell, Guillermo. 1979. *Modernization and Bureaucratic-Authoritarianism*, 2d ed. (Berkeley: Institute of International Studies, University of California).

―――. 1994. "Delegative Democracy," *Journal of Democracy* 5: 55–69.

―――. 1996. "Illusions About Consolidation," *Journal of Democracy* 7 (2): 34–51; see also related debate in *Journal of Democracy* 7 (4): 151–168.

O'Donnell, Guillermo, and Philippe Schmitter. 1986. *Tentative Conclusions About Uncertain Democracies,* vol. 4 of O'Donnell, Schmitter, and Laurence Whitehead, eds., *Transitions from Authoritarian Rule* (Baltimore: Johns Hopkins University Press).

O'Donnell, Guillermo, Philippe Schmitter, and Laurence Whitehead, eds. 1986. *Transitions from Authoritarian Rule* (Baltimore: Johns Hopkins University Press).

Oppenheim, Lois Hecht. 1993. *Politics in Chile: Democracy, Authoritarianism, and the Search for Development* (Boulder: Westview).

Oquist, Paul. 1980. *Violence, Conflict, and Politics in Colombia* (New York: Academic Press).

Osorio, Jaime. 1990. *Raíces de la democracia en Chile, 1850–1970* (México: Ediciones Era).

Ostrogorski, M. 1974. *Democracy and the Organization of Political Parties* (New York: Ayer).

Oxhorn, Philip. 1995. *Organizing Civil Society: The Popular Sectors and the Struggle for Democracy in Chile* (University Park: Pennsylvania State University Press).

Pacheco Méndez, Guadalupe. 1995. "El nuevo mapa electoral: Dos partidos y medio," *Nexos* 18 (209): 14–17 (May).

Paine, Thomas. 1995. *Collected Writings* (New York: Library of America).

Palmer, David Scott. 1980. *Peru: The Authoritarian Tradition* (New York: Praeger).

Pangle, Thomas. 1992. *The Ennobling of Democracy: The Challenge of the Postmodern Era* (Baltimore: Johns Hopkins University Press).

Panizza, Francisco. 1990. *Uruguay: Batllismo y después* (Montevideo: Ediciones de la Banda Oriental).

Pareto, Vilfredo. 1984. *The Transformation of Democracy*, Charles Powers, ed. (New Brunswick, N.J.: Transaction).

Pastor, Robert. 1992. *Whirlpool: U.S. Foreign Policy Toward Latin America and the Caribbean* (Princeton: Princeton University Press).

―――, ed. 1989. *Democracy in the Americas: Stopping the Pendulum* (New York: Homes and Meier).

Pastrana Borrero, Misael. 1991. "La Constituyente de la Paz," *Revista Javeriana* 59 (578): 165–173 (September).

Paternostro, Silvana. 1995. "Mexico as a Narco-Democracy," *World Policy Journal* 12 (1): 41–48 (Spring).

Payne, Stanley. 1973. *A History of Spain and Portugal*, 2 vols. (Madison: University of Wisconsin Press).

Paz, Juan Gervasio. 1995. "La hegemonía conservadora en la Argentina de los '90," *Realidad Económica* 132: 22–27 (May–June).

Paz Aguilar, Ernesto. 1992. "The Origin and Development of Political Parties in Honduras," in Louis W. Goodman, William LeoGrande, and Johanna Mendelson Forman, eds., *Political Parties and Democracy in Central America* (Boulder: Westview), pp. 161–174.

Peckenham, Nancy, and Annie Street, eds. 1985. *Honduras: Portrait of a Captive Nation* (New York: Praeger).

Peeler, John A. 1976. "Columbian Parties and Political Development," *Journal of Interamerican Studies and World Affairs* 18: 203–224.

———. 1985. *Latin American Democracies: Colombia, Costa Rica, Venezuela* (Chapel Hill: University of North Carolina Press).

———. 1992. "Elite Settlements and Democratic Consolidation: Colombia, Costa Rica, and Venezuela," in John Higley and Richard Gunther, eds., *Elites and Democratic Consolidation in Latin America and Southern Europe* (Cambridge: Cambridge University Press), pp. 81–112.

———. 1995a. "Decay and Renewal in Democratic Regimes: Colombia and Venezuela," *MACLAS Latin American Essays* 9: 135–152.

———. 1995b. "Elites and Democracy in Central America," in Mitchell A. Seligson and John A. Booth, eds., *Elections and Democracy in Central America Revisited* (Chapel Hill: University of North Carolina Press), pp. 244–263.

Perelli, Carina, Sonia Picado S., and Daniel Zovatto, eds. 1995. *Partidos y clase política en América Latina en los 90* (San José: IIDH/CAPEL).

Pérez, Louis. 1995. *Cuba: Beween Reform and Revolution,* 2d ed. (New York: Oxford University Press).

Pérez, Orlando. 1995. "Elections Under Crisis: Background to Panama in the 1980s," in Mitchell A. Seligson and John A. Booth, eds., *Elections and Democracy in Central America Revisited* (Chapel Hill: University of North Carolina Press), pp. 123–147.

Pérez Brignoli, Héctor. 1987. *Breve historia de Centroamérica* (Madrid: Alianza).

Pérez-Stable, Marifeli. 1993. *The Cuban Revolution: Origins, Course, and Legacy* (New York: Oxford University Press).

———. 1994. "Ciento veinticinco años de lucha: El nacionalismo cubano y la democracia política hacia el siglo XXI," *Estudios Internacionales* 27 (107–108): 335–348 (July–December).

Petras, James. 1969. *Politics and Social Forces in Chilean Development* (Berkeley: University of California Press).

Petras, James, and Fernando Ignacio Leiva, with Henry Veltmeyer. 1994. *Democracy and Poverty in Chile: The Limits to Electoral Politics* (Boulder: Westview).

Phelan, John. 1978. *The People and the King: The Comunero Revolt in Colombia, 1781* (Madison: University of Wisconsin Press).

Pimenta, Cornelio Octavio Pinheiro. 1989–1990. "Estudo Comparativo da Constituição de 1988," *Revista de Ciencia Politica*, pt. 1, 32 (3): 67–93 (May–July 1989); pt. 2, 32 (4): 123–169 (August–October 1989); pt. 3, 33 (1: 102–152 November 1989–January 1990).

Pizarro, Eduardo, and Ana María Bejarano. 1994. "Colombia: Neoliberalismo moderado y liberalismo socialdemócrata," *Nueva Sociedad* 133: 12–19 (September–October).

Plato. 1983. *The Republic,* Benjamin Jowett, trans. (New York: Random House).

Pole, J. R., ed. 1987. *The American Constitution, For and Against: The Federalist and Anti-Federalist Papers* (New York: Hill and Wang).

Polity Forum. 1995. "Institutions and Institutionalism," *Polity* 28: 81–140.

Pool, John, Patrice Franko-Jones, and Stephen Stamos. 1991. *The ABCs of International Finance,* 2d ed. (Lexington, Mass.: Lexington Books).

Pottenger, John. 1989. *The Political Theory of Liberation Theology* (Albany: State University of New York Press).

Prevost, Gary. 1991. "The FSLN as Ruling Party," in Thomas W. Walker, ed., *Revolution and Counterrevolution in Nicaragua* (Boulder: Westview), pp. 101–116.

Priestley, George. 1986. *Military Government and Popular Participation in Panama: The Torrijos Regime, 1968–1975* (Boulder: Westview).

Przeworski, Adam. 1991. *Democracy and the Market: Political and Economic Reforms in Eastern Europe and Latin America* (Cambridge: Cambridge University Press).

Przeworski, Adam, et al. 1996. "What Makes Democracies Endure?" *Journal of Democracy* 7 (1): 39–55.

Puryear, Jeffrey. 1994. *Thinking Politics: Intellectuals and Democracy in Chile, 1973–1988* (Baltimore: Johns Hopkins University Press).

Putnam, Robert. 1993. *Making Democracy Work: Civic Traditions in Modern Italy* (Princeton: Princeton University Press).

Quintero, Rafael, and Erika Silva. 1995. *Ecuador: Una nación en ciernes* (Quito: Editorial Universitaria).

Ramírez Necochea, Hernán. 1985. *Fuerzas Armadas y política en Chile* (Havana: Casa de las Américas).

Reed, Gail. 1995. "Elections in Cuba," Peacenet, Reg. Cuba, 13 July.

Reiter, Frederick. 1995. *They Built Utopia: The Jesuit Missions in Paraguay, 1610–1768* (Potomac, Md.: Scripta Humanistica).

Remmer, Karen. 1984. *Party Competition in Argentina and Chile* (Lincoln: University of Nebraska Press).

———. 1990. "Democracy and Economic Crisis: The Latin American Experience," *World Politics* 42: 315–335.

———. 1991a. "New Wine or Old Bottlenecks? The Study of Latin American Democracy," *Comparative Politics* 23: 479–495.

———. 1991b. "The Political Impact of Economic Crisis in Latin America in the 1980s," *American Political Science Review* 85: 777–800.

———. 1993. "The Political Economy of Elections in Latin America, 1980–1991," *American Political Science Review* 87: 393–407.

Restrepo, Darío. 1992. "El trasfondo político de la constitución política de Colombia," *Revista Interamericana de Planificación* 25 (99–100): 17–43 (July–December).

Rial, Juan. 1986. "The Uruguayan Elections of 1984: A Triumph of the Center," in Paul Drake and Eduardo Silva, eds., *Elections and Democratization in Latin America, 1980–1985* (San Diego: Center for Iberian and Latin American Studies), pp. 245–272.

Richard, Patricia Bayer, and John A. Booth. 1995. "Election Observation and Democratization: Reflections on the Nicaraguan Case," in Mitchell A. Seligson and John A. Booth, eds., *Elections and Democracy in Central America Revisited* (Chapel Hill: University of North Carolina Press), pp. 202–223.

Riemer, Neal. 1996. *Creative Breakthroughs in Politics* (Westport, Conn.: Praeger).

Rizzo de Oliveira, Eliézer. 1988. "O papel das forças armadas na nova constituição e no futuro da democracia no Brasil," *Vozes* 82 (2): 21–27 (July–December).

Rock, David. 1987. *Argentina, 1516–1987* (Berkeley: University of California Press).

Roett, Riordan, ed. 1995. *The Challenge of Institutional Reform in Mexico* (Boulder: Lynne Rienner).

Roett, Riordan, and Richard Scott Sacks. 1991. *Paraguay: The Personalist Legacy* (Boulder: Westview).

Rohter, Larry. 1996a. "Cables Show U.S. Deception on Haitian Violence," *New York Times*, 6 February, p. A8.

———. 1996b. "Cuban Communists Take Harder Line," *New York Times*, 31 March, pp. 1, 12.

———. 1996c. "Guatemalans Formally End 36-Year Civil War," *New York Times*, Internet edition, 30 December.

Rojas Aravena, Francisco, and Luis Guillermo Solís. 1988. *¿Súbditos o aliados? La política exterior de Estados Unidos y Centroamérica* (San José: FLACSO).

Rojas Bolaños, Manuel, and Carlos Sojo. 1995. *El malestar con la política* (San José: FLACSO).

Roman, Peter. 1995. "Workers' Parliaments in Cuba," *Latin American Perspectives* 22 (4): 43–58 (Fall).

Romero, Aníbal. 1996. "Venezuela: Democracy Hangs On," *Journal of Democracy* 7 (4): 30–42.

Ropp, Steve C. 1982. *Panamanian Politics* (New York: Praeger).

———. 1996. "Panama: Cycles of Elitist Democracy and Authoritarian Populism," in Howard Wiarda and Harvey Kline, eds., *Latin American Politics and Development*, 4th ed. (Boulder: Westview), pp. 507–517.

———. 1997. "Panama: Tailoring a New Image," *Current History* 96 (607): 55–60 (February).

Rosada Granados, Héctor. 1992. "Parties, Transitions, and the Political System in Guatemala," in Louis W. Goodman, William LeoGrande, and Johanna Mendelson Forman, eds., *Political Parties and Democracy in Central America* (Boulder: Westview), pp. 89–110.

Rosario Adames, Fausto. 1996a. "Old Enemies Unite," *Latinamerica Press*, 13 June, p. 5.

———. 1996b. "A New Era Begins," *Latinamerica Press*, 11 July, p. 5.

Rosen, Fred. 1996a. "The PRI's Protection Racket: Maintaining Control at the Grassroots," *NACLA Report on the Americas* 29 (5): 10–13 (March–April).

———. 1996b. "Zapatistas' New Political Organization Prompts Realignments on the Left," *NACLA Report on the Americas* 29 (5): 2, 45 (March–April).

Rosenberg, Mark. 1989. "Can Democracy Survive the Democrats? From Transition to Consolidation in Honduras," in John A. Booth and Mitchell A. Seligson, eds., *Elections and Democracy in Central America* (Chapel Hill: University of North Carolina Press), pp. 40–59.

———. 1995. "Democracy in Honduras: The Electoral and the Political Reality," in Mitchell A. Seligson and John A. Booth, eds., *Elections and Democracy in Central America Revisited* (Chapel Hill: University of North Carolina Press), pp. 66–83.

Rottenberg, Simon, ed. 1993. *Costa Rica and Uruguay* (New York: World Bank).

Rouquié, Alain. 1990. *Extremo occidente: Introducción a América Latina* (Buenos Aires: Emecé).

———. 1994. *Autoritarismos y democracia: Estudios de política argentina* (Buenos Aires: Edicial).

Rovira Mas, Jorge. 1987. *Costa Rica en los años 80* (San José: Ed. Porvenir).

———. 1988. *Estado y política económica en Costa Rica, 1948–1970* (San José: Ed. Porvenir).

———. 1992. "Elecciones y democracia en Centroamérica y República Dominicana: Un análisis introductorio," in Rodolfo Cerdas-Cruz, Juan Rial, and Daniel Zovatto, eds., *Una tarea inconclusa: Elecciones y democracia en América Latina, 1988–1991* (San José: Instituto Interamericano de Derechos Humanos/Centro de Asesoría y Promoción Electoral).

———. 1994. "Costa Rica 1994: ¿Hacia la consolidación del bipartidismo?" *Espacios: Revista Centroamericana de Cultura Política* 7: 38–47 (July–September).

Ruchwarger, Gary. 1987. *People in Power: Forging a Grassroots Democracy in Nicaragua* (South Hadley, Mass.: Bergin and Garvey).

Rudolph, James D. 1992. *Peru: The Evolution of a Crisis* (Westport, Conn.: Praeger).

Rueschemeyer, Dietrich, Evelyne Huber Stephens, and John Stephens. 1992. *Capitalist Development and Democracy* (Chicago: University of Chicago Press).

Ruhl, J. Mark. 1997. "Doubting Democracy in Honduras," *Current History* 96 (607): 81–86 (February).

Saffirio S., Eduardo. 1994. "El sistema de partidos y la sociedad civil en la redemocratización chilena," *Estudios Sociales* 82: 63–113 (October–December).

Sagasti, Francisco, and Max Hernández. 1993–1994. "La crisis de gobernabilidad democrática en el Perú," *Debate* 16 (75): 24–28 (December–January).

Salamanca, Luis. 1994. "Venezuela: La crisis del rentismo," *Nueva Sociedad* 131: 10–19 (May–June).

Salcedo-Bastardo, J. L. 1979. *Historia fundamental de Venezuela* (Caracas: Fundación Gran Mariscal de Ayacucho).

Salom, Roberto. 1987. *La crisis de la izquierda en Costa Rica* (San José: Ed. Porvenir).

———. 1996. "Costa Rica: Ajuste y pacto político," *Nueva Sociedad* 142: 11–15 (March–April).

Salomón, Leticia. 1996. "Honduras: Los retos de la democracia," *Nueva Sociedad* 141: 10–14 (January–February).

Sánchez Parga, José. 1993. "Ecuador en el engranaje neoliberal," *Nueva Sociedad* 123: 12–17 (January–February).

Santamaría S., Ricardo, and Gabriel Silva Lujan. 1986. *Proceso político en Colombia: Del Frente Nacional a la Apertura Democrática* (Bogotá: Fondo Editorial CEREC).

Schemo, Diana Jean. 1997. "Ecuadorian Crisis over Presidency Ends Peacefully," *New York Times,* Internet edition, 10 February.

Schifter, Jacobo. 1979. *La fase oculta de la Guerra Civil en Costa Rica* (San José: EDUCA).

———. 1986. *Las alianzas conflictivas* (San José: Libro Libre).

Schlesinger, Stephen, and Stephen Kinzer. 1982. *Bitter Fruit: The Untold Story of the American Coup in Guatemala* (Garden City, N.Y.: Anchor).

Schmidt, Gregory. 1996. "Fujimori's 1990 Upset Victory in Peru: Electoral Rules, Contingencies, and Adaptive Strategies," *Comparative Politics* 28: 321–354 (April).

Schmidt, Samuel. 1986. *El deterioro del presidencialismo mexicano: Los años de Luis Echeverría* (México: Edamex).

Schneider, Ronald. 1996. *Brazil: Culture and Politics in a New Industrial Powerhouse* (Boulder: Westview).

Schoultz, Lars. 1981. *Human Rights and United States Policy Toward Latin America* (Princeton: Princeton University Press).

———. 1987. *National Security and United States Policy Toward Latin America* (Princeton: Princeton University Press).

Schulz, Donald E., and Edward J. Williams, eds. 1995. *Mexico Faces the 21st Century* (Westport, Conn.: Praeger).

Schumpeter, Joseph. 1950. *Capitalism, Socialism, and Democracy,* 3d ed. (New York: Harper).

Scully, Timothy R. 1992. *Rethinking the Center: Party Politics in Nineteenth- and Twentieth-Century Chile* (Stanford: Stanford University Press).
———. 1995. "Reconstituting Party Politics in Chile," in Scott Mainwaring and Timothy Scully, eds., *Building Democratic Institutions: Party Systems in Latin America* (Stanford: Stanford University Press), pp. 100–137.
Selbin, Eric. 1993. *Modern Latin American Revolutions* (Boulder: Westview).
Seligson, Mitchell A., and John A. Booth, eds. 1995. *Elections and Democracy in Central America Revisited* (Chapel Hill: University of North Carolina Press).
Sharpless, Richard. 1978. *Gaitán of Colombia: A Political Biography* (Pittsburgh: University of Pittsburgh Press).
Silva, Eduardo. 1996. "From Dictatorship to Democracy: The Business-State Nexus in Chile's Economic Transformation, 1975–1994," *Comparative Politics* 28: 299–320 (April).
Silva Michelena, José A. 1971. *The Illusion of Democracy in Dependent Nations*, Vol. 3 of Frank Bonilla and Silva Michelena, eds., *The Politics of Change in Venezuela* (Cambridge: Massachusetts Institute of Technology Press).
Simons, Geoff. 1996. *Cuba: From Conquistadors to Castro* (New York: St. Martin's).
Skocpol, Theda. 1994. *Social Revolutions in the Modern World* (Cambridge: Cambridge University Press).
Small, Melvin, and William Hoover, eds. 1992. *Give Peace a Chance: Exploring the Vietnam Antiwar Movement* (Syracuse: Syracuse University Press).
Smith, Adam. 1952. *An Inquiry into the Nature and Causes of the Wealth of Nations* (Chicago: Encyclopaedia Britannica).
Smith, David. 1992. "Panama: Political Parties, Social Crisis, and Democracy in the 1980s," in Louis W. Goodman, William LeoGrande, and Johanna Mendelson Forman, eds., *Political Parties and Democracy in Central America* (Boulder: Westview), pp. 213–233.
Smith, Lois, and Alfred Padula. 1996. *Sex and Revolution: Women in Socialist Cuba* (New York: Oxford University Press).
Smith, William C., Carlos H. Acuña, and Eduardo A. Gamarra, eds. 1994a. *Democracy, Markets, and Structural Reform in Latin America: Argentina, Bolivia, Brazil, Chile, and Mexico* (New Brunswick, N.J.: Transaction).
———. 1994b. *Latin American Political Economy in the Age of Neoliberal Reform* (New Brunswick, N.J.: Transaction).
Soares, Glaucio Ary Dillon. 1986. "Elections and the Redemocratization of Brazil," in Paul Drake and Eduardo Silva, eds., *Elections and Democratization in Latin America, 1980–1985* (San Diego: Center for Iberian and Latin American Studies), pp. 273–298.
Sojo, Carlos. 1995a. *Al arbitrio del mercado: Reformas económicas y gobernabilidad en Centroamérica* (San José: FLACSO).
———. 1995b. "Gobernabilidad y ajuste en Centroamérica," *Nueva Sociedad* 138: 6–16 (July–August).
Sondrol, Paul C. 1992. "The Emerging New Politics of Liberalizing Paraguay: Sustained Civil-Military Control Without Democracy," *Journal of Inter-American Studies and World Affairs* 34 (2): 127–163.
Spinoza, Benedict de. 1951. *Chief Works*, 2 vols. (New York: Dover).
Stallings, Barbara, and Robert Kaufman, eds. 1989. *Debt and Democracy in Latin America* (Boulder: Westview).
Stamos, Stephen C., and John Pool. 1989. *International Economic Policy: Beyond the Trade and Debt Crisis* (Lexington, Mass.: Lexington Books).
Stein, Eduardo, and Salvador Arias Peñate, coords. 1992. *Democracia sin pobreza: Alternativa de desarrollo para el istmo centroamericano* (San José: DEI).

Stepan, Alfred. 1978. *The State and Society: Peru in Comparative Perspective* (Princeton: Princeton University Press).
———. 1988. *Rethinking Military Politics: Brazil and the Southern Cone* (Princeton: Princeton University Press).
Stepan, Alfred, and Cindy Skach. 1993. "Constitutional Frameworks and Democratic Consolidation: Parliamentarism Versus Presidentialism," *World Politics* 46: 1–22.
———. 1994. "Presidentialism and Parliamentarism in Comparative Perspective," in Juan Linz and Arturo Valenzuela, eds., *The Failure of Presidential Democracy* (Baltimore: Johns Hopkins University Press), pp. 119–136.
Stepan, Alfred, ed. 1989. *Democratizing Brazil: Problems of Transition and Consolidation* (New York: Oxford University Press).
Stephen, Lynn. 1995. "The Zapatista Army of National Liberation and the National Democratic Convention," *Latin American Perspectives* 22 (4): 88–100.
Stokes, Susan. 1997. "Democratic Accountability and Policy Change: Economic Policy in Fujimori's Peru," *Comparative Politics* 29: 209–228.
Stone, Samuel. 1975. *La dinastía de los conquistadores: La crisis de poder en la Costa Rica contemporánea* (San José: Ed. Universidad de Costa Rica).
Tarrow, Sidney. 1994. *Power in Movement: Social Movements, Collective Action, and Politics* (Cambridge: Cambridge University Press).
Thibaut, Bernard. 1993. "Presidencialismo, parlamentarismo y el problema de la consolidación democrática en América Latina," *Estudios Internacionales* 26 (102): 216–252 (April–June).
Thoumi, Francisco. 1995. *Political Economy and Illegal Drugs in Colombia* (Boulder: Lynne Rienner).
Tirado López, Victor. 1986. *Nicaragua: Una nueva democracia en el tercer mundo* (Managua: Vanguardia).
Tocqueville, Alexis de. 1980. *Alexis de Tocqueville on Democracy, Revolution, and Society: Selected Writings,* John Stone and Stephen Mennell, eds. (Chicago: University of Chicago Press).
———. 1988. *Democracy in America* (New York: Harper and Row).
Tonkin, John. 1971. *The Church and the Secular Order in Reformation Thought* (New York: Columbia University Press).
Tönnies, Ferdinand. 1971. *Ferdinand Tönnies on Sociology* (Chicago: University of Chicago Press).
Torres, Rosa María, and José Luis Coraggio. 1987. *Transición y crisis en Nicaragua* (San José: DEI).
Torres Rivas, Edelberto. 1993. *History and Society in Central America* (Austin: University of Texas Press).
Trend, David, ed. 1996. *Radical Democracy: Identity, Citizenship, and the State* (New York: Routledge).
Trindade, Hélgio, org. 1992. *Reforma eleitoral e representação política* (Porto Alegre: Ed. da Universidade).
Truman, David. 1951. *The Governmental Process: Political Interests and Public Opinion* (New York: Knopf).
Tucker, Robert C., ed. 1978. *The Marx-Engels Reader,* 2d ed. (New York: Norton).
Tulchin, Joseph, ed. 1995. *The Consolidation of Democracy in Latin America* (Boulder: Lynne Rienner).
U.S. Senate. 1975. *Covert Action in Chile, 1963–1973 (Staff Report, Select Committee on Governmental Operations with Respect to Intelligence Activities)* (Washington: Government Printing Office).
Vacs, Aldo C. 1987. "Authoritarian Breakdown and Redemocratization in Argentina," in James Malloy and Mitchell Seligson, eds., *Authoritarians and*

Democrats: Regime Transition in Latin America (Pittsburgh: University of Pittsburgh Press), pp. 15–42.

Valenzuela, Arturo. 1978. *The Breakdown of Democratic Regimes: Chile* (Baltimore: Johns Hopkins University Press).

———. 1989. "Chile: Origins, Consolidation, and Breakdown of a Democratic Regime," in Larry Diamond, Juan J. Linz, and Seymour Martin Lipset, eds., *Democracy in Developing Countries* (Boulder: Lynne Rienner), pp. 159–206.

Valenzuela, Arturo, and J. Samuel Valenzuela, eds. 1986. *Military Rule in Chile: Dictatorship and Oppositions* (Baltimore: Johns Hopkins University Press).

Van Parijs, Philippe. 1995. *Real Freedom for All: What (If Anything) Can Justify Capitalism?* (Oxford: Clarendon).

Vanger, Milton. 1980. *The Model Country: José Batlle y Ordóñez of Uruguay, 1907–1915* (Hanover, N.H.: University Press of New England).

Vanhanen, Tatu. 1994. "Global Trends of Democratization in the 1990s: A Statistical Analysis," paper presented at the International Political Science Association meeting, Berlin.

Vargas, Oscar René. 1995. "Nicaragua: Peligra la consolidación democrática," *Nueva Sociedad* 137: 10–16.

Veblen, Thorstein. 1934. *The Theory of the Leisure Class* (New York: Modern Library).

Vega Carballo, José Luis. 1982. *Poder político y democracia en Costa Rica* (San José: Ed. Porvenir).

———. 1992. "Party Systems and Democracy in Costa Rica," in Louis W. Goodman, William LeoGrande, and Johanna Mendelson Forman, eds., *Political Parties and Democracy in Central America* (Boulder: Westview), pp. 203–212.

Velarde, Federico. 1995. "Perú: La reelección de abril," *Nueva Sociedad* 139: 13–18.

Vélez Rodríguez, Ricardo. 1987. "Constituinte e Tradições Politicas Brasileiras," *Convivium* 30 (2): 150–161 (March–April).

Véliz, Claudio. 1980. *The Centralist Tradition of Latin America* (Princeton: Princeton University Press).

Vilas, Carlos. 1993. "The Hour of Civil Society," *NACLA Report on the Americas* 27 (2): 38–42.

———. 1995a. "Economic Restructuring, Neoliberal Reforms, and the Working Class in Latin America," in Sandor Halebsky and Richard Harris, eds., *Capital, Power, and Inequality in Latin America* (Boulder: Westview), pp. 137–164.

———, coord. 1995b. *Estado y políticas sociales después del ajuste* (Caracas: Nueva Sociedad).

von Mettenheim, Kurt, ed. 1997. *Presidential Institutions and Democratic Politics: Comparing Regional and National Contexts* (Baltimore: Johns Hopkins University Press).

Vunderink, Gregg. 1991. "Peasant Participation and Mobilization During Economic Crisis: The Case of Costa Rica," *Studies in Comparative International Development* 25 (4): 3–34.

Wahl, Rainer. 1986. "A Primazia da Constituição," *Revista de Ciencia Politica* 29 (3) 9–34 (July–September).

Waisman, Carlos. 1992. "Capitalism, the Market, and Democracy," in Gary Marks and Larry Diamond, eds., *Reexamining Democracy* (Newbury Park, Calif.: Sage), pp. 140–155.

Walker, Thomas W., ed. 1986. *Nicaragua: The First Five Years* (New York: Praeger).

———. 1991. *Revolution and Counterrevolution in Nicaragua* (Boulder: Westview).

Wallerstein, Immanuel. 1974. *The Modern World-System* (New York: Academic Press).

Walsh, Edward T. 1996. "An Embargo's Devastating Impact on Higher Education in Cuba," *Chronicle of Higher Education,* 22 March, pp. B1–2.

Walton, John. 1984. *Reluctant Rebels: Comparative Studies of Revolution and Underdevelopment* (New York: Columbia University Press).

Walzer, Michael. 1965. *The Revolution of the Saints: A Study in the Evolution of Radical Politics* (Cambridge: Harvard University Press).

Warren, Mark. 1992. "Democratic Theory and Self-Transformation," *American Political Science Review* 86: 8–23 (March).

———. 1996. "Deliberative Democracy and Authority." *American Political Science Review* 90: 46- 60 (March).

Weaver, Eric, and William Barnes. 1991. "Opposition Parties and Coalitions," in Thomas W. Walker, ed., *Revolution and Counterrevolution in Nicaragua* (Boulder: Westview), pp. 117–142.

Weaver, Frederick Stirton. 1994. *Inside the Volcano: The History and Political Economy of Central America* (Boulder: Westview).

Weber, Max. 1983. *Max Weber on Capitalism, Bureaucracy, and Religion,* Stanislav Andreski, ed. (London: Allen and Unwin).

Weeks, John. 1995. "The Contemporary Latin American Economies: Neoliberal Reconstruction," in Sandor Halebsky and Richard Harris, eds., *Capital, Power, and Inequality in Latin America* (Boulder: Westview), pp. 109–136.

Weinstein, Martin. 1988. *Uruguay: Democracy at the Crossroads* (Boulder: Westview).

———. 1995. "Uruguay: The Legislature and the Reconstitution of Democracy," in David Close, ed., *Legislatures and the New Democracies in Latin America* (Boulder: Lynne Rienner), pp. 137–150.

Whitehead, Laurence. 1994. "Liberalización económica y consolidación de la democracia," in Georges Couffignal, comp., *Democracias posibles: El desafío latinoamericano* (Buenos Aires: Fondo de Cultura Económica), pp. 129–148.

———, ed. 1996. *The International Dimensions of Democratization: Europe and the Americas* (Oxford: Oxford University Press).

Wiarda, Howard. 1990. *The Democratic Revolution in Latin America: History, Politics, and U.S. Policy* (New York: Holmes and Meier).

———, ed. 1992. *Politics and Social Change in Latin America: Still a Distinct Tradition?* (Boulder: Westview).

Wiarda, Howard, and Harvey Kline, eds. 1996. *Latin American Politics and Development,* 4th ed. (Boulder: Westview).

Wickham-Crowley, Timothy. 1991. *Exploring Revolution: Essays on Latin American Insurgency and Revolutionary Theory* (Armonk, N.Y.: M. E. Sharpe).

———. 1992. *Guerrillas and Revolution in Latin America: A Comparative Study of Insurgents and Regimes Since 1956* (Princeton: Princeton University Press).

Wilkinson, Bertie, ed. 1972. *The Creation of Medieval Parliaments* (New York: Wiley).

Williams, Eric. 1984. *From Columbus to Castro: The History of the Caribbean* (New York: Vintage).

Williams, Philip J. 1994. "Dual Transitions from Authoritarian Rule: Popular and Electoral Democracy in Nicaragua," *Comparative Politics* 26: 169–185.

Williamson, Edwin. 1992. *The Penguin History of Latin America* (London: Penguin).

Williamson, John, ed. 1990. *Latin American Adjustment: How Much Has Happened?* (Washington: Institute for International Economics).

Wilson, Woodrow. 1885. *Congressional Government* (Boston: Houghton Mifflin).

Winson, Anthony. 1989. *Coffee and Democracy in Modern Costa Rica* (New York: St. Martin's).

Woldenburg, José. 1995. "México: Los partidos en un momento de transición política," in Carina Perelli et al., eds. *Partidos y clase política en América Latina en los 90* (San José: IIDH/CAPEL), pp. 415–436.

Wollstonecraft, Mary. 1929. *A Vindication of the Rights of Woman* (New York: Dutton).

Wolter, Matilde. 1993. "Chile renueva su democracia," *Nueva Sociedad* 128: 6–11.

Woodward, Ralph Lee. 1993. *Rafael Carrera and the Emergence of the Republic of Guatemala* (Athens: University of Georgia Press).

World Bank. 1991. *World Development Report: The Challenge of Development* (New York: Oxford University Press).

Wynia, Gary W. 1986. *Argentina: Illusions and Realities* (New York: Holmes and Meier).

———. 1995. "Argentina's New Democracy: Presidential Power and Legislative Limits," in David Close, ed., *Legislatures and the New Democracies in Latin America* (Boulder: Lynne Rienner), pp. 71–88.

Yashar, Deborah. 1995. "Civil War and Social Welfare: The Origins of Costa Rica's Competitive Party System," in Scott Mainwaring and Timothy Scully, eds., *Building Democratic Institutions: Party Systems in Latin America* (Stanford: Stanford University Press), pp. 72–99.

———. 1997. *Demanding Democracy: Reform and Reaction in Costa Rica and Guatemala, 1870s–1950s* (Stanford: Stanford University Press).

Zeitlin, Maurice. 1984. *The Civil Wars in Chile* (Princeton: Princeton University Press).

Zeitlin, Maurice, and Richard Ratcliff. 1988. *Landlords and Capitalists: The Dominant Class of Chile* (Princeton: Princeton University Press).

Zermeño, Sergio. 1995. "Zapatismo: Región y nación," *Nueva Sociedad* 140: 51–57 (November–December).

Index

Absolutism, 5, 6, 26–28, 33–34
Action, xii, 21, 30, 97, 160–162, 190–191
AD. *See* Democratic Action
ADN. *See* National Democratic Alliance
Alessandri, Arturo, 45–46, 67
Alfonsín, Raúl, 79, 82, 94, 98, 143, 147
Allende, Salvador, 61, 145, 151
Almond, Gabriel, 15
American Popular Revolutionary Alliance
  (APRA) (Peru), 177
APRA. *See* American Popular Revolutionary
  Alliance
Aquinas, Thomas, 3, 22(n3), 33
Arbenz, Jacobo, 89
ARENA. *See* National Renewal Alliance
Arévalo, Juan José, 71(n11)
Argaña, Luis Maria, 112
Argentina, 43, 68, 72(n31), 79, 94–95, 167,
  191; Austral Plan, 143, 147; economy,
  143, 147, 152, 176; extrication model,
  80, 82; Malvinas/Falklands War, 94, 98,
  147; party system, 175–176; Peronists,
  94–95, 175–176
Arias, Arnulfo, 77, 78, 178
Arias Sánchez, Oscar, 63, 72(n23), 174
Aristide, Jean-Bertrand, 81, 93, 103(n45),
  178–179
Aristotle, 1–2, 3, 41(n22), 155, 196
Arzú, Alvaro, 90
Augustine, 2–3
Auténtico Party (Cuba), 126, 139(n26)
Authoritarian regimes, 14, 105, 137(n1);
  armed forces, 76-77; destabilization and,
  106; extrication model, 79–80, 82, 107;
  of 1970s, 75–78; nineteenth-century
  roots, 43–44; positivism and, 29–31;
  social movements and, 156–157. *See also*
  Caudillismo
Authority: institutionalization and, 181–182;
  liberal democracy and, 12, 29; medieval

tradition, 26, 33, 34; popular resistance to,
  35–40
Aylwin, Patricio, 85, 142, 146

Bachrach, Peter, 15
Balaguer, Joaquín, 76, 92–93, 143, 178
Banzer, Hugo, 76, 77, 80, 85, 144, 177
Barber, Benjamin, 17
Barco, Virgilio, 172
Barrios, Justo Rufino, 31
Batista, Fulgencio, 125–126
Batlle y Ordóñez, José, 48, 67
Belaúnde, Fernando, 177
Bengelsdorf, Carollee, 133, 135
Bentley, Alfred, 15
Bernstein, Eduard, 13
Betancur, Belisario, 66
Bielous, Silvia Dutrénit, 168
Blanco party (Uruguay), 47–50, 68, 169
Bolívar, Simón, 53, 57
Bolivia, 68, 76, 79, 95, 130, 167; economy,
  144–145; elite pacts, 84, 85–87, 191;
  extrication model, 80; Left, 86–87;
  parliamentarism and, 183; War of the
  Pacific and, 44–45; Workers' Central,
  144
Bordaberry, Juan María, 61, 62, 186(n9)
Bosch, Juan, 92, 178
Brazil, 28, 35–36, 41(n25), 44, 80, 158, 191;
  clientelism, 100; constitution, 35, 183;
  economy, 143, 145, 148–149; elite settle-
  ment, 84; Old Republic, 176; parliamentarism and, 183; party system, 176– 177;
  quilombos, 36; Real Plan, 145
Breakdown of Democratic Regimes, The,
  21
Britain, 5, 30, 33, 44–45
Broad Front (FA) (Uruguay), 61–62,
  147–148, 169, 186(n5)
Bucaram, Abdalá, 143, 144

233

About the Book

This innovative book provides a comprehensive, comparative analysis of the democratic experience in Latin America.

Peeler first discusses the major elements of democratic theory within the context of the Latin American tradition. Following a review of early examples of liberal democracy in Latin America, the core of his book traces democratic transitions during the 1980s. A wealth of empirical data illustrates how differing regimes have dealt with challenges to their consolidation and stability. Peeler's conclusions suggest that if liberal democracy is to survive in the region, it may be in spite of the very elites who were essential to its establishment.

John Peeler is professor of political science at Bucknell University. He is author of *Latin American Democracies: Colombia, Costa Rica, Venezuela.*